★★★★ UNITED STATES ★★★★
AIRBORNE
★★ FORCES ★★

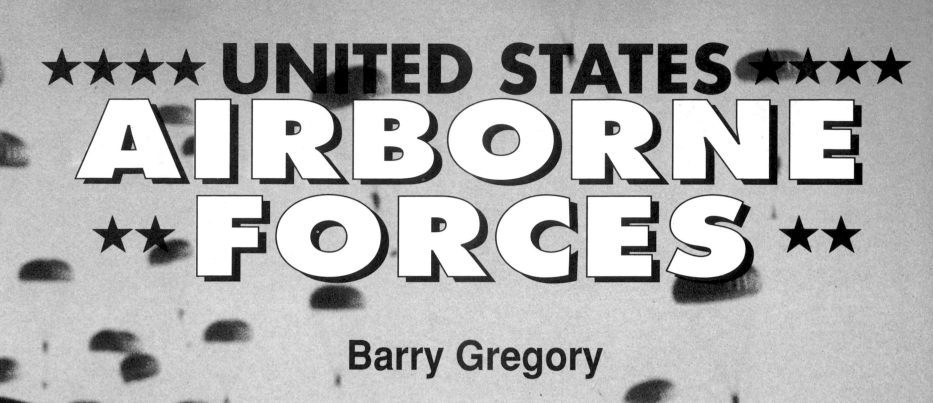

★★★★ UNITED STATES ★★★★
AIRBORNE
★★ FORCES ★★

Barry Gregory

Brian Trodd Publishing House Limited

Photographic Acknowledgments
All photographs supplied by Brian Trodd Publishing
House Ltd with the exception of the following.
Irvin GB Ltd: 18 right.
TRH Pictures: 9, 10, 12,14, 15 top, 39, 40, 58, 60, 61
top, 65, 73, 75 top, 77 bottom, 79 top, 87, 107, 110,
111 top, 116, 132, 143, 147 top, 149, 158 left and right,
160, 161, 163, 169, 170/171, 171, 176, 188, 192, 192/
193, 193 top and bottom, 195, 197 top, 198/199, 203,
206, 207 top and bottom, 208 top and bottom, 209,
211, 212, 213, 220, 222, 227, 228/229.
TRH Pictures/A Landau: 162, 182/183

Front cover: A Drop Zone Controller relays information
up to the Jump Master, during a routine Airborne
training exercise.
Back cover: Airborne troops check their equipment
while waiting to board a C-47 in North Africa, 1943.
Endpapers: Airborne troops board a C-141 bound for
Grenada.
Half-title: 2nd Battalion, 503rd Airborne at Hungerford,
Berkshire, England, 1942.
Title: Nearly 2,000 jumpers fill the skies above Fort
Bragg, as the 82nd Airborne Division return from
Operation "Just Cause," in Panama.

The Publishers would like to thank the staff of the 82nd
Airborne Division War Memorial Museum, the Department of Defense Still Media Record Center, the Library
of Congress and the United States National Archives
for their help and assistance in the production of this
book.

Published in 1990 by
Brian Trodd Publishing House Limited
27 Swinton Street, London WC1X 9NW

ISBN 1 85361 167 0

Printed in Portugal

CONTENTS

Foreword

FOREWORD

Fifty years ago, airborne forces demonstrated that vertical deployment of ground forces was practical. That innovation substantially enhanced the strategic and tactical advantages of military offense – by decreasing time, increasing distance and extending the selectivity for attack – against vital battlefield objectives.

U.S. Airborne exploited those advantages extensively and pervasively throughout World War II. In Europe, starting with a long-range, battalion parachute assault into North Africa in 1942, they progressed continuously and successfully with regimental, division and corps airborne operations into Sicily, Holland, Belgium, France and Germany. In the Pacific, they spearheaded the return of General MacArthur's forces into Manila and they recaptured Corregidor.

Following World War II, U.S. Airborne did combat in Korea, Vietnam, Grenada and Panama. Over a fifty-year span, a small Parachute Test Platoon activated at Fort Benning, Georgia became the precursor of a fully fledged, combat-ready airborne corps now based at Fort Bragg, North Carolina.

At the outset of World War II the newly-created airborne forces had no history. But they did "have a rendezvous with destiny," as Major General William Lee, who was later to be recognized as "The Father of U.S. Airborne," perceptively proclaimed.

Throughout the past half-century, U.S. Airborne have kept their rendezvous with destiny faithfully, gallantly and bravely. In the process they developed a history and created an Airborne spirit that is uniquely their own. Their Airborne spirit is derived from, and manifested by, the individual paratrooper's strong confidence in self, his unyielding faith in his comrades-in-arms and his fierce pride in his unit.

A half-century's overview of such an innovative, colorful and complex military arm as Airborne demands exhaustive research of a tremendous volume of data. It entails the collection, collation and analysis of a vast array of official and personal records and documents assembled from diverse sources. It requires judgements to be made on varying accounts of events experienced within common arenas, but under differing perspectives and emotional environments.

For years to come, historians, researchers, critics, analysts and veterans will likely discuss and debate the Airborne's contributions to World War II and subsequent Allied and American military operations, in terms of casualties saved, combat time reduced and decisive influences on pivotal campaigns. But all should agree that those contributions were not only substantial but significantly vital to ultimate victory.

And all Airborne enthusiasts should agree that Barry Gregory merits highest commendations for the dedicated, painstaking and exhaustive efforts he obviously devoted to preparing and presenting his overview of Airborne history. One senses that, like his subject, Barry Gregory is "Airborne All the Way."

W. T. Ryder
Brig. Gen. (U.S. Army Rtd.)
(Former Commander U.S. Army Parachute Test Platoon)

The New York Times.

"All the News That's Fit to Print."

LATE CITY EDITION
POSTSCRIPT
Fair, not much change in temperature today. Tomorrow cloudy.

Copyright, 1940, by The New York Times Company.

VOL. LXXXIX...No. 30,057.   NEW YORK, FRIDAY, MAY 10, 1940.   THREE CENTS

NAZIS INVADE HOLLAND, BELGIUM, LUXEMBOURG BY LAND AND AIR; DIKES OPENED; ALLIES RUSH AID

U.S. FREEZES CREDIT

President Acts to Guard Funds Here of Three Invaded Nations

SHIP RULING TODAY

Envoy Reports to Hull on Germany's Attacks by Air and Land

WASHINGTON, Friday, May 10—President Roosevelt early today ordered the freezing of all credits held by Belgium, the Netherlands and Luxembourg in this country.

He called a conference for 10:30 A. M. of heads of the State, War and Navy Departments to consider pressing problems of neutrality.

The President acted swiftly after news of Germany's invasion of the three European neutral countries reached Washington and galvanized high officials into action. His order with regard to the freezing of all the invaded countries' credits and cash balances here was a counter-part of the action taken after Germany invaded Norway and Denmark.

Congress this week completed action on legislation that specifically authorizes the President by decree to freeze all such cash and credits of any belligerent. The object is to prevent these resources from falling into the hands of the invading power.

Ships to Be Considered

The President's order directed Secretary of the Treasury Henry Morgenthau Jr. to freeze all Belgian, French and Luxembourg credits before the markets open this morning.

It was announced also that the conference is to be held at 10:30 will consider the question of Belgian and Netherland ships that may be attend this conference.

The White House, meanwhile, indicated some skepticism of the official explanation of the invasion given by German Propaganda Minister Joseph Goebbels, who was reported to have said that the Germans moved because of information that Great Britain and France intended to invade the countries involved.

"Nevertheless," said Stephen T. Early, Presidential secretary, after he had quoted the Goebbels statement, "it remains to be seen who invaded who."

It was announced that the President would remain awake throughout the night, if necessary, to receive reports and consult with officials. Sumner Welles, Under-Secretary of State, at 1:40 A. M. joined the group of State Department officials who remained on duty at the department.

Report From Ambassador

A general invasion of the three neutrals by heavy German land and air forces was reported to the State Department and Mr. Roosevelt early today by Ambassador John J. Cudahy at Brussels.

The International Situation

In the midst of Britain's Cabinet crisis Germany struck another powerful blow early this morning by invading the Netherlands, Belgium and Luxembourg.

After swarms of planes had engaged in air fights over Amsterdam, parachute troops, some of them clad in Netherland uniforms, descended at strategic points while planes bombed air fields. The Netherlands resisted the incursion and promptly opened the dikes that are part of her water defense system. [Page 1.]

Parachute troops likewise made surprise landings in Belgium and bombs from 100 planes blasted the Brussels airport. [Page 1.]

Appeals for help were dispatched to the Allies by the invaded countries and it was understood that machinery of assistance was being set in motion. Queen Wilhelmina in a proclamation issued at The Hague declared, "I and my government will do our duty." [Page 1.]

As in the case of Norway, Berlin explained that the German action had been taken to forestall the Allies; an announcement said that an attack on German territory through the Low Countries. What the Reich was doing, it was declared, was safeguarding the neutrality of those countries. [Page 1.]

President Roosevelt lost no time in acting on the new situation. After night conferences he ordered the freezing of credits of the three invaded countries. Further measures are to be taken today. [Page 1.]

London, meanwhile, announced that British troops had occupied Iceland to prevent a possible German seizure of that former Danish possession. [Page 1.]

Before all these happenings Neville Chamberlain had appeared to be on his way out as Prime Minister, but today it was expected the new developments might save him.

Following upon his relatively narrow escape in the House of Commons vote on Wednesday night, Mr. Chamberlain set about yesterday to see what could be done to satisfy his critics. He offered Cabinet posts to two leaders of the Labor Opposition, but they refused to serve under him. As to whether they would serve under another Conservative, they delayed their reply. If Mr. Chamberlain steps out of office, it is thought probable his

Bombs Drop on Swiss Soil

By The United Press

BERNE, Switzerland, Friday, May 10—The army staff announced today that foreign airplanes had dropped bombs in the Berne Jura Alpine district between Delemont, near the frontier, and Mount Terr, damaging a railroad.

Traffic continued over the road, the army said. It added that other foreign planes were flying over Swiss territory near Basle but that no details had been received.

place will be taken by the present Foreign Secretary, Viscount Halifax, with Winston Churchill acting as government spokesman in the Commons, from the floor of which the peer would by tradition be barred. [Page 1.]

Moreover, the Allies' Narvik campaign seemed to be making progress. From that far northern area it was reported that two Allied columns closing in on the railway to the port were within ten miles of each other near the Swedish border; their intention apparently was to join and drive westward along the railroad to Narvik itself, which is held by the Nazis. The Germans, in their effort to thwart the besiegers, were said to be landing parachute troops and supplying them by air. [Page 4.]

In the aftermath of the campaign in the south of the country Foreign Minister Koht disclosed that four of Norway's six divisions had been, hors-killed, wounded or captured by the Nazis or interned by Sweden. [Page 6.]

Allies Visible to Planes

The biggest handicap to the British and French was in the timing of the German thrust at dawn. This prevented the Allies moving troops under cover of darkness, and since hundreds of German planes already had flown over practically all of Netherland and Belgian territory for some hours, the disposition of Allied troops and their every movement must have been known to the German High Command.

Wireless to THE NEW YORK TIMES.

LONDON, Friday, May 10—The Germans crossed the Belgian frontier at four points this morning, according to an announcement over

Continued on Page Two

MUSSOLINI TO LET 'ONLY FACTS' SPEAK

Press Assures Yugoslavia, but Reminds Her of Fate of Poland and Norway

By HERBERT L. MATTHEWS
By Telephone to THE NEW YORK TIMES.

ROME, May 9—The fourth anniversary of the founding of the new Italian Empire was celebrated today in an atmosphere of warlike preparation. The army was honored, Italian armed strength was glorified and the country was told by its leading commentators that the em-

ICELAND OCCUPIED BY BRITISH FORCE

Secret Expedition Is Justified as Thwarting Action There by Germany

Special Cable to THE NEW YORK TIMES.

LONDON, Friday, May 10—Forestalling a possible German swoop on the strategically valuable former Danish dominion of Iceland, the British have landed an expeditionary force there, it was announced this morning by the Foreign Office here.

Chamberlain Saved by Nazi Blow In Low Countries, London Thinks

By RAYMOND DANIELL
Special Cable to THE NEW YORK TIMES.

LONDON, Friday, May 10—The first effect of the German attack on the Low Countries is expected to be

ALLIED HELP SPED

Netherland and Belgian Appeals Answered by British and French

TACTICS ARE WATCHED

London Thinks Move an Effort to Get Bases to Attack Britain

Italians Reported Massing

By The United Press

BUENOS AIRES, Argentina, Friday, May 10—The Madrid radio was heard broadcasting today that the British had closed the Strait of Gibraltar and that Italy was massing troops on the French frontier.

Special Cable to THE NEW YORK TIMES.

LONDON, Friday, May 10—The British Government received appeals for help early today from both the Netherlands and Belgium.

The British and French reply to the Netherland-Belgian appeals was prompt. Representatives of the respective governments here were told by 6:30 A. M. (1:30 A. M. New York time) they could expect all the help Britain could give them.

The Netherland Legation here received assurance that its country and Belgium were now regarded as Allies of Britain and France.

Within a few minutes after receipt of official news of the invasion of the Low Countries, the British Cabinet was called to 10 Downing Street and was in session throughout the country with the appearance of the first planes.

According to information here, the Belgian Cabinet was in Brussels and Premier Hubert Pierlot conferred with King Leopold.

The German invasion of the Low Countries had been expected in London, and it must be presumed the Allies were ready for it in some extent.

BRUSSELS IS RAIDED

400 Reported Killed— Troops Cross Border at Four Points

PARACHUTE INVASION

Mobilization Is Ordered and Allied Aid Asked— Luxembourg Attacked

Wireless to THE NEW YORK TIMES.

LONDON, Friday, May 10—The invasion Belgium had feared came with the outbreak of the European war some hours before dawn this morning. About a hundred German planes flew over this city and bombed the airport.

The airfield at Antwerp also was bombed. Parachute troops were landed at Hasselt in Eastern Belgium. Artillery fire was reported heard along the German and Luxembourg frontiers.

Anti-aircraft guns at the airport commenced firing with the appearance of the first invaders and kept up a steady barrage. Those in the center of the city went into action at 2:30 A. M.

Above the drone of airplanes engines could be heard the staccato of machine guns. Bombs wrecked many houses in the vicinity of the airport and caused some loss of life. [Exchange Telegraph (British news agency) said 400 persons had been killed in the first raid.]

Reports from Antwerp and other parts of the country said German planes had flown constantly over since 4:30 A. M., keeping anti-aircraft batteries steadily in action. Premier Hubert Pierlot and Foreign Minister Paul-Henri Spaak conferred with King Leopold and then called an emergency meeting of the Cabinet. The radio broadcast repeated summonses to all soldiers to join their unit at once. A "state of alarm" was decreed throughout the country with the appearance of the first planes.

The Belgian radio also stated German parachute troops had fluttered down at Nivelles, less than twenty miles south of Brussels, and at Saint Trond, about thirty-five miles east of the capital. The broadcast stated that Germany had made no demarche in Brussels before the invasion.

Wireless to THE NEW YORK TIMES.

LONDON, Friday, May 10—The Germans crossed the Belgian frontier at four points this morning, according to an announcement over

Continued on Page Two

NAZIS SWOOP ON THE LOW COUNTRIES
By land and air German troops descended this morning upon the Netherlands, Belgium and Luxembourg. The principal land incursion into the Netherlands was at Roermond.

Ribbentrop Charges Allies Plotted With the Lowlands

By GEORGE AXELSSON
Wireless to THE NEW YORK TIMES.

BERLIN, Friday, May 10—Foreign Minister Joachim von Ribbentrop at 9 o'clock this morning announced that Reich forces had launched military operations against Holland, Belgium and Luxembourg to "protect their neutrality."

Earlier it was reported that German troops had occupied Maastricht, the Netherlands, and had "landed" contingents in Brussels, probably meaning parachute troops.

Herr von Ribbentrop said that Germany had received unimpeachable proof that the Allies were engineering an imminent attack through the Lowlands into the German Ruhr district therefore the Germans felt compelled to take corresponding measures. He said the time had come for settling the final account with the "Franco-British leaders."

And thus the war is a decisive finish has at last started in the West. This was the assumption when Herr von Ribbentrop informed the world through newspaper men that the German action meant that she had decided to settle all accounts with the Allies.

"France and Britain dropped their mask," said Herr von Ribbentrop. "The alarm in the Mediterranean was a faint behind which the Allies were preparing an onslaught on German territory which the Reich could not tolerate."

The notes—handed to The Hague and Brussels simultaneously with a shorter note to the Grand Duchy of Luxembourg just prior to their invasion by Germany—accused the Lowlands with having been overwhelmingly partial toward the Allies, adding that the attitude of the press was objectionable to the Reich.

HOLLAND'S QUEEN PROTESTS INVASION

Wilhelmina Vows She and the Government Will Do Duty— Bars Negotiation With Foe

By The United Press

THE HAGUE, the Netherlands, Friday, May 10—Queen Wilhelmina said today in a statement on the German invasion of the country that "I and my government will do our duty."

The Queen, in a proclamation addressed to "my people," said:

"After our country, with scrupulous conscientiousness, had observed strict neutrality during all these months, and while Holland had no other plan than to maintain strictly this attitude, Germany last night made a sudden attack on our territory without any warning.

"This was done notwithstanding a solemn promise that the neutrality of our country would be respect-

AIR FIELDS BOMBED

Nazi Parachute Troops Land at Key Centers as Flooding Starts

RIVER MAAS CROSSED

Defenders Battle Foe In Sky, Claim 6 Planes as War Is Proclaimed

First Bombing in France

Special Cable to THE NEW YORK TIMES.

PARIS, Friday, May 10—The Bron airdrome, a big airport near Lyon, was bombed by German planes today. One German aircraft was shot down. The alarm was first given at 4:32 A. M. The all-clear signal was given at 6:45 A. M.

WASHINGTON, Friday, May 10—United States Ambassador William C. Bullitt telephoned the State Department from Paris at 4 A. M. today that the Germans had bombed a number of fortified towns in France, "such as Colmar and others."

By THE UNITED PRESS.

AMSTERDAM, The Netherlands, Friday, May 10—Germany invaded the Netherlands early today, and troops being pressed by widespread air attacks as announced by the landing of parachute troops.

The Netherlands resisted and announced she was at war with Germany. Anti-aircraft batteries and fighter planes engaged swarms of German aircraft when they appeared simultaneously over a score of Netherland cities.

An official proclamation said: "Since 3 A. M. German troops have crossed the Netherland frontier and German planes have tried to attack airports. Inundations are effective according to plan. The army anti-aircraft batteries were found prepared. So far as is known six German planes have been shot down."

[French, Belgian and British planes were sighted over the Netherlands this morning, a Reuters (British news agency) dispatch said in quoting the Netherland radio station at Hilversum, near Amsterdam.]

German troops went first reported crossing the Netherland frontier near Roermond, eight miles north of the Belgian frontier, German planes landed troops by parachute at strategic points near Rotterdam, The Hague, Amsterdam and other large cities.

A large number of the German troops landed by parachute were said to be dressed in Netherland military uniforms.

Other Germans crossed the Maas River in rubber boats to attack Netherland territory. They were said to be reaching the Netherland side on "considerable numbers."

A fierce air battle raged over Amsterdam as Netherland fighter planes dived repeatedly on German

In the spring of 1940 few Americans seriously thought that they would be involved in a world war. Post-World War I reaction in the U.S.A. had led to two decades of pacifism and isolation. In the early 1920's, Brigadier General William ("Billy") Mitchell, chief of the United States Air Service (from 1926 the United States Army Air Corps), provoked worldwide repercussions by challenging the traditional American naval and military hierarchy, and by his advocacy of the theories of the Italian air force general Giulio Douhet, shared also by the professional head of the British Air Force, Sir Hugh Trenchard. These views in outline presented a seemingly persuasive case for winning wars by the use of airpower to break the enemy's will through violent and destructive bombardment of enemy cities. Later Mitchell charged the War and Navy Departments with "incompetency, criminal negligence and almost treasonable administration of the national defense." By order of President Calvin Coolidge, Mitchell was court-martialed for his trouble, which included warning the U.S.A. of the possibility of a war with Japan, and ordered to be suspended from rank and duty for five years. In January 1926, the outspoken Army Air Corps general, who was deemed by many to be an egocentric publicity seeker, resigned from the service.

The period of military retrenchment in the U.S.A. ended on 12 January 1939, when President Franklin Delano Roosevelt, spurred by the Munich crisis of the previous year, asked the Congress for $552 million for defense spending. On 5 September 1939, two days after the U.K. joined France in declaring war on Nazi Germany, in one of his fireside chats over the radio the president stated: "This nation will remain a neutral nation, but I cannot ask that every American remain neutral in thought as well." Roosevelt proclaimed a limited national emergency on 8 September. Still, as the months went by the war in Europe seemed a long way off. True, American lives had been lost when on 3 September the *Athenia*, a British passenger liner bound from Liverpool to Montreal, had been sunk without warning by a German U-boat; Poland had been devastated by 1,250,000 German invaders, and the country was divided between Nazi Germany and the U.S.S.R., the Red Army having swept in from the east. But what most caught the average American's imagination in the winter of 1939-1940 were the thrilling newspaper accounts of the war between Finland and the U.S.S.R. in which the Finnish troops outmatched "Ivan" on skis and ice skates, but not ultimately in firepower. Mountain resorts in Colorado were reported to be doing good business as young Americans took to skis for the first time, an indispensable skill no doubt if the U.S.A. went to war. At that time a certain complacency reigned in "wartime" Britain and France: after all, the Germans had advanced east and not west and probably had no designs on the western Allies. This over-optimistic mood was shattered when, on 10 May 1940, 2,500,000 Germans invaded the Netherlands, Belgium and France. The advancing armies destroyed all in their paths with the combination of tank and dive-

Above: General William ("Billy") Mitchell (right) in 1918. "Billy" Mitchell had a plan to drop the American 1st Division from British Handley Page bombers behind the enemy lines to capture Metz.

Far left: The front page of The *New York Times*, 10 May 1940, announcing the German invasion of the Low Countries.

bomber, generally known as the *Blitzkrieg* (lightning war) tactics which had been used so successfully in the invasion of Poland and on the side of the Nationalists in the Spanish Civil War (1936-1939). But for all the startlingly innovative nature of the *Blitzkrieg*, those Americans who sat up and took notice were more intrigued by the Germans' use of parachute and gliderborne troops in the assault on the Netherlands and Belgium.

German parachutists had already seen action a month earlier – on 9 April – when units of the 1st Parachute (Fallschirmjäger regiment Nr 1, or FJR 1) were committed in company strength in Denmark at Aalborg and Vordingborg for minor but decisive actions to secure strategically important bridges and airfields. Denmark fell on the same day, almost without bloodshed. Bad weather on 9 April prevented a projected attack by parachutists from FJR 1 on Oslo airport in support of the German seaborne invasion of Norway but the city later fell to air-transported mountain units. The German *Fallschirmjäger* arm finally saw Norwegian action in mid-April at Dombas in central Norway, where, leaping from Junkers Ju 52/3m transport aircraft into deep snow, they reinforced German mountain troops in a four-day engagement with Norwegian troops, who were fighting to link up with the British

forces that had been landed from the sea at Andalsnes. The parachutists were obliged to surrender when new airborne supplies of ammunition were delayed by adverse weather conditions.

When Hitler turned his attentions to the Low Countries on 10 May, the Luftwaffe's 7th Air Division, which had been in the process of training and development since 1936, was to be thoroughly tested for the first time. Key bridges, airfields and fortifications in Belgium and the Netherlands were to be seized by units operating in battalion and company strength. Capture of these vital objectives was essential to the successful advance of Army Groups "A" and "B" across the Belgian and Dutch frontiers. The idea was largely Hitler's own, but the operational plan was shaped and carried out by the Luftwaffe's Generalleutnant (Lieutenant General) Kurt Student, who had conceived the German airborne division. Some 4,500 trained parachutists were ready for action, the bulk of them supported by an air-transported 22nd Infantry Division, whose 12,000 men would be sent into the Netherlands.

Before first light on 10 May, the initial day of Operation *Fall Gelb*, the *Sturmabteilung* (Assault Group), commanded by Hauptmann Walther Koch was lifted in 11 DFS 230

Right: German *Fallschirmjäger* in action in Holland on 10 May 1940. This posed shot of a machine-gun position was taken by another parachutist, who was captured by the Dutch and sent to England as a prisoner of war.

gliders towed by Ju 52/3m aircraft from their operational base at Köln-Wahn, setting a course for the Belgian frontier fortress at Eben-Emael. The Germans' main objective was to capture the fortress, but three adjacent bridges spanning the Albert Canal were also to be seized. Eben-Emael stood at the northern end of the Liège fortified system. Its machine-guns covered the nearby crossings of the Albert Canal, including the nearest bridge at Canne. Artillery batteries covered the roads leading westward from Maastricht, and also the key bridges farther north at Vroenhoven and Veldwezelt. The seizure of the Eben-Emael fortress and the three bridges by Hauptmann (Captain) Walther Koch's assault group greatly accelerated the entry of Army Group "A" into the Low Countries.

The gliders bearing a single company of paratroopers (Company FJR 1) and a parachute engineer platoon were released by their tug aircraft before crossing the Belgian frontier, and seven of them sailed over the 10m (33 ft) high walls into the center of the fortress compound. The engineers immediately got to work blowing in the exits of the fortress and destroying two 120mm (4.7 in) cannon and nine 75mm (2.95 in) guns with explosive charges before the Belgian soldiers, who had been aroused from their beds, surrendered. Meanwhile, the paratroopers who had landed near the bridges captured two of their objectives intact, but Belgian engineers got to the Canne bridge first and blew it up in the face of the assault party.

In the Netherlands the strategic intention of the German general staff was to paralyze resistance as swiftly as possible and disrupt the movement of Dutch reserves by capturing The Hague, Rotterdam and a few other vital communications centers. Both the 7th Air Division and the 22nd Division were assigned on 10 May within the operational framework of an *ad hoc* air-landing corps under Student. In the south, Student would personally lead the 7th Air Division from headquarters set up at Waalhaven airport, later to be established in Dordrecht in the southern Netherlands, while to the north Generalleutnant (Lieutenant General) Hans Graf von Sponeck, commander of the 22nd Division, would seize vital objectives once the paratroopers of FJR 2 had taken the landing zones. The air-landed infantry were additionally ordered to seize the Dutch government offices at The Hague and, on personal instructions from Hitler, arrest the Dutch royal family, which as it happened escaped the country with the help of the U.K.'s Royal Navy.

Four days after nearly 600 Ju 52/3m transport aircraft had crossed over the Dutch frontier, it was almost all over. The Dutch troops had fought bravely, but in spite of French intervention in the south there was no effective help from the Allies. By the end of June the Netherlands, Belgium and France had fallen to German military might. The U.K., supported by her Commonwealth, now stood alone against the Nazi aggressor but was too busy organizing its defenses under the direction of a forceful new prime minister, Winston Churchill, to make any official studies of the Germans' brilliant deployment of their Panzer columns, outflanking the Maginot Line by advancing through the wooded terrain of the Ardennes and the new concept of "vertical envelopment" by airborne assault in the Netherlands. British intelligence officers were totally lacking in appreciation of the tactical doctrine and strengths of German airborne troops, which contributed in some measure to the defeat of British and Commonwealth troops when *Fallschirmjäger* struck again a year later on the Mediterranean island of Crete.

At the time of the invasion of the Low Countries, British and American newspaper and radio reports carried many wild and completely inaccurate stories about how the German paratroopers operated. One "eye-witness" in a widely circulated account published immediately after the fall of the Netherlands and sub-titled "I saw them drop" writes:

"Transport planes were landing on every beach, every football ground, every open space and were pouring out troops. A great majority of them were disguised – as civilians, Dutch soldiers, as policemen and railwaymen. Thousands of Dutchmen, hailing them as comrades, were losing their lives at the hands of these men, who had been ordered to stop at nothing."

No photographs are in existence to support this intrepid observer's assertions, but some reports stated that parachutists were dropped in large numbers disguised as nuns and might be expected to function more as "fifth columnists" than conventional soldiers. They were expected to carry street maps marked with the names of Nazi sympathizers. Consequently, elaborate precautions were taken in the U.K. to render farmland and other open spaces unsuitable for landing operations by parachutists, transport aircraft and gliders. (Although there was little substance to the rumors of the rather theatrical behavior of the *Fallschirmjäger*, it can be reliably reported that a small unit of the *Abwehr* (German military intelligence) did operate in civilian clothes near the Venlo area, where it was said two British officers were engaged in sabotaging a bridge.)

Churchill reacted to the German parachute drop in the Netherlands in two memorable ways. One was the raising of the Local Defence Volunteers (L.D.V.) from male aspirants who were too young, too old or in too poor a medical category to be drafted, along with others who had found a comfortable niche in reserved occupations. The L.D.V. established posts to defend factories that were essential to the war effort, likely landing zones for a parachute drop, road junctions and other strategic centers on lines of communication. The *Fallschirmjäger* were guaranteed a hot reception from the L.D.V., at first armed only with sticks and umbrellas, every bit as bruising as the fate that awaited the French *Aërostiers* (balloon troops) at the hands of the English militia had these adventuresome airborne soldiers crossed the British coast — as was threatened in the Napoleonic Wars! The L.D.V. units are better known today by their later name, the Home Guard.

Churchill's other brainwave, and directly relevant to the Allied "airborne effort" (as the forming of parachute and glider forces and the mounting of airborne operations was to be termed in top American military circles) was the formation of the first British paratroop unit. This event was preceded in early June 1940, however, by the prime minister's order to the Commander-in-Chief Home Forces that 10,000 men must immediately be drawn from existing units to form "Storm Troop" or "Leopard" battalions. The officers and men should be lightly armed with automatic weapons and grenades for small boat cross-Channel raids, and in addition should be supplied with motor-cycles and armored cars for lightning action on the home beaches in the event of invasion. The Commando groups, to use their long-enduring name, had an original establishment of 500 men each, and were raised from the Regular Army and Royal Marines.

On 22 June the prime minister brought up the business of parachute troops, not for the first time, with the Joint Chiefs-of-Staff in a communication tabbed ACTION THIS DAY. "We ought to have a corps of at least 5,000 parachute troops... I hear that something is being done already to form such a corps but only, I believe, on a very small scale. Advantage must be taken of the summer to train these forces, who can none-

theless play their part meanwhile as shock troops in home defense." Manchester Corporation's civil airport, Ringway, was chosen as the site of the Parachute Training School. R.A.F. Ringway was to be a combined services establishment with the title Central Landing School, and the Royal Air Force and Army were to work together on the staff. No. 2 Commando was assigned to Ringway for jump training, along with six obsolete Armstrong Whitworth Whitley bombers which were to be converted to drop parachutists, but the most the R.A.F. would undertake in "Britain's darkest hour" was a battle commitment to drop 720 fully armed men. The British response to Hitler's *Fallschirmjäger* was under way, and Ringway did not close for business for five long, thrill-packed, and often emotional years.

After the conquest of Greece in 1941, during which German paratroopers were employed to capture the vital bridge over the Corinth canal, Hitler turned his attention to Crete. Student put a case to the Führer which suggested that given the strength of the Royal Navy in the Mediterranean, a seaborne invasion might well prove disastrous. Hitler agreed, but with some misgivings, to allow Student to assemble his XI Air Corps, which had been formed in the summer of 1940, for a mass parachute and glider assault on the island. The airborne corps (7th Air Division with the 5th Mountain Division) was duly assembled in the neighborhood of Athens where seven airfields were chosen as departure points. Ten air transport groups of KGzbV 1, 2 and 3 (mustering roughly 500 Ju 52/3m aircraft) and three glider-towing groups were assigned to Operation "Mercury," which was scheduled to commence on 20 May 1941.

Even so the air transport allocation was insufficient to make the assault in one lift, and when the day came the Ju 52/3m aircraft made their drops and then had to return to the Greek airfield to pick up more paratroopers. Crete is a mountainous island 260km (160 miles) long by 65km (40 miles) broad, but its centers of population lie on the narrow northern littoral. Malème and Canea were the objectives for the first lift in the morning, while the four landing zones were to be reinforced by a third lift. The 5th Mountain Division was to be flown into an airfield west of Malème on the north-western corner of the coastal strip. Responsibility for bomber and fighter support was given to VIII Air Corps. The backbone of the corps were the Junkers Ju 87 dive-bomber squadrons,

Above: German Junkers Ju 52 transport planes drop paratroopers over the island of Crete on 20 May 1941. The German airborne conquest of Crete was a Pyrrhic victory; the loss of life was so great that Hitler never again risked his beloved *Fallschirmjäger* in a major action.

numbering some 150 machines.

The Greek airfields were quickly enshrouded in dust clouds rising from the runways as the air transports took off. The Germans expected that the fighting on Crete would be all over in one day, but in the event the first day did not go according to plan. Although the airborne assault came as a complete surprise to the defenders, the British and imperial garrison, consisting of 28,000 troops, was larger and more effective than the Germans had anticipated. In addition, Greek battalions and Cretan irregulars were distributed among the various sectors. The total strength under the command of New Zealand Major General Sir Bernard Freyberg, V.C. was about 42,000 men. The battle opened before the first German parachutist touched the ground. As the DFS 230 gliders floated loose and massive waves of paratroopers appeared in the sky, they were greeted by lethal machine-gun and rifle fire.

The design of the German RZ parachute was not one of the more inspired examples of craftsmanship. When the *Fallschirmjäger* made his exit from the Ju 52/3m, he dived head first with his arms extended before being sucked into the prop wash of the aircraft. The Allied practice was to jump feet first in an upright position: when the prop wash trailed away and the parachutist heard the canopy of his parachute open after activation by the static lines, he was able to some extent to control his direction of flight by pulling down on his risers, which were attached to the parachute harness on his shoulders and connected with the canopy's rigging lines. Once his parachute was open, the German found himself suspended from a rope attached to his harness in the middle of his back; as a consequence he made his descent "on all fours" and was thus totally unable to correct his drift. Marksmen in Crete took a heavy toll of the *Fallschirmjäger*, and many more were severely injured on hitting the hard earth strewn with stones.

The gliderborne troops also came in for some rough landings, and many gliders broke up on landing. Both the parachutists and the gliders were widely scattered and the fighting on the first day was largely between small *ad hoc* groups of *Fallschirmjäger* and the island defenders, who became increasingly disorganized. Fortunately for the Germans, the 5th Mountain Division landed at Malème intact and started its advance eastward. By 24 May, Freyberg had abandoned hope of holding Crete, and three days later his decision was made to abandon the island. The Germans had won a considerable victory, but only at a price. The 7th Air Division had taken heavy casualties and Hitler, for whom the German paratroopers were the embodiment of military perfection, was filled with despair.

Two months after the battle, at his Wolfschanze headquarters, Hitler declared to Student: "The day of the parachutist is over. The parachute arm is a surprise weapon and without the element of surprise there can be no future for airborne forces." Although the Germans went on to form ten parachute divisions, the *Fallschirmjäger* were never again deployed in their true role of assault from the sky. Hitler was wrong in his assessment of the worth of airborne forces

but, as the Allies were to discover as the war progressed, it takes more than the element of surprise and muscle-bound paratroopers to make an airborne division. Prime considerations are "air power" and control of the skies, and – although lightly armed with a reduced scale of support weapons as compared with the average infantryman – a well-oiled war machine to fight on the ground.

Above: A German DFS-230 glider has taken a hard knock on sailing to earth in Crete.

Below: Three of R.A.F. Ringway's Whitleys on a parachute training flight. The jumpers can be seen exiting from a hole in the center of the fuselage. The men sat on the edge with their feet in the hole before pushing off.

At the time of the fall of Crete, James M. Gavin was a regular officer serving on the staff of the United States Military Academy, West Point. Gavin was 34 years of age, and was already a veteran with 16 years service. He had enlisted as a private soldier way back in 1925 and later applied for entry to West Point, from which he graduated on 13 June 1929 with a Bachelor of Science degree, and was commissioned as a 2nd lieutenant in the infantry. The 1930's were not busy years for the U.S. Army and promotion was consequently slow. When the war broke out in Europe in 1939, Jim Gavin took a deep interest in the military events. Technical officers at West Point were usually more concerned with discipline than teaching the cadets battlefield tactics, but Gavin wasted no time in apprising his students of what was going on in Europe and the kind of enemy the U.S. Army might well be fighting in the near future. Gavin made a special study of the German airborne operations and after reading accounts of the assault on Crete decided to become a paratrooper himself. "Jumping Jim" Gavin was not the first American soldier to make that decision, but he did more than most to shape the destiny of the U.S. airborne forces. By 1944 he had advanced through the grades from captain to major general in command of the U.S. 82nd Airborne Division, at 37 the youngest general in the Allied armies.

Although parachute troops did not figure in U.S. military thinking until after the Munich crisis of 1938, the U.S.A. had a long history of parachuting for pleasure and profit dating back to a day in 1887 when Tom Baldwin leapt by parachute from the wicker basket of the balloon *Eclipse* before a sellout crowd at Golden Gate Park in San Francisco. The jump altitude was 1,525m (5,000 ft) and when Baldwin dropped into the roar of applause from the spectators, he must have felt more than lucky to be alive. On 28 February 1912 Albert Berry became the first man in history to make a parachute jump from an aeroplane. On that day Berry took off from Kinloch Field, Missouri, aboard a Benoist pusher-type aeroplane and made a safe descent from just over 305m (1,000 ft). By this time stunt parachuting at carnivals was a favorite attraction for young and old.

Early in 1919, a special board of officers was established at McCook Field for the purpose of testing the best type of escape parachute to issue to U.S. Army pilots. Leslie T. Irvin of Buffalo, New York, was one of several contenders for the order. In addition to being a designer of parachutes, Irvin was an experienced jumper. He had made his first parachute descent at 16 years of age. Since then he had made numerous exhibition jumps from balloons at carnivals. He had also been employed as a circus high diver and was known throughout the circus profession as "Sky High" Irvin. The parachute that "Sky High" designed and brought to McCook Field represented a totally new concept in parachuting. It was not opened automatically by a rope attached to the aeroplane or balloon basket but by the jumper himself – and at a height of his choosing. The free-fall type parachute had arrived.

Above: This member of the Parachute Test Platoon is using a dummy 'chute to practice pulling in his canopy on landing in windy conditions.

Far left: An American parachutist has made his exit from a Curtiss bomber over Sky Harbor airfield in 1929. He has fallen through the prop wash and as his rigging lines are twisted, he needs to kick round in circles, to adopt a good parachuting position for a forward descent.

Above: A parachutist after landing at Kelly Field, Texas, in October 1918.

Above right: Leslie Irvin, the American parachute pioneer. A barnstorming circus tightrope performer and Hollywood aviation stuntman, he spent most of his career in Britain where he established Irvin G.B. Ltd. in Letchworth, Hertfordshire, to supply the R.A.F. with emergency 'chutes. During World War II, Irvin, with the help of the G.Q. Company, designed the X-type parachute, which was used by all British paratroopers. He also initiated the famous "Golden Caterpillar Club" for downed crew, whose lives had been saved by the Irvin escape 'chute.

On 28 April 1919, Irvin approached McCook Field in the back seat compartment of a de Havilland biplane cruising along at a altitude of 455m (1,500 ft). After receiving a prearranged "get ready" hand signal from the pilot, Irvin made his final safety checks and stood up into the blast of rushing wind. When the aeroplane passed over the jumping field, Irvin dived head first out into space. When after a lengthy period of freefall, he pulled his ripcord, a small parachute popped out of his backpack, followed by a stream of silk instantly inflating into a perfectly shaped parachute which supported him as he made his descent to the ground. Irvin's free-fall parachute was adopted as the standard parachute for use by American military aviators and the U.S. Post Office Department's airmail pilots. It was not until 1922, however, that a regulation was published which required U.S. Army air crew to wear parachutes at all times while in flight. "Sky High" Irvin's 1919 model parachute would remain in service for the next 50 years.

Irvin also supplied parachutes to the Royal Air Force and he shortly went to England where he set up a factory to manufacture them and where he remained until he retired after World War II. In 1940, when British troops commenced training at Ringway, 135 successful parachute jumps were made before a recruit fell to his death after his parachute

canopy tangled with the rigging lines and failed to develop correctly. Irvin was called in and in collaboration with Raymond Quilter of the GQ Company experimented with packing the Irvin parachute in a GQ bag in such a way that when the static line, which was attached to a rail in the aeroplane, ripped off the packing bag within seconds of the paratrooper making his exit, the rigging lines paid out before the canopy, a reversal of the procedure that had caused the fatality. The experiment was a success and the Irvin X-type parachute has remained in service ever since. A small, bespectacled man, "Sky High" was a popular figure at Ringway during the war years and is remembered with great affection also by aircrew of the R.A.F. who were forced to bail out of their aircraft. All the flyers had to do was write a letter to Leslie Irvin at his office in Letchworth, Hertfordshire and they would receive a gold caterpillar badge, and a personal letter from the boss. The former circus performer from New York was one of the great unsung heroes of World War II.

American airborne troops may be said to have made their debut in the Civil War (1861-1865) when the Union forces used observation balloons, which appeared again in World War I. Captive balloons were widely used by the opposing armies of the Western Front spotting targets for the artillery.

Supported by 1,043m³ (37,000 cu ft) of hydrogen contained in a gas bag made of rubberized cloth, two officers slung in a look-out basket could, on a fine day, comfortably observe activity on the ground from an altitude of up to 1,525m (5,000 ft) over a radius of 16km (10 miles) or more. The operational life of an observation balloon was reckoned to be 15 days; and German airmen rated balloon-busting as being worth 1.5 aircraft per balloon for the record. But for the parachute, casualties among balloon spotters would have been enormous. The primitive parachutes were packed in containers and hung on the side of the basket. The harnesses were not adjustable and the spotters made their own with rope. When a balloon was set on fire the time margin for escape was negligible. No small amount of nerve was necessary, however, to make the effort and escapees were usually unmercifully strafed in mid-air by the attacking fighter.

Although the U.S. Marines made an experiment in dropping parachutists in the early 1920's and the Army Air Corps dropped a machine-gun and crew during the same period, it was not until the 1930's that albeit sporadic thought was given to the "airborne effort" in the U.S.A. In 1931 Major General Preston Brown, Commanding General of the Panama Canal Department, moved Battery "B" of the 2nd Field Artillery from France Field across the Isthmus to Rio Hato, Canal Zone, a distance of 145km (90 miles) by air transport. The following year Captain (later Lieutenant General) George C. Kenney

astounded his colleagues during maneuvers at Fort Dupont, Delaware, by air-landing an infantry detachment "behind enemy lines." In 1933 Batteries "A," "B," and "C" (and Headquarters) of the 2nd Field Artillery were transported by air from Bejuca to Cherrara, Panama, a distance of 56km (35 miles). On 6 May 1939 the Executive in the Office of the Chief of Infantry suggested to the G-3 of the War Department General Staff that consideration be given to the organization of a small detachment of Air Infantry. It was envisaged that these troops would be used as saboteurs and demolition crews, and were to be termed Air Grenadiers.

Above: America's first airborne troops, Civil War (1861-65).

Below: Doughboys handle a French "Kite" balloon on the Verdun sector in 1919. These balloons were used by artillery spotters, perched in crude baskets.

Below left: Marine Corps parachutists jumping from a Marine Corps de Havilland DH.4 at North Island, San Diego, in 1929.

Nothing came of this scheme, but on 25 June 1940 the War Department directed the formation of a parachute test platoon, to be drawn from the 29th Infantry Regiment at Fort Benning, Georgia. The 29th Infantry was being used to demonstrate tactics at Fort Benning, but in summary did not know the first thing about parachuting. Qualifications for joining the unit were very rigid: a) a minimum of two years service; b) a weight of no more than 84 kg (185 lb); and c) excellent physical condition. The directive ended with the following statement: "Because of the high degree of risk associated with parachute jumping, all those volunteering must understand that duty with the Parachute Test Platoon is strictly voluntary. It will require frequent jumps from airplanes in flight at various altitudes, which may result in serious injury or death. Therefore, only unmarried men may volunteer." As a result of the announcements that were made immediately after reveille in the pre-dawn darkness of 26 June, 200 men handed their names in to the regimental sergeant major by 8.30 a.m.

The initial experiments were made using a standard rifle platoon, which at that time consisted of one officer and 39 enlisted men. However, to allow for anticipated jump casualties, an additional nine men were added to the test platoon. Two officers were needed to lead the platoon and the volunteers were required to take a two-hour written examination, especially prepared by the Infantry Board on the subject of parachute troops. Fortunately for Lieutenant William T. Ryder, he had already studied the subject and passed the exam way ahead of his rivals. Lieutenant James A. Bassett was selected as assistant platoon leader. With the help of a flight surgeon from Maxwell Field, the process of the selection of the other ranks began and once completed the test platoon moved into a tent camp located near Lawson Field where the jumps were to be made. An abandoned corrugated iron hangar was made available, and this was put into service as a combined training hall and parachute packing shed. Warrant Officer Harry "Tug" Wilson, an experienced Army Air Corps parachutist, arrived from Kelly Field, Texas, to act as the chief jump instructor, and he was joined by a sergeant and two corporals, all three experienced Army Air Corps parachutists and riggers from Wright Field, Ohio.

The training schedule embraced a strenuous physical fitness program consisting of calisthenics, hand-to-hand combat, tumbling and a daily 4·8km (3 mile) run, which was interlaced with parachute instruction to cover jump and landing techniques. All this was combined with rigorous infantry training to accustom the men to fight as a team on the ground. Everywhere the men went they did so "on the double," which never let up in the intense heat of the Georgia summer. During the first day in the hangar, the Army Air Corps instructors lectured the platoon on the T-4 static-line parachute. Wilson showed movies of himself parachuting out

Below: The Parachute Test Platoon practice tumbling from a low ramp. The man on the ground is attempting to roll over, "gripping" his risers with his elbows in. This parachute training device was one of several copied from German photographs taken at the *Fallschirmjäger's* parachute training school at Stendal, near Berlin. The high tower is in the background – it took a lot longer to climb up it than to jump down!

Below right: Two instructors give a demonstration on landing technique. The near man is about to hoist his colleague onto the wooden framework before releasing him to make a forward landing with a firm grip on his riser straps.

of various U.S. Army aircraft at Kelly Field. Ryder and his platoon of volunteers watched and listened to their instructors with great interest. None of them had ever seen a parachute before, or ridden in an aeroplane.

Outside the hangar the men were taught what to do on hitting the ground after a parachute descent. On landing the parachutists were taught to keep their feet and knees together and arms and elbows in, so that on impact with the ground the shock was taken on the flats of the feet and up through the body while the jumper tumbled, or rolled over in the direction of his flight drift. With arms and elbows tucked in the danger of breaking arms was reduced. When the trainees had mastered the art of jumping off stationary platforms, realism was injected into the training by requiring them to jump off trucks that were being driven slowly across grassy areas. After making the leap, each man was expected to pick himself up and stand rigidly to attention for several minutes. No man ever made a perfect tumble – in the opinion of the instructors – and the ritual usually ended with the men being ordered to make ten press-ups. Early in July Lieutenant Colonel (later Major General) William C. Lee, who as a major in the Office of the Infantry had rendered valuable service in fostering the parachute project, and Infantry Board representatives witnessed controlled parachute jumps being made from a 76m (250 ft) tower at the New York World's Fair. Impressed with these demonstrations and visualizing the use of such towers as valuable training aids in the early stages of parachute training, Lee recommended that the Parachute Test Platoon be moved to Hightstown, New Jersey, for a week's training on these towers, which were the property of the aptly named Safe Parachute Company. Such a tower was (and still is) the first test of a volunteer's aptitude for heights.

One of the towers at Hightstown was rigged for controlled parachute descents. It had four steel cables which extended from its outstretched arm down to cement blocks enclosed in the ground. The student jumper was strapped into a body harness suspended beneath an open parachute that was fastened inside a huge metal hoop. Sewn into the periphery of the parachute were small metal rings that rode freely up and down the four steel cables. A fifth steel cable was attached to the top of the hoop holding the parachute. This cable was used to haul the jumper to the top of the tower, from which he was released to fall beneath the parachute, straight down the guiding wires to a slow-motion landing. The other tower was the same as the first except that it had no guide wires. On this tower, the open parachute was hauled to the top of the tower and then released from its restraining hoop, allowing the jumper to float freely away and down to a more realistic landing.

On 21 August 1940 the Chief of Infantry directed the parachutists be trained under the following instructions. "The initial jump

Below left and right: The Parachute Test Platoon pioneers make controlled jumps from the high tower. This was and still is the first real test of a potential parachutist's aptitude for heights.

Above: A Douglas B-18 bomber was used in 1940-41 for dropping parachutists.

Inset: Geronimo! The Parachute Test Platoon is about to make one of its qualifying jumps.

for each individual will be made at an altitude of not less than 1,500 feet; thereafter the altitude to be determined by the officer conducting the training, but not less than 750 feet without further authority." This revision provided the authority under which jumps could be made at altitudes considered practical and commensurate with those made in combat. Returning to Lawson Field after training on the towers, two of which were later purchased by the U.S. Army and installed at Fort Benning, the men of the Parachute Test Platoon were soon briefed for their first aircraft jumps. The first two jumps, explained the platoon officer, were to be "tap-outs," when each individual would jump only on the command of the warrant officer jump master, who would give the students a short kick on the leg. The third jump would be rapid exits following the first man out, and two more jumps would be made with the entire platoon jumping simultaneously from three aircraft to assemble on the ground and attack a simulated enemy position.

The first descents by the Parachute Test Platoon from aircraft in flight were made on 13 August 1940, from Douglas C-33 twin engine, low-wing cargo aircraft. Each man was issued with a jump suit and jump boots, and as headgear wore the standard khaki A-2 flying helmet. Each parachutist wore the Army Air Corps T-4 static line back pack parachute and, in addition, an emergency test-type parachute strapped to his chest. On the first day, the first man out of the B-18 flying at 455m (1,500 ft) over Lawson Field was Ryder. The second man was paralyzed with fear when he got to the exit door and nothing or no one could persuade him to jump, but the other men of the Parachute Test Platoon made their jumps without further incident. On the next jump, one paratrooper to prove he meant business when he reached the door yelled "Geronimo," a catchword that has stuck with American paratroopers ever since. The initial "mass jump" was made on 29 August before an imposing assembly of high-ranking officers at Lawson Field. All were agreed that the "airborne method" would work, and the Parachute Test Platoon was to comprise the first intake of the U.S. Army's first parachute unit, the 501st Parachute Infantry Battalion, which was shortly to be assembled at Fort Benning. Major (later Major General) William W. Miley was selected as battalion commander.

Probably the greatest single impetus to airborne development in the U.S.A. was provided by the German invasion of Crete in May 1941. Within two months the Army Air Forces (renamed from the Army Air Corps in June 1941) began experimenting with gliders for the transportation of men and matériel, and the following month the War Department G-3 called on the Army Air Forces to develop new cargo aircraft for an airborne combat team, to consist of an infantry battalion, an anti-tank company, a field artillery battery and a medical detachment. The first air-landing unit of the U.S. Army was activated on 1 July 1941 at Fort Kobbe, Panama Canal Zone, and was designated as the 550th Infantry Airborne Battalion, with an authorized strength of 22 officers and 550 enlisted men. Lieutenant Colonel (later Major General) Harris M. Melaskey was selected as the first commanding officer of the unit. A short time later, the 550th was reinforced by the attachment of Company "C," 501st Parachute Infantry Battalion, which had completed its training at Fort Benning.

In these early days assault maneuvers concentrated on dropping the parachute element first followed by air-landing troops. Only a limited number of aircraft were available for training purposes, these being B-18s, B-18As and Douglas C-39s. In August 1941, the reinforced 550th emplaned in 74 B-18s and four C-39s at Howard Field, Canal Zone, moving in two lifts, with the parachute element spearheading the attack echelon. The objective was to "capture" an auxiliary field near Rio Hato. By the time the air-landing element reached the target area (one hour after the parachute drop), the airfield had been "secured" by the parachutists and was held for the landing of the transport aircraft. The entire operation was termed "a complete success" by the many high-ranking officers and notables present. On 16 October 1941, a special unit – the 88th Infantry Battalion – was assigned for the study of the testing, organization, equipment, logistics, training and development of airborne units.

Meanwhile, Lieutenant Colonel William C. Lee was assigned to the command of the Provisional Parachute Headquarters, whose task it was to raise the parachute battalions. "Bill" Lee is regarded as the "father of U.S. airborne forces," and he and his team made a vigorous search of U.S. Army infantry units in training to enlist parachute volunteers. Commanding officers were more than reluctant to lose their best officers and NCOs but Lee had succeeded in raising the 501st, 502nd, 503rd and 504th Parachute Battalions by the end of the year. The Parachute Group devised an intensive technical parachute training course. This course was divided into two phases:

1) parachute maintenance, which included folding, packing, inspection and repair; and

2) jump training, which included proper exit from the aeroplane, manipulations of the parachute in the air and on the ground, and safe landings in water, on trees, etc. The second phase, or battalion training, included field exercises in which the battalion operated on independent missions.

Early in 1941 Miley was hell-bent on proving that his paratroopers of the 501st Parachute Infantry Battalion were different from other foot-sloggers in the U.S. Army. The only recognition each man had for having completed parachute training was a certificate, signed by Miley himself, attesting to the fact that this holder was jump-qualified. Army uniform regulations in force at the time required all ranks to wear low-cut shoes and the round "flying saucer" service hat with the Class A or dress uniform. In an effort to raise morale and give his battalion something no other infantry outfit had, Miley issued orders authorizing his troops to wear their jumping boots in place of the regulation low-cut shoes with their dress uniform. He also authorized them to tuck the trouser legs into the tops of the boots, so that the entire boot could be seen. And officers of the battalion were permitted to wear the numerals "501" atop the brass crossed-rifle infantry insignia on their uniforms. Later, Miley also authorized wearing of the foldable "overseas" hat, with a special circular-shaped cloth insignia a little larger than a silver dollar sewn on the left front of it. This insignia, which became known as the hat patch, consisted of a large white parachute emblazoned on a solid field of infantry blue.

The Army's Department of Heraldry came up with an idea for a brevet for parachute-qualified troops. Miley did not like the design, so he delegated one of his officers, Lieutenant William P. Yarborough, to try some recommendations and sketches. The best of these was that of a bold parachute with strong eagle-like wings extending from the base of the parachute and curving upward to touch the canopy. With the help of Lee, Yarborough went to Washington and cutting through the red tape did not return to the battalion until he had 350 silver badges in his suitcase. Yarborough also suggested a cloth, oval-shaped wing background bearing the battalion's colors of blue and red to be placed under the wings on the uniform to make the small badge stand out and, at the same time,

give regimental identity to the wearer. Initially, these wing backgrounds were not officially sanctioned by the U.S. Army. As new units were formed, they adopted the practise of wearing backgrounds bearing their unit colors. Eventually, U.S. Army uniform and insignia regulations were modified to acknowledge and authorize the backgrounds.

Yarborough next designed a smart two-piece jump suit combat uniform to replace the standard Army Air Forces one-piece mechanic's coveralls with which the 501st had been issued as a training and field uniform. The main deficiency in these coveralls was a lack of suitable pockets. In his design, Yarborough slanted the pockets downward, so they could be accessible even while the jumper was wearing his parachute harness. The two large pockets on the trouser legs would later serve as the paratrooper's combat pack – to be stuffed full of everything from socks to hand grenades. Yarborough's jump suit was issued to parachute troops until 1945, when it was replaced by the standard U.S. Army-issue combat fatigues that came into being in 1944. It was later resurrected in 1963, at Fort Bragg, for issue to the U.S. Army "Green Beret" Special Forces, whose commander by no form of coincidence was Major General William P. Yarborough. Earlier that same year, and with the approval of President John F. Kennedy, Yarborough had introduced the green beret for wear by Special Forces.

Yarborough also designed the American paratrooper's jump boots, regarded by all as

Right: The basic American paratrooper's brevet designed in 1941 by William Yarborough and still worn today.

Facing page: The paratrooper, 1941-style; the static-line parachute on his back is a T-3 model.

even more of a status symbol than the jump-qualified wings. The boots first used by the 501st were borrowed from the artillery, and their main danger was a buckle and strap that crossed the main instep. If the straps became undone there was a danger of entanglement with the paratrooper's rigging lines as he fell from the aeroplane before his canopy was fully developed. The buckle and strap were replaced with heavy-duty stitching, which also had the effect of strengthening the instep. Yarborough now added a slightly bubble-shaped, leather-covered metal toe to the boot for additional safety. Finally, he cut back the leading edge of the heel to a 45-degree angle. This new streamlined version of the jump boot was much safer to wear.

Lee's assignment at Fort Benning was to jump-train each new parachute battalion the U.S. Army formed. He was also charged with developing suitable tables of organization and equipment, and a practical doctrine for the employment of parachute troops. At that time Lee took a crash course in parachute jumping from his own staff of instructors. Con-struction of the 76m (250 ft) steel jumping towers transferred from Hightstown was well under way at Fort Benning when the U.S. Army came into possession of a copy of the German parachute training handbook. The Germans had built a same-size wooden mock-up of the aft section of the Ju 52/3m, complete with open jumping door. In using the aircraft mock-up at their parachute school at Stendal near Berlin, German student paratroopers were required to jump out of its door and down onto a tumbling mat positioned a few feet below the door.

The Americans went one better by constructing the framework of a door along a platform supported by 10·4m (34 ft) tele-phone poles. Having climbed a ladder onto the platform of the mock-up, an instructor connected his two long riser straps to a metal wheel resting atop a steel cable, which extended from the jumping door out horizontally some 46m (150 feet) to where it was anchored to the top of a shorter telephone pole. The canopy had been re-moved from the parachute harness, and on the word "Go" the student jumped out of the door and fell nearly three-quarters of the way to the ground. At that point, the fully extended risers abruptly stopped his fall, simulating the parachute's opening. The wheel to which his risers were connected then began riding down the slanting cable, carrying him to a pile of earth at the end of the cable just in front of the anchor pole.

82D Airborne Division

SHOULDER SLEEVE INSIGNIA

Approved by telegram from the Adjutant General, A.E.F. 21 October 1918 and 21 February 1919.

DESCRIPTION

Upon a red square 2⅝ inches on a side a blue disc 1¾ inches in diameter with the letters AA in white. The inner elements of the two A's vertical lines and the outer elements arcs of a circle 1⅝ inches in diameter, elements of letters ⅛ inch in width. On a tab placed above the square the word "Airborne" in white on a blue background.

DISTINCTIVE UNIT INSIGNIA

Approved 23 October 1942

DESCRIPTION

A silver color metal and enamel device 1⅛ inches in height consisting of a pair of blue enamel stylized wings, tips down, surmounted by a white enamel fleur-de-lis supported by a blue enamel scroll inscribed 'In Air, On Land' in silver color metal letters.

SYMBOLISM

The fleur-de-lis is representative of the battle honors earned in France during World War I. The wings are symbolic of the Division's mission. The motto is expressive of the personnel of the organization either on land or in the air.

NON-COLOR BEARING UNITS OF THE DIVISION

Headquarters and Headquarters Company
Administration Company
Brigades of the Division

Military Police Company
Support Command of the Division
Chemical Company

The Sky Legions

On 30 January 1942, the War Department directed that four parachute regiments be constituted. The 503rd Parachute Infantry Regiment was formed from the 503rd and 504th Parachute Battalions, and received priority on personnel and equipment during the formation. The 502nd Parachute Infantry Regiment had an initial strength of less than 900 men and did not reach its authorized strength until enough men had completed basic parachute training to make up the numbers. Lieutenant Colonel George P. Howell became commander of the 502nd Regiment and Colonel Miley was appointed to the command of the 503rd Regiment, leaving his 501st Battalion which was concentrated in Panama. The 504th Parachute Infantry Regiment was formed on 1 May under Lieutenant Colonel Reuben H. Tucker, and on 6 July the 505th Parachute Infantry Regiment followed under Lieutenant Colonel James M. Gavin. By this time Airborne Command had been set up, by order of Lieutenant General Leslie J. McNair, commander of U.S. Army Ground Forces. Colonel "Bill" Lee was named its commander. All parachute units in existence, plus the 88th Infantry Airborne Battalion, were made part of Lee's command formation.

One of Lee's objectives was to form an airborne division, and he hastened to Washington with Gavin – Lee's plans and training officer before Gavin was appointed to the 505th – but the Washington staff seemed rather skeptical about the whole idea. Finally it was agreed that the formation of an airborne division was feasible from an existing division which had completed its basic training and which was stationed in an area near one or two airfields where flying weather was generally good. The one division that met all these requirements was the 82nd Division stationed at Camp Claiborne, Louisiana, which turned "airborne" on 26 March 1942. At that time the division, which had previously been assigned to the armored role, was commanded by Major General Omar N. Bradley. The 82nd already had a great reputation: recruited from all states of the Union in World War I, it was designated the 82nd "All American" Infantry Division.

The 82nd Division was to be converted by the addition of two parachute infantry regiments, making one of the infantry regiments glider-borne, and replacing all heavy equipment throughout the division with lighter substitutes that could be delivered by glider or parachute. From the division a cadre was set aside for the 101st Airborne Division. The two new parachute regiments scheduled for the 82nd were the 504th and 505th. After a few months Bradley went on to another division and Major General Matthew B. Ridgway succeeded to the command on 26 June 1942. On 15 August the 82nd was formally designated as an airborne division. The 82nd surrendered at least half its strength to form the 101st Airborne Division. Those personnel of the 82nd who did not care for the idea of jumping out of aircraft were transferred to the 98th Infantry Divison. The 82nd "All American" Airborne Division moved to Fort Bragg, North Carolina, and was in full training with the glider elements so far assembled by

Above: America's original paratroopers demonstrate their paces in Washington D.C. in 1941. The parachute arm of the Army had come a long way from the early days of the Parachute Test Platoon in 1940.

Far left: The official certificate from the Institute of Heraldry, U.S. Army, authorizing the 82nd Airborne Division's "All American" sleeve patch, 23 October 1942.

October 1942. The Parachute Training School was at Fort Benning.

Shortly after the establishment of Lee's Airborne Command at Fort Benning, the Army Air Forces established their counterpart, Air Transport Command, at Short Field, near Indianapolis, Indiana. The Army Air Forces named Colonel Fred C. Borum as the commanding officer of Air Transport Command: his task was to train the pilots who would fly the aircraft and gliders used by the airborne troops. Borum started off with only 56 transport aircraft, but he was promised 600 transports and 2,000 gliders in the immediate future. The aeroplane to be used by the pilots of the Troop Carrier Command in World War II was the Douglas C-47 Skytrain, or Dakota as it was universally known. The C-47, which had a payload capacity of 2,722 kg (6,000 lb), carried 28 paratroopers who jumped through one door situated on the port side of the fuselage. The Curtiss C-46 Commando came on the scene in mid-1942, and had a payload of 4,763 kg (10,500 lb) and jump doors on both sides of the fuselage. Because of its greater lift capacity and vulnerability to ground fire, the C-46 was employed mainly as a supply type, but it did drop paratroopers on the Rhine-crossing operation in March 1945.

Lee attached great importance to the development of glider-borne forces. The glider was seen as the means of carrying not only airborne infantry but support weapons and equipment such as the 75mm pack howitzer, a mountain gun which was to be ideal as airborne artillery and as an anti-tank gun, as well as the soon-to-be-famous Willys Jeep. Many glider prototypes were tried out at Wright Field, Ohio but the model finally settled on was the Waco XCG-4, which entered production as the CG-4A. The fuselage was constructed of small-gauge steel tubing with plywood flooring and a thin canvas skin covering its entire body. Just slightly smaller than its C-47 tow ship, its entire load-carrying capacity was 1,724 kg (3,800 lb) of cargo or 15 fully equipped combat soldiers (including the crew of two). Troops entered the glider through a small door positioned at the port side. The glider's hinged nose section, containing the pilot and co-pilot's compartment, could be raised to facilitate loading of the heavier weapons and equipment. A typical mixed load was six men and one 1/4-ton Jeep.

Like many other aspects of the great American war production effort on the Home Front, some unlikely manufacturers turned their hands to turning out war machines and

Right: A Waco CG-4A glider tries a landing with parachute arrester gear, Clinton County Air Base, Ohio, 1942. This was the standard U.S. glider in World War II.

Left: G.I.s demonstrate loading a jeep through the nose-opening of a Waco CG-4A glider. The jeep was the Airborne man's only means of transport.

equipment. Furniture factories, as it happened, proved to be very suitable for the production of gliders, and some 13,900 CG-4As were produced between 1942 and 1945. Glider training centers were established at Sedalia, Missouri, at Alliance, Nebraska, and at Laurinburg-Maxton Army Air Base in North Carolina. The North Carolina base became the largest of the three and was the center of all U.S. Army glider training activities. Infantry units were stationed at each of the three bases to receive instruction in the use of the flimsy aircraft. Altogether some 10,000 American glider pilots were trained during the war. Most experienced airborne men of the World War II era considered that riding in a glider was more hazardous than jumping by parachute. Unlike paratroopers, glider troops were not volunteers, and it was not until July of 1944 that "the Glider Riders" (the title of a popular song dedicated to these troops) were given equal special duty pay as the jumpers – $50 per month for enlisted men and $100 per month for officers.

The first U.S. Army organization designated as a glider infantry unit was the 88th Infantry Airborne Battalion. While at Fort Bragg this battalion was enlarged to 1,000 men in May of 1942 and renamed the 88th Glider Infantry Regiment. Eleven glider infantry regiments, plus one separate glider infantry battalion, were formed by the U.S. Army during the

war. Compared with the parachute regiments, which had 1,958 men organized into three battalions apiece, the glider regiments were smaller. Each had 1,605 men organized into only two battalions. When the 82nd Airborne Division commenced training in earnest at Fort Bragg, the formation consisted of the 325th and 326th Glider Field Artillery Battalions, the 504th Parachute Infantry Regiment, and the 376th Parachute Field Artillery Battalion. The engineer element was constituted by two companies of glider troops and one of parachutists. On 12 February 1943, the 505th Parachute Infantry Regiment replaced the 326th Glider Infantry Regiment, and Company "B" of the 307th Airborne Engineer Battalion was converted from glider to parachute status; the 456th Parachute Field Artillery was also added to the division's order of battle.

When he first reported to Camp Claiborne as Bradley's assistant, Ridgway admitted that he did not know the first thing about airborne warfare, but quickly impressed his personality on the 82nd Airborne Division. Ridgway had the noble air of a Shakespearean actor; deeply religious, his mild and graceful manners belied the ruthless thoroughness with which he

Left: Major General Matthew B. Ridgway, the first commanding general of the 82nd Airborne Division in 1942.

pursued the soldier's trade. He had been born at Fort Monroe, Virginia, in 1895. He was the son of Colonel Thomas Ridgway, who in 1900 had gone out to China during the Boxer Rebellion to take over a battery of horse-drawn guns in the siege of Peking. Young Ridgway entered West Point on 14 June 1913, but after graduating in the class of 1917 he did not go overseas in World War I. In the inter-war years, Ridgway climbed through the grades as was usual for an officer destined for top command. At the time of Pearl Harbor in December 1941, Major Ridgway was serving in the War Plans Division of the War Department in Washington.

Shortly after he took over the 82nd Airborne Division, Ridgway decided it was time he reported to Fort Benning to make his first parachute jump. Brigadier General Joe Swing, the 82nd's artillery commander, went with him for the same purpose. At Bragg they met "Bud" Miley, who promised to check them out as parachutists. In *Soldier: The Memoirs of Matthew B. Ridgway*, the general recounts his first experience of the noble art of parachuting:

"Many men have described the wonderful sensation of a parachute drop – the leap into the roaring wind, the hard shock of the opening that is like the blow of a club across the shoulders, and after that the wonderful silence, the motionless hanging in the sky while the earth swims up beneath you – trees and rocks growing bigger and nearer. And then – Wham! – the tumbling, bruising roll of the landing. Whatever the sergeant had told me about guiding my body straight down, stopping oscillation by pulling on the risers, I had forgotten. I hit going backward and went over on my head with a tooth-rattling crash. I made quite a speech to my officers later about the beautiful feeling of serenity and peace you feel while going down. I didn't mention that the landing was about like jumping off the top of a freight car, traveling at thirty-five miles an hour, on to a hard clay roadbed."

Lee, who had just returned from England after studying airborne training methods, was given command of the 101st Airborne Division on the same day that the 82nd went airborne, namely 15 August 1942. Lee's chief-of-staff was Colonel Maxwell D. Taylor, who spoke fluent Japanese and who had made a special study of the Japanese military machine but who would find no use for this particular expertise where the "Screaming Eagles" were

destined to serve. The 101st's assistant division commander was Brigadier General Don F. Pratt. When Lee first arrived at Camp Claiborne to review his volunteers, he announced:

"The 101st . . . has no history, but it has a rendezvous with destiny. Like the early American pioneers whose invincible courage was the foundation of this Nation, we have broken with the past and its traditions to establish our claim to the future. Due to the nature of our armament and the tactics in which we shall perfect ourselves, we shall be called upon to carry out operations of far-reaching military importance, and we shall habitually go into action when the need is immediate and extreme."

The "Screaming Eagles" were initially allocated the 502nd Parachute Infantry Regiment and two glider regiments, and in October 1942 moved with the 82nd to Fort Bragg where the two airborne divisions were given intensive combat training. The month of October also witnessed the departure of the first parachute unit to the war: the 503rd Parachute Infantry Regiment, which headed to the Pacific theater and was first stationed in Australia. In March of 1943, Fort Bragg was visited by Anthony Eden (the British Foreign Secretary), Field Marshal Sir John Dill (a former Chief of the Imperial General Staff and at that time heading the British joint staff mission in Washington), and General George Marshall (the American Chief-of-Staff). The visitors witnessed the 82nd and 101st Airborne Divisions make a simulated "attack" in the Fort Bragg area. Gavin later recalled an especially warm handshake and "good luck" from Eden. Unlike Gavin, Eden knew where the 82nd's first combat posting would be and that the division's first operational jump would be over the American beach-heads in Sicily a few months later.

On 25 February the 11th Airborne Division was formed at Camp Mackall, Hoffman, North Carolina. Major General Joseph M. Swing was transferred from the 82nd to be its commander. Like the 82nd and 101st, the 11th Airborne was initially composed of only one parachute and two glider infantry regiments. These units were the 511th Parachute Infantry Regiment, and the 187th and 188th Glider Infantry Regiments. The "Angels," as the 11th Airborne Division was called, was shortly joined at Camp Mackall by the Headquarters Airborne Command, which moved from Fort Bragg. The second division to be born at Mackall was the 17th "Thunder from Heaven" Airborne Division, which was also known as the "Talons." Under the command of newly promoted Major General William M. Miley, the 17th was activated on 15 April 1943. Major maneuver elements of the division were the 513th Parachute Infantry Regiment, and the 193rd and 194th Glider Infantry Regiments, both born on the same day as the division.

Now with four divisions, the American "airborne effort" had come a long way since the Parachute Test Platoon days of 1940. A tract of land had been purchased in Alabama, across the border from Fort Benning, Georgia, for training maneuvers, and this area included target ranges and jump grounds. Most people who soldiered at Fort Benning called it the "Frying Pan." Situated near the Chattahoochee River, the training ground abounded in tall pine trees, swamps and waterways. At Fort Benning itself there were two rows of wooden barracks and some tented accommodation. The two barracks faced each other, forming a street down the center. At one end, the mess hall ran at right angles with the company street, forming a large "T." At the other end, and set apart from the company street, were the latrines; then farther down the hill, and closer to the blacktop road, was the P.X. complete with one-armed bandits.

If the recruits were looking for a more exciting time than the P.X. could provide during training breaks, they caught a bus to Phoenix City. On one occasion a squad of troopers was involved in a brawl at a roadside inn called Cotton Fish Camp and escorted at gun point to the camp by state police. It was a Saturday evening, and Lieutenant Colonel Gavin assembled the entire 505th and led them on an all-night march down through the canebrakes in the bottoms of the Chattahoochee. At daylight Gavin organized a supply drop and that evening marched them back to the camp. The Battle of Cotton Fish Camp might be said to be the 505th's first campaign honor. The soil in the area was almost grassless and the sandy surfaces caused much aggravation to the troopers. Training runs and press-ups for dereliction of duty were the orders of the day. As one trooper who joined the "Screaming Eagles" later wrote:

"Five o'clock the following morning we fell out, stripped to the waist, to begin our first day as paratroopers. Every morning after this, rain or shine, we fell out, wearing only jump boots and pants, naked from the waist up. It was still dark as we answered to roll call, and after everyone was accounted for, we were told that this was the first step in separating the men from the boys. We were then given the order to double-time, and we started running in step to the cadence count of the T-shirted sergeant, down the sandy road of the Frying Pan and onto the black top road leading toward the Alabama Ferryboat landing on the Chattahoochee River. After a while I began to breathe pretty hard, but I knew that my second wind would come soon and running would seem easier. We all expected the non-com to give quick march pretty soon, but we kept going on and on without any sign of the break we were used to getting in the regular infantry. Our feet beat a steady slapping tattoo on the asphalt, and with the sergeant setting the pace, we moved as a single body over the road through the early hours of the morning. After a few more miles my body seemed to be operating on its own, my legs driving a steady rhythm, my chest sucking in and letting out deep lungfuls of air, while I retreated mentally to the inner corner of my brain to relax in thought and go along for the ride. "Making a wide circuit of the countryside, we were heading back toward the Frying Pan when the man in front of me began to weave back and forth a little; this brought me back to reality. In a little while he began to stagger quite a bit. Suddenly he pitched forward on his face and rolled over on his back. The men behind him spread out and ran by on either side while the sergeant yelled for us to keep going and not pay any attention to him. Two more men fell out long before we reached the center of the field, and the same orders were given – keep going and leave him alone. Once in the field we were immediately formed into ranks and began calisthenics, starting with side-straddle hops and going the full course to push-ups and other exercises, to cool off after our six-mile run. "Double-timing back to the company area, we fell out for breakfast . . ." (Donald Burgett. *Currahee: We Stand Alone*)

Each trooper was taught how to pack his own parachute for his five qualifying parachute jumps. After the first phase of intensive training the next stage was to better acquaint the men with getting out of the aeroplane, controlling the parachute in the air, and landing without getting hurt. This was achieved jumping from a series of

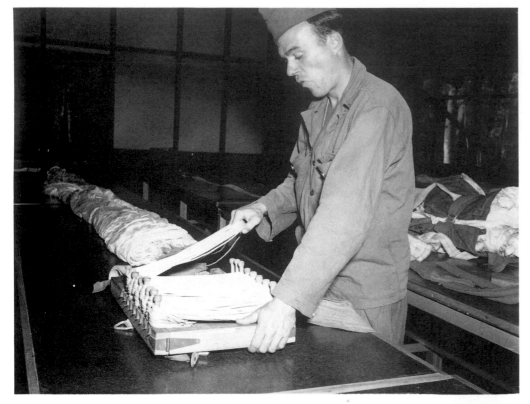

platforms starting with a controlled jump in a harness from 4·6m (15 ft) to the 76m (250 ft) tower jump first tried out by the Parachute Test Platoon. Before the first aircraft jump each man took a turn at putting on a parachute, lying on the ground and being blown across the field after the canopy was filled by wind from an aero engine propeller. This was to teach them how to react if, when after making a real jump, the canopy was inflated by the wind causing the man to be dragged along the ground. This could be a painful experience and was avoided by a swift twist and tap on the harness release box, thus releasing the man from the whole parachute outfit.

Once a stick of paratroopers was aboard the C-47 and the aeroplane was approaching the dropping zone, the jump master wearing a rip-cord parachute gave the order "Stand up and hook up." The troopers rose from the benches and attached the D-ring on the end of the static line to a clip on an overhead rail beneath the ceiling of the fuselage. "Check equipment" was the next order. The jumpers went through the formalities of checking that the release boxes of their harnesses were firmly closed and the ties of the parachute pack of the man in front were not broken. "Sound off" came next and the last man in the stick nearest the cockpit yelled "Twelve O.K." (or whatever number he happened to be) and slapped the man ahead of him on the shoulder. He in turn called out "Eleven O.K." and so on. This routine was not easy to achieve with the men staggering as the aircraft lurched from side to side, and the roar of the engines made voices difficult to hear.

When the pilot switched on a red light, the jump master barked "Stand in the door, close it up tight." The first man pivoted into the doorway, placed his hands on either side of the opening and extended his left foot forward. After one of the Parachute Test Platoon had refused to jump in 1940, paratroopers were always told to look ahead and never down at the ground. The next man put his right foot against the first trooper's right foot and his left in behind the lead man. This way he would be ready to pivot to his right into the door as soon as the first man jumped and be ready to go as soon as the jump master tapped his leg. Receiving the signal, he would leap out of the door, turning left toward the tail of the aeroplane at the same time. Now the jump master was kneeling by the lower right side of the door looking at the ground. "Is everybody happy," he yelled. "Yeh," all yelled back.

On the green light signal, the jump master tapped the first man on the calf of the leg, and the man shot through the opening like a bullet. (It was important for the parachutist to push off with a very determined leap, as otherwise the prop wash of the aeroplane might drag him along the fuselage to the tail, causing painful burns to arms and legs.) The jumper's static line snapped taut and vibrated, like a hangman's rope on the gallows, and the parachute pack was left dangling from the aeroplane. The next man did a quick right pivot and snapped into the doorway; another tap on the leg, a whispered command "Go" and he too disappeared from sight. The men in the stick were moving forward, each keeping his left foot forward, the right one behind, like a boxer – never crossing the two. The next man went out, then the next until the entire stick had been despatched in a matter of seconds. The jumper experienced his first sense of relief when as in an instant the prop wash trailed away and his parachute canopy snapped open. He instantly reached for the risers and looked up – no blown panels, or broken or snarled rigging lines; if there were, or the canopy had just not developed, it was time to pull the free-fall parachute.

The jumper still had plenty to think about once the canopy had opened and the ground started rushing up to him. At worst he could be in a strong wind swinging from side to side through a half circle of 180 degrees, at best in a soft wind he could be suspended vertically making a gentle descent. Oscillation and drift direction could be controlled by manipulation of the appropriate risers. Having "looked up" the jumper had then to jerk his harness around to "make all round observation" and to take evasive action if there was a danger of collision between two or more of the parachutists. If the jumper was making a normal descent his companions in the air would appear to be going neither up nor down. Wind drift could be checked by watching the feet in relation to the ground. During training the jumper was coached down by an instructor with a megaphone who made terse but often reassuring comments about the trooper's antics in the air. Adopting what (under advice) he thought to be a good body position, the jumper hit the ground and tumbled over less than a minute after leaving the aeroplane. Four more jumps and the trooper was a fully-fledged paratrooper, and he would receive his wings. No matter what happened from then on, no one could take that away from him.

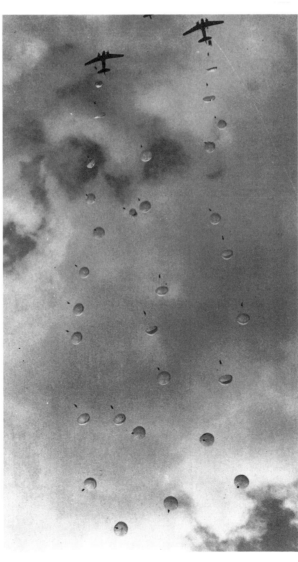

Facing page, top: Packing a T-5 parachute (1944).

Facing page, below: A stick of 82nd Airborne Division paratroopers emplane in a C-47 for a jump rehearsal in French Morocco during June 1943 for the invasion of Sicily.

Above: The 82nd Airborne Division in training in North Africa in 1943. General Ridgway shows how it is done but he does not have far to fall.

Left: Dropping from C-47s on the same exercise.

The American T-type Parachute in World War II

The paratrooper's most essential item of equipment was unquestionably the parachute itself. In 1940 the Test Platoon jumped with the Army Air Corps T-4 parachute which was opened by a static line. This was an Irvin design with the then current three-hook fastening to the harness, and a large square back pack containing the canopy and rigging lines. The canopy was 8·53m (28 ft) in diameter, flat circular, and of conventional design and performance. The reserve was a large chest pack hooked to the front of the harness with snap hooks. The rigging lines came out of the top of the pack and ran to the shoulders of the main harness where they joined to it. The handle was on the right. The T-4 worked well even though it was of the type in which the canopy opened first, as were all aircrew life-saving parachutes at that time.

The T-5 assembly consisted of a 8.53m (28 ft) diameter canopy with as many panels, each panel being made up of four panel sections. The top or center of the canopy, which was known as the apex, contained a 0·46m (18 in) diameter hole to let the surplus air escape and keep the parachute from oscillating; it was supposed to, that is. Twenty-eight suspension (or rigging) lines, each 6·7m (22 ft) long, ran from the canopy to the four cotton-web risers; they were attached, seven each, to the risers by metal rings called connector links. The risers were actually the ends of the harness that were constructed in such a way as to loop around the body, pass through the crotch and back up to the shoulders again.

The unique construction of the harness had a tightening effect around the body much like Chinese finger cuffs, which absorbed the shock, rather than yanking up through the crotch. The harness also had a bellyband that

held the smaller reserve parachute in front of the wearer, and the wide part that fitted the seat was appropriately called the "saddle." A canvas-covered rectangular wire frame on the back, in which the canopy, suspension lines and part of the risers were stored, was called the pack tray. A 4·57m (15 ft) static line, attached from a cover on the pack tray to a cable inside the aeroplane, ripped the pack cover off as the trooper jumped free of the ship, pulling out the contents of the pack tray. The prop blast would then blow the parachute open and snap the break cord, tied between the static line and the apex of the canopy. The opening time for the parachute was not more than three seconds, which permitted paratroopers to make low altitude jumps in mass formation.

The T-7 replaced the T-5. Also designed from the start to be a static-line parachute, the T-7 demonstrated improved reliability in opening. It had a three-point harness, using snap hooks, and a wide canvas waistband to hold the pack close to the back. However, it was still canopy-first opening, and the shock was still there. The canopy was retained in the pack by a sort of canvas lid, which was held to the outer cover by a breakable line running around the flaps. The lid was firmly sewn to the static line, and the apex of the canopy was tied to it with a breakable line. The static line was stowed outside the pack and, on extending, pulled the canopy clear of the pack by breaking the retaining line around the pack. On a windy drop zone, the T-7 could be difficult to get out of. It did not have the shoulder releases of the later T-10, and required three separate snap hooks to be undone before the jumper was free. This was not easy to do when being dragged at speed along rough ground. The T-7, which in World War II was the standard American

Below left: Paratroopers based near Hungerford in Berkshire, England, October 1942. They will soon be leaving for North Africa.

Below center: Lone descent.

Below right: A mass training drop by the 82nd Airborne Division in North Africa in 1943. This photograph demonstrates the dangers of collision and entanglement in mid-air.

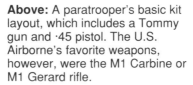

Above: A paratrooper's basic kit layout, which includes a Tommy gun and ·45 pistol. The U.S. Airborne's favorite weapons, however, were the M1 Carbine or M1 Gerard rifle.

Above right: 503rd Parachute Infantry in action on Noemfoor Island in December 1944.

parachute, was modified, however, to take a single release box.

The U.S. parachute infantry were more lightly armed than their "penguin" counterparts. The U.S. airborne favored carrying a ·45 caliber Thompson sub-machine gun behind the reserve parachute, tilted at an angle. The gun was ready when the men landed and could even be fired on the way down. The favorite weapon of the American paratrooper was, however, the ·30 caliber M1 carbine. This little rifle was not specifically intended for airborne use, but it was immediately adopted by the airborne arm and huge numbers were produced by American arms firms. In early 1942 a folding butt was introduced so that it could be carried on a parachutist and not interfere with his landing, and by 1945 some 150,000 of this type had been made. The M1 was easy to carry and to fire. It weighed only 2·47kg (5 lb 7 oz), yet it could be fitted with a 30-round magazine and was semi-automatic.

Later models were capable of firing automatic also, though the weapon was so light that on auto it could scarcely be held on target. The only drawback to the M1 was its lightweight bullet, which limited its effective range to about 180m (590 ft). Colt ·45 caliber pistols were drawn by officers, selected N.C.O.s and signalers.

The parachute infantrymen were also armed with the ·30 caliber Browning Automatic Rifle (BAR), the ·30 caliber M1 rifle, which like the M1 carbine was on wide distribution to the division, and the ·30 caliber M1C sniper rifle.

Heavier platoon support was provided by the ·30 caliber Browning light and heavy machine-guns, the 0·5 caliber Browning heavy machine-gun, and bazookas. These last were used to knock out armored vehicles. The 60mm (2·36 in) standard infantry mortar was cut down by exactly half to 29·9 kg (66 lb) for airborne use. The modified version of the 81mm (3·2 in) mortar was in fact designed for jungle use but the reduced range caused by the reduction in weight was a handicap both on jungle and airborne operations. As anti-tank artillery the towed 37mm gun was used by paratroopers, although it was not officially allocated to the division. The towed 57mm gun does appear in the official listing, however, as does the 75mm high-speed howitzer, introduced into service as a mountain weapon.

U.S. Army drop containers for weapons and equipment were used from the very beginning of the formation of airborne forces. The first models were rolled bundles. That type, together with variations on the basic theme, continued for many years. At the same time numerous experiments were tried in the search for the best design, and containers (usually made of metal in all shapes and sizes) appeared in the years between 1940 and 1943. The drawback of the system, which forced the soldier to find a container – dropped from specially fitted aircraft "bomb-racks" – before he was properly armed and equipped was quickly appreciated. The container could easily get hooked up under its aeroplane and carried back to base, or it might be dropped by some mishap miles away from the man's drop zone and fall into the hands of the enemy. Even in the best circumstances he

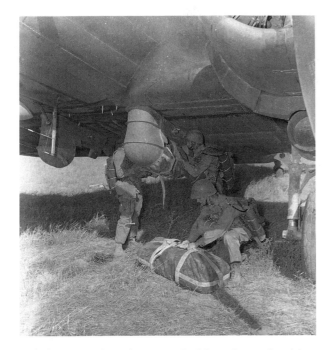

might spend as long as half an hour looking for it, and at night the task was virtually impossible.

When the British Army in 1940 experimented with the means of dropping weapons and equipment on the paratrooper, it devised the airborne kitbag and a weapons valise. The canvas kitbag would contain a sleeping bag, spare clothing, washing materials etc. or heavy items such as a 6-volt battery, and the valise either a rifle or the Bren light machine-gun, each of ·303 caliber. The kitbag was laced down the side for ease of opening, and the weapon valise was an envelope of thick felt material, roughly sewn along the seams and fitted with straps. A 6·1m (20 ft) rope was attached from the parachute harness to the top of the kitbag or to the center of the valise, so that it hung horizontally in mid-air. Either a kitbag or valise was strapped to the man's leg and the rope was paid out in mid-air, the jumper first making sure that there was no one beneath him. The "Prepare for action" drill, when the paratrooper secured his equipment, struggling down the aeroplane one man behind the other, clutching his kitbag or valise and keeping a firm grip on it, could be a strenuous and rather tiresome business. Carrying equipment did have one advantage, however. Since the container on the end of the rope hit the ground first and took part of the load off the parachute, the parachutist's own impact with the ground was considerably softened.

Like the British, the U.S. Army reckoned that a man should be able to carry at least 36·3 kg (80 lb) of equipment. The personal carrier handled by the American paratrooper was not, however, dropped by him on the end of a rope, but carried down on the man all the way. The Griswold container might aptly be described as a bundle and two could be carried, one to the front beneath the reserve parachute and one in the vicinity of the rear quarters. The U.S. T-type parachute allowed a slow enough rate of descent for this to be safe, and on landing the American paratrooper simply rolled over with his heavy encumbrances.

In World War II, as we have learned, heavier weapons and equipment were delivered mainly by glider, but some progress was made by the British airborne forces in dropping heavy items by parachute. The ultimate success did not come until long after the war, but by 1945 a certain amount of groundwork had been completed. Jeeps and anti-tank guns were dropped from Stirling bombers using special 9·75m (32 ft) diameter canopies in clusters. The jeep was fitted with elaborate frames above and below the vehicle to take the strains of both the parachute opening and landing. Various connectors helped the chassis to accept the unexpected shocks, and crash pans were rigged below to absorb the landing. The British 6-pounder anti-tank gun was rigged in the same way, though as its construction was more robust a simpler framework could be used.

Both jeep and gun were hung in the bomb bay of a Stirling from which the bomb doors had been removed. They hung well out into the slipstream making plenty of drag with the square shapes, and because of this shape they did not always fall straight. There was a tendency to somersault, and many tricks were tried to overcome this. One evil effect of a somersault was the cutting of rigging lines, and sometimes the collapse of a canopy. On rare occasions the entire suspension system was cut away and the whole load dropped to destruction into the drop zone. All manner of methods were used in combating the somersault menace, the most obvious one being to round off all the corners on the load so that rigging lines did not catch, and the somersault became harmless. A better idea was to tilt the load slightly forward and use the slipstream to correct the first tendency to roll. Jeep trailers were especially prone to somersaulting, and the cure was not found until after the war.

The Dakota, which was essentially a cargo-lifting aeroplane, could, of course, carry jeeps and other items of light equipment inside the fuselage, but this assignment was for air-landing, transportation purposes only.

Left: Loading bundles onto the specially fitted bomb racks of a C-47 in North Africa. When bundles and metal containers were dropped on the Sicily operation in July 1943, they were so widely dispersed on the ground that the U.S. Airborne resolved never to use this method of supply dropping again. After Sicily they carried heavy weights on their bodies and relied on gliders to bring in what they could not carry themselves.

Into the Wild Blue Yonder

When the independent 509th Parachute Infantry Battalion, commanded by Lieutenant Edson D. Raff, departed the U.S.A. in June 1943 for England in the converted luxury liner *Queen Mary*, the mission of these crack paratroopers was cloaked in secrecy. Raff, who was of stocky, diminutive stature – of ideal size and weight for a paratrooper in fact – was known as "Little Caesar" to his men. For the journey from Fort Bragg, all personnel took down their wings and airborne patches but somehow the news of their status got around and on docking in England they were greeted as a parachute battalion over Radio Berlin by the Anglo-Irish traitor, William Joyce ("Lord Haw-Haw"). The 509th set up a base on a country estate at Chilton Foliat in Wiltshire and participated in jump training with British airborne troops, who during 1943 formed two formations, the 1st and 6th Airborne Divisions. While Raff's men were busy jumping on drop zones in the north of England, Scotland and across the water in Northern Ireland, the Allied commanders were equally busy planning their next moves in the war against Germany and Italy.

Lieutenant General Dwight D. Eisenhower had been in England since 1942, and in company with President Roosevelt and the Chief-of-Staff, General George Marshall, he favored supporting Soviet demands for a "Second Front" in Europe by an all-out assault on the French coast. After November 1942, when the British 8th Army broke out from its positions at El Alamein in Egypt and advanced rapidly across the Western Desert, the British campaigned for an Allied amphibious landing in French North Africa to effect a link-up with the 8th Army in eastern Tunisia. The on-going objective was the invasion first of Sicily, then of Italy as the "soft underbelly" of Europe. After acrimonious debate, the Americans acceded to British demands, and in August of 1942 Eisenhower was appointed to the command of a considerable task force heading for the French colonies of north-west Africa, which were defended by military forces loyal to the pro-German Vichy government.

The plan for Operation "Torch" envisaged seizing Morocco, Algeria and Tunisia. The operation was divided into three elements. Direct from the U.S.A. came Major General George S. Patton's Western Task Force of 35,000 men in 39 vessels, escorted by a powerful U.S. naval squadron; its main target was Casablanca on the Moroccan Atlantic coast. U.S Major General Lloyd R. Fredendall's Central Task Force of 39,000 men in 47 ships, escorted by a strong British naval squadron came from the U.K.; its goal was Oran, on the Mediterranean coast. The Eastern Task Force, under Major General Charles W. Ryder, of 33,000 men in 34 ships, also arrived from England and was escorted by another naval force under British command; its objective was Algiers. Except for a British contingent – shortly after the invasion expanded into the British 1st Army– all troops in the initial assault were American. The British element included the British 1st Parachute Brigade (the 1st, 2nd and 3rd Battalions, the Parachute Regiment), scheduled to make drops as fighting developed.

Above: Landing barges operate from American transport ships off Fedala, French Morocco, during Operation "Torch," the Allied invasion of North Africa in November 1943.

Far left: Glider troops ride in a Waco CG-4A. The "glider riders" were not volunteers like the paratroopers but they were an essential, hard-hitting element of an airborne division.

Above: U.S. infantry waiting to go ashore in French Morocco during Operation "Torch." In the foreground a light infantry support gun is prepared for off-loading.

During the planning for "Torch," Major General Mark W. Clark, Eisenhower's deputy, called in his airborne advisor in London to assess the practicability of dropping American parachute troops in North Africa. The airborne staff officer was Major William P. Yarborough, newly arrived from Fort Bragg. After giving Yarborough the operational outline, Clark pointed a finger to a map of the French military airfields at La Senia and Tafaraoui, and the major agreed that the capture of these targets was within the capability of the 509th Parachute Infantry Battalion. Yarborough left London to apprise Raff of his mission. At Chilton Foliat, Raff learned that the destination of his battalion was Algeria and that his paratroop task force would fly over neutral Spain to make a night drop at Tafaraoui to destroy all French fighter planes which could oppose Allied amphibians and shipping at daybreak. Once Tafaraoui had been captured, one parachute company was to march north to La Senia before dawn and destroy all aircraft parked on the ground there.

Yarborough, who was to drop with the 509th, was responsible for the detailed pre-planning. One logistical problem was that the C-47 aircraft would run out of fuel just before reaching their target, so Yarborough directed that the aircraft would first land in the mud flats east of Oran. There they were to await a resupply of aviation fuel, to be brought ashore by U.S. ground units. Another problem was navigational. After taking off again, how would the pilots find their way in the dark to Tafaraoui? The answer to this tricky problem lay with a device called the "Rebecca-Eureka" radar aircraft guidance system. The "Rebecca" receiver was designed to be mounted in the aircraft while the suitcase-size "Eureka" transmitted a radar beam to be picked up by the airborne receiver unit. But how to place "Eureka" on the ground? This would be accomplished by an American officer making his entry into Algeria, using diplomatic credentials obtained from the Vichy French by the U.S. State Department. On the night of the drop, the officer would put "Eureka" into operation at Tafaraoui and send the critical radar guidance beam from the portable unit to the aircraft.

In the event, when the paratroopers were ready to emplane in their C-47s in England on 7 November, a signal from Gibraltar indicated that as the French were unlikely to resist Operation "Torch," the 509th was to air-land at La Senia, a shorter distance away than Tafaraoui. At 9.30 pm on 7 November 1942, the Paratroop Task Force (39 C-47 aircraft with 556 paratroopers on board) took off into the cold, overcast sky on the first leg of its 2,400 km (1,490 mile) aerial journey to Africa. In those days aircraft interiors were never very warm, and G.I. blankets were issued in case the heaters did not work. Turbulent headwinds were encountered over the Spanish mountains, and the C-47 formation became slightly dispersed. Colonel William C. Bentley, the overall U.S.A.A.F. commander, considered that his pilots would drift further apart in the darkness, and he made an attempt to coordinate their southward approach to North Africa.

This proved to be a forlorn hope, and Yarborough awoke at dawn to find that his aeroplane was over Spanish Morocco, some 320km (200 miles) west of Oran. Moreover, the aircraft was alone in the sky! Soon it was joined in flight by another lost C-47 and then by a third, which had landed in a field, then taken off hotly pursued along the ground by Spanish horsemen. The three-plane armada then flew eastward along the coast of Africa looking for Oran. A large bunch of 21 C-47s managed to regroup over the Mediterranean and made it to La Senia only to find that on the run-in, the French were far from friendly. Evading anti-aircraft fire, the paratroop aircraft flew a short distance away and landed on a dry salt lake, called Sebkra d'Oran, west of Oran. Meanwhile Raff's command ship was approaching La Senia, followed by five other C-47s. The paratroopers at Sebkra d'Oran came under fire from surrounding hills and two squads were despatched to deal with the snipers. Raff and his six-aircraft group were about to arrive over the fray when three tanks were observed lumbering in the general direction of the grounded aircraft.

Raff made an instant decision to jump with his stick, ordering the men in the other aircraft to follow suit. The terrain was hilly and very rocky, but the paratroopers landed safely with the exception of the colonel, who cracked two ribs on impact with a jagged rock. As luck would have it the three tanks were American, the ground forces having already taken Tafaraoui airfield. Now Yarborough's three-aircraft group arrived overhead and, spotting the C-47s at Sebkra d'Oran, the

major ordered his aircraft to land. Contacting Raff, who was writhing in pain with his injury and spitting blood, all the two American officers could conclude from their unsuccessful mission was that the French had after all decided to resist the invasion. Of the paratroop aircraft unaccounted for, two C-47s that had attempted to land at La Senia earlier that morning had been driven off by anti-aircraft fire, and after landing nearby all aboard had been taken prisoner by French soldiers. Two other planeloads landing at Fez aerodrome in French Morocco suffered the same fate. The remaining four aircraft were down in Spanish Morocco; the Spanish authorities quickly rounded up these paratroopers and air crews and hustled them off to gaol.

After surviving a hail of French bombs, shells and bullets at Tafaraoui, Raff was ordered to fly to Maison Blanche airfield, near Algiers, where he was to receive orders for his next mission. His instructions were received from the British commander, General Kenneth Anderson, whose brief for the 509th Battalion was to jump near the Tunisian border to secure the French airfield at Tebéssa. German parachute units were known to be reinforcing in the area of this airfield. The timing of the jump would be Sunday, 15 November. Early on the day before his battalion was to jump at Tebéssa, Raff learned from two friendly Frenchmen, who were paid in francs for their trouble, that there was a larger French airfield at Youks les Bains, also near the Tunisian border. On relaying this information to Anderson's headquarters, the American battalion was ordered first to drop on, and capture, Youks les Bains, detaching one company on landing to march eastward to occupy Tebéssa.

On the morning of 15 November, the men of the 509th rose, washed and shaved, breakfasted, checked their weapons and 'chuted up in the darkness. At 7.30 a.m. sharp, the first of the 22 C-47s was roaring down the runway at Maison Blanche. Soon the entire flight formed up into a V of Vs with an escort of British Supermarine Spitfires, heading out to sea following the coastline before the aircraft turned landward in a south-easterly direction toward the target area. Eight British Hawker Hurricane fighters joined the formation for the last leg of the journey. Over land again, the aircraft encountered thick clouds. With decreasing altitude on the fly-in to Youks les Bains, the men who had time to look out of the aircraft windows, spotted that they were flying over mountainous terrain.

On the red light signals, crew chiefs opened the doors of C-47s to be greeted by ice-cold blasts of air. On the green light signals, 350 men, including Jack Thompson, a civilian war correspondent who had not undergone jump training, parachuted onto a drop zone just short of the main runway at Youks les Bains. Fifteen troopers were injured on the drop, but Thompson emerged unscathed!

The French had sited their machine-guns and 75mm cannon around the airfield to afford interlocking fields of fire. The 509th would almost certainly have been annihilated but for the fact that the Germans had not, as expected, put in an appearance, and the French troops at Youks les Bains had decided to disregard Marshal Pétain's orders from Vichy and thus not fight. A French colonel of Zouaves approached Raff and, pinning his badge on the American officer's jacket, put his regiment at the disposal of the 509th. When the Americans reached Tebéssa that airfield, too, was taken without opposition. To the disappointment of Raff's men, the German *Fallschirmjäger* were nowhere to be seen. The American paratroopers, however, inflicted their first casualty on the enemy when a pilot of a Junkers Ju 88 attempted to land his bomber at Tebéssa. Unaware that the American paratroopers were dug in around the airfield, the German aeroplane flew into a withering blast of rifle fire and

burst into flames on landing.

With the winter rains turning the roads into muddy quagmires, the Allies thrust eastward in North Africa to meet the British 8th Army advancing across the Western Desert in Tunisia ground to a halt. Although Raff objected to the idea, his battalion during this period was fragmented and assigned piecemeal to tough infantry missions. (It is worth noting that at this time the Italian *Arditi*, who have received little mention in World War II annals, were wreaking havoc behind the Anglo-American lines, blowing up bridges, railway lines and attacking bridges, playing a similar role to the British Special Air Service Regiment [S.A.S.] which had been formed at Kabrit in Egypt in mid-1941.) On 21 December 1942 a bridge-busting mission was assigned to the 509th, and on that day Raff briefed 2nd Lieutenant Dan A. Deleo to lead a raiding party to blow up a bridge at the city of El Djem, spanning Tunisia's north-south coastal railroad line.

At 90 minutes to midnight on Christmas Eve, two C-47s carrying Deleo and his raiders took off from Maison Blanche airfield, bound for the drop zone 8km (5 miles) north of the El Djem bridge. Attached to the belly of each plane was a 91kg (200 lb) parachute bundle containing blocks of T.N.T. explosives. The paratroopers smoked as the two C-47s flew through the night and when the aircraft began

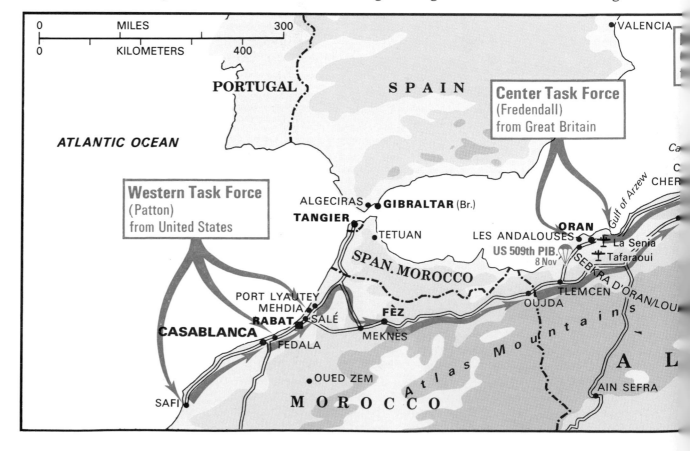

to lose height they knew they were approaching the target. It was midnight – Christmas Day – and when the green lights flashed on the C-47s discharged their human cargoes into the pitch darkness. Hitting the ground in the uncanny silence was welcome respite from the roar of the engines and the apprehension in the aircraft. Half an hour after the drop Deleo had accounted for all his men and detailed the parachutes to be buried. It took a party of raiders an hour to find one of the T.N.T. bundles but at 1.30 a.m. Deleo and his men were ready to move off on the approach march to the bridge. The raiders started marching south beside the tracks, their jump suit trousers pockets bulging with blocks of T.N.T.

After marching until daybreak, Deleo discovered the awful truth: the party had been dropped in the wrong place and was now located 32km (20 miles) south of the bridge. The lieutenant told his men that it was out of the question for them to march the distance back north to the bridge. Deleo spotted a small building, which he decided to blow across the track and at the same time take out a stretch of track. Demolition men quickly set to work rigging the building and all machinery in it for destruction. Meanwhile, several paratroopers placed blocks of T.N.T. at key points of track. All the explosives were linked together with a single length of

detonation cord, so that everything would go up at the same time. Just as the last few blocks of T.N.T. were put in place, look-outs reported that there were Germans approaching on foot from both directions. The demolition men hastened to complete their work, the ensuing deafening explosion rending the morning calm.

The plan to evacuate the 33 Americans was deceivingly simple on paper. They would simply walk back to the American lines, a distance of some 177km (110 miles) from the El Djem bridge! Breaking up into small teams, they shed all but their essential loads and made their way west. The Germans and Italians mounted a strenuous operation to hunt them down. Some Americans chose to walk by night and sleep by day but for others that slowed the pace, so they walked by daylight as well. At one point, Deleo and his party hijacked an Italian truck but after a journey of a couple of hours, the engine failed, so the fugitives were obliged to resume their journey on foot. Of the 33 men that started out on the El Djem bridge raid, only eight, including Deleo, ever made it back to friendly lines in Tunisia. Sixteen of the raiders were taken prisoner and eventually returned to their homes, some of them having made daring escapes from P.O.W. camps. The remaining nine men were never heard of again.

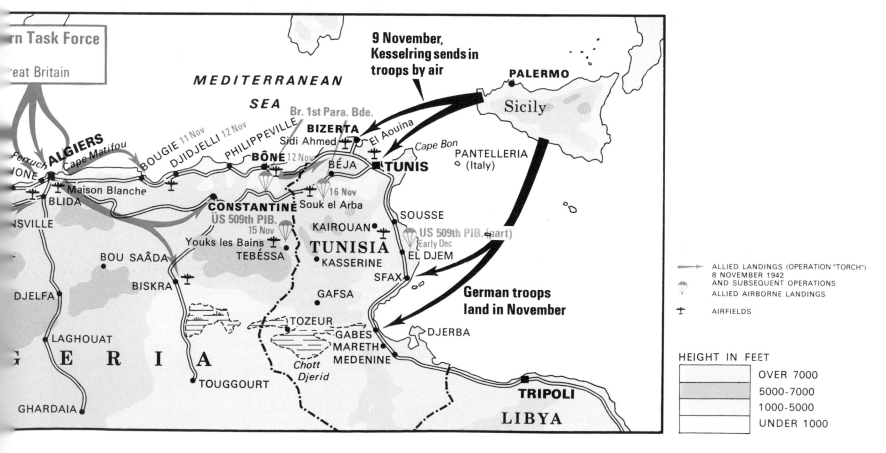

The Invasion of Sicily

A month before the termination of hostilities in Tunisia during May 1943, the 82nd Airborne Division commanded by Major General Matthew B. Ridgway departed from Fort Bragg and set sail for North Africa. The voyage was uneventful and the convoy came to a halt in Casablanca harbor, after a journey of 12 days on the high seas. Stepping ashore humping their heavy packs and weapons, the "All Americans" found Casablanca a city of contrasts, where east does meet west in head-on collision. While posters now proclaimed "Vive De Gaulle," continental Frenchmen, sitting in street cafés, sipped their wine and read their newspapers as if the war was hundreds of miles away. Moroccan soldiers mingled in the streets with Arabs, turbanned and clad in flowing white tunics, going about their business selling their wares.

After only a few days in Casablanca, the 82nd Airborne Division moved by aircraft, train and truck to Oujda. The parachutists of the division bivouacked at Oujda and the glider troops at Marnia near the Algerian border. The train ride from Casablanca to Oujda, a journey of eight days, was accomplished by the G.I.s in a depressing lack of style. The train was specially furnished with a series of well-ventilated boxes stuck on wheels. The cars had been built for transporting war materials, and were labeled "Forty Men or Eight Horses." The journey time was spent playing poker and crap, and eating C-rations liberally washed down by French wine. The Americans were of the opinion that Oujda was worth seeing, if there was nothing else to do and if life had become so unbearable

that one did not care what happened. Oujda and Marnia brought the division its first taste of extended field conditions. Troops lived in long straight rows of pup tents, interspersed with slit trenches. They slept on the ground or upon mattresses filled with straw. They squatted on the ground and ate from mess kits. They bathed under an open-air shower at the water point, and their steel helmets were especially useful for sponge baths, washing and shaving. They worked through the heat of the African days on the rolling treeless plain, and welcomed the cool of the evening.

Despite the climatic conditions, Oudja was turned into a spit and polish parade ground. On 18 May, the division's colors were dipped for Lieutenant General Mark Clark, Commanding General of the U.S. 5th Army, and the following day the men were filed again for Lieutenant General Carl "Tooey" Spaatz, who commanded the U.S.A.A.F. forces operating in the Mediterranean theater. Other VIPs followed, Generals Eisenhower, Patton and Bradley among them. Seven weeks were filled with long route marches, live-fire tactical training, hand-to-hand combat drills, parachute jumps and glider landings. Before the glider men of the 325th Glider Infantry Regiment, who had assembled under Brigadier General Charles L. Keerans, could conduct their airborne maneuvers, they had first to reconstruct their CG-4As, which had been delivered to North Africa stripped down and packed in wooden cases.

The British scheme to delay the launching of the "Second Front" in 1942 had worked.

Above: Parachute troops man a defensive position in Sicily.

Far left: American generals confer in North Africa in 1943. (Left to right) George Patton, Omar Bradley, Matthew Ridgway and Maxwell Taylor, who was artillery commander of the 82nd Airborne Division.

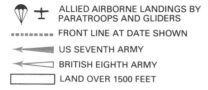

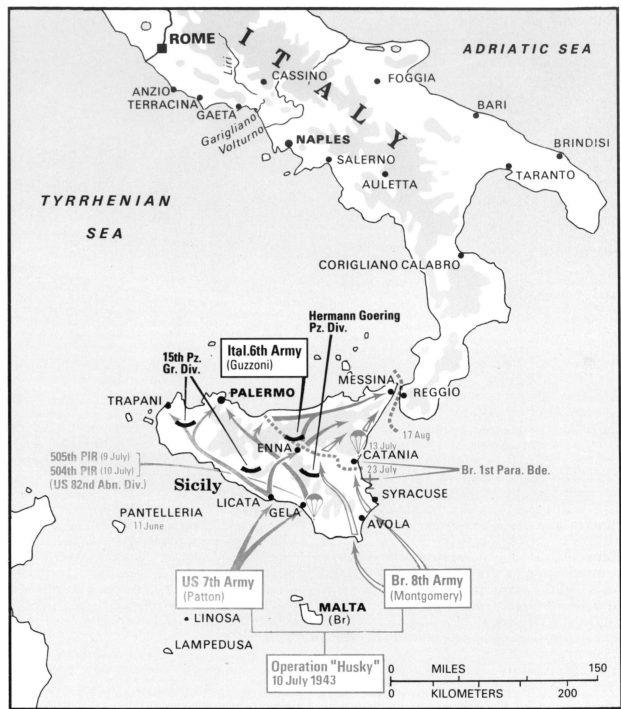

ALLIED AIRBORNE LANDINGS BY PARATROOPS AND GLIDERS

FRONT LINE AT DATE SHOWN

US SEVENTH ARMY

BRITISH EIGHTH ARMY

LAND OVER 1500 FEET

More time could be given to mounting the gigantic operation which would take place on 6 June 1944 – the invasion of Normandy by the largest amphibious force with air cover ever assembled in world history. Meanwhile with the eviction of the Axis forces from North Africa in May 1943, the Allies were ready to strike back into Europe, via the southern route into Sicily and then Italy. Some 200,000 Allied troops would participate in the initial assault on Sicily, which would take place before dawn on 10 July under a full moon. Paratroopers and glider troops would start landing a few hours before midnight on 9 July in order to be well in position before amphibious assault troops waded ashore the next morning. Operation "Husky" called for four separate airborne operations. Two of them were British by the 1st Airborne Division, including attached glider infantry battalions. The remaining two would be executed by the U.S. 82nd Airborne Division.

On 16 June, the 82nd left Oujda and Marnia for Kairouan in Tunisia, the third-ranking city in all Islam. In Tunisia, the Americans of the 82nd Division got a closer look at the war, for here the desert was strewn with the

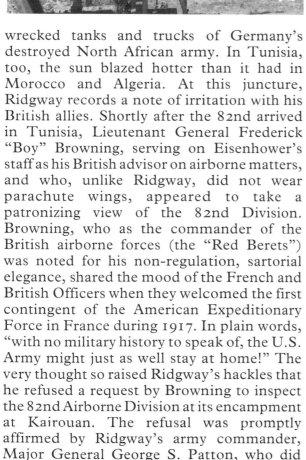

wrecked tanks and trucks of Germany's destroyed North African army. In Tunisia, too, the sun blazed hotter than it had in Morocco and Algeria. At this juncture, Ridgway records a note of irritation with his British allies. Shortly after the 82nd arrived in Tunisia, Lieutenant General Frederick "Boy" Browning, serving on Eisenhower's staff as his British advisor on airborne matters, and who, unlike Ridgway, did not wear parachute wings, appeared to take a patronizing view of the 82nd Division. Browning, who as the commander of the British airborne forces (the "Red Berets") was noted for his non-regulation, sartorial elegance, shared the mood of the French and British Officers when they welcomed the first contingent of the American Expeditionary Force in France during 1917. In plain words, "with no military history to speak of, the U.S. Army might just as well stay at home!" The very thought so raised Ridgway's hackles that he refused a request by Browning to inspect the 82nd Airborne Division at its encampment at Kairouan. The refusal was promptly affirmed by Ridgway's army commander, Major General George S. Patton, who did not like the British anyway.

Browning's attitude or motive was partly arrogant and partly patriotic. British parachute and glider troops, who were to land on the south-east coast of Sicily, in support of General Bernard Montgomery's 8th Army, were to play as large a part in the initial assault as the American airborne troops, who were to land ahead of the U.S. 1st Division of Patton's 7th Army on the south coast of the island. But the Royal Air Force was desperately short of parachute and tug aircraft. (Although the Red Berets had ridden in C-47s since mid-1942, they relied mainly on converted bombers such as the Armstrong Whitworth Whitley, Armstrong Whitworth Albemarle, Handley Page Halifax, Vickers Wellington and finally the Short Stirling for parachute descents and as tugs.) In short, Browning was out to obtain a larger share of the C-47s than he might freely be given!

The plan for Operation "Husky" called for the Red Berets to lead the attack against Sicily with an operation codenamed "Ladbroke" – a glider-landing just below Syracuse by 1,600 men of the 1st Air Landing Brigade. Their main objective was a bridge needed by Montgomery's troops for their advance into Syracuse. Hard on the heels of "Ladbroke" would come "Husky Number One," the first American airborne operation of the Sicilian campaign. About one hour after British glider troops had landed on the east coast, Colonel James Gavin and his reinforced 505th Regimental Combat Team would make a parachute assault into a large oval-shaped area that extended between Niscemi and Gela on Sicily's southern shores. Gavin's mission was to block all roads leading to beaches around Gela, and to occupy key points within the DZ so that it could be used again by the other parachute regiment of the division.

Above left: Paratroopers get into shape in the burning sun in preparation for airborne operations in Sicily.

Above: Parachute troops of the 82nd Airborne Division assemble at Kairouan airfield in Tunisia prior to the Sicily landings in July 1943. Waco CG-4A gliders are seen in the background.

"Husky Number Two" also involved the American troops, and was scheduled to take place after beach-heads had been well established on the island. Tentatively planned for the night of 11 July, this operation involved the parachute delivery of Colonel Reuben H. Tucker's 504th Regimental Combat Team into the DZ being secured by Gavin's force. The fourth and final large airborne operation, known as "Fustian," was to be a jump on the east coast by British paratroopers of the 1st and 2nd Parachute Brigades. Slated for the night of 13 July, this operation's primary purpose was to capture the Primosole bridge over the Simento River, north of Lentini. The overall British objective was to race across the Catania plain and capture Messina, thereby cutting off the only escape route to the mainland for the German and Italian troops. The U.S. 7th Army's overall objective was to proceed from the beach-heads along the southern coast before following the western and northern littorals to meet the British 8th Army in Messina.

The success of the British glider operation involving 2,000 troops depended on surprise. After taking off from Tunisian airfields on 9 July, to avoid enemy radar the R.A.F. tug pilots followed a devious route making for Delimara Point on the south-east coast of Malta, passing Cape Passero and from there onto the neighborhood of Cape Murro di Porco. Some 4km (2·5 miles) short of this promontory, the gliders were to be released. Seven of the gliders did not even make it over the North African coastline, but about 90 per cent of the tugs entered the second leg of their journey from Malta with their charges unscathed.

The wind had begun to rise from the south-east before the airborne formation passed Malta, and soon it increased to gale proportions. Conditions were made worse by the need to fly low to escape radar detection. Wind speeds reached 72km/h (45 mph), but then moderated to around 48km/h (30 mph) as the tugs approached Cape Passero. Several adverse factors led to about 60 per cent of the gliders being prematurely parted from the tugs. The sparse light of the quarter-moon was of little help to the tug navigators, but as the tug-glider combinations flew along the coast a wall of dust raised by the offshore wind blotted out the landmarks completely. Many of the tugs turned away too soon, the glider pilots blindly slipping their tow ropes before crash-landing in the sea. The more fortunate of the troops clinging to the floating wooden wreckages were picked up by the

Right: Another airborne rehearsal in North Africa for the Sicily drop.

passing assault craft; others, including the 1st Air Landing Brigade's commander, swam for the shore. Altogether 252 men were drowned. Only 52 of the gliders made landfall, and only 12 of them landed anywhere near the target.

As the men from the 505th Regimental Combat Team donned their parachutes, the more inquisitive among them must have been wondering where they would next set foot on land. This important piece of information was printed on a small slip of paper handed to each paratrooper before emplaning. This read:

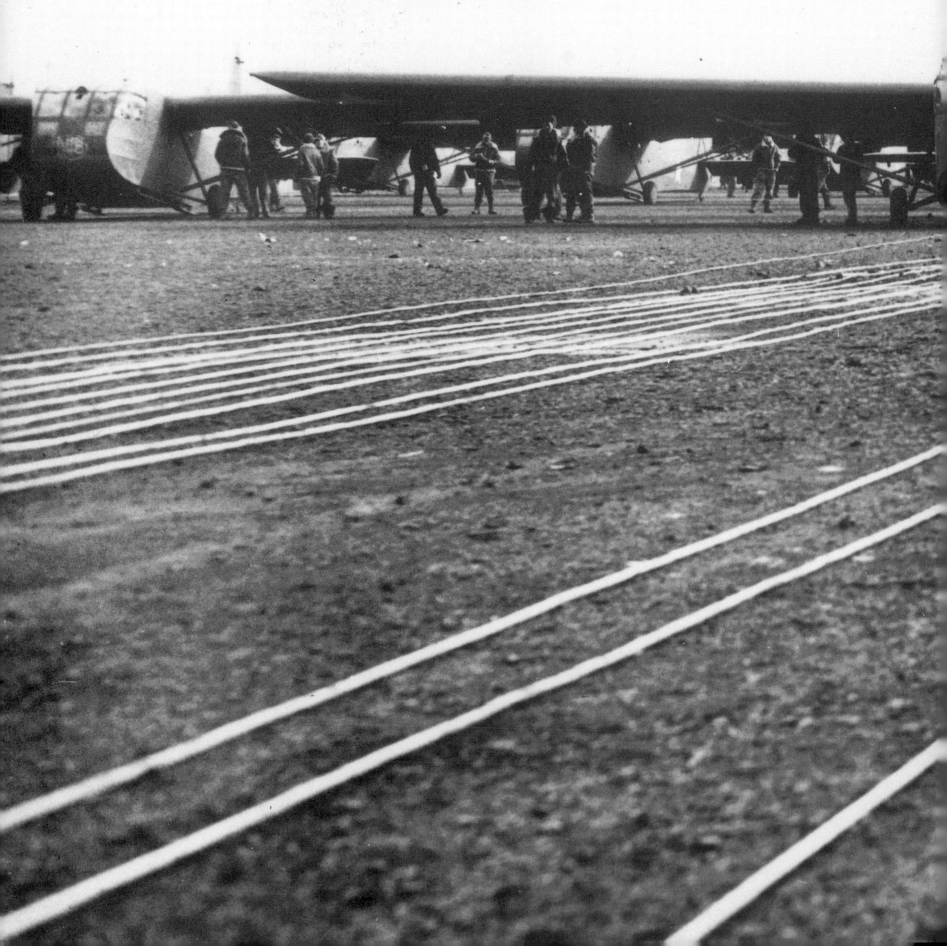

"Soldiers of the 505th Combat Team. Tonight you embark on a combat mission for which our people and the free people of the world have been waiting for two years.

"You will spearhead the landing of an American Force upon the Island of SICILY. Every preparation has been made to eliminate the element of chance. You have been given the means to do the job and you are backed by the largest assemblage of airpower in the world's history.

"The eyes of the world are upon you. The hopes and prayers of every American go with you."

James M. Gavin

Below: Waco CG-4A gliders being prepared for aerial towing.

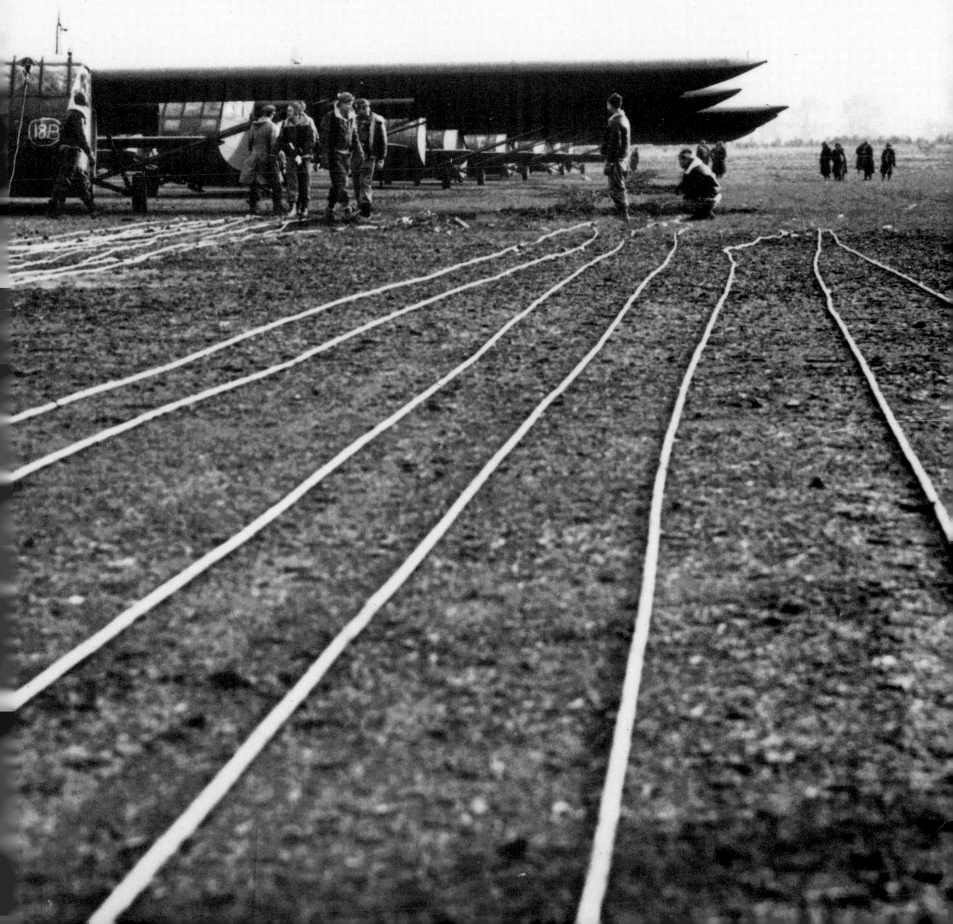

Main picture: A C-47 tows a Waco CG-4A into the air in North Africa for another practice run.

Individual equipment was given a final check and loading began. The equipment consisted of a rifle or carbine, rations, water cans, knife, grenades, a compass, and here and there a bazooka, which would be the only weapon available to fight tanks. Before take-off Gavin was informed that ground winds over the objective were blowing at 56km/h (35 mph). This gave the colonel cause for concern as these wind speeds were over twice the maximum permissible wind speed on a training drop, but there was nothing he could do about it. Some two hours after the British glider troops had begun taking off, 266 C-47s carrying Gavin and his men began rising into the dark sky from airfields around Kairouan.

The air armada was soon blown hopelessly off course by the increasingly strong winds, and many of the pilots failed to see the brightly burning signal lights on Malta. There was

no hope of maintaining the proposed V of Vs formation, and the C-47s began to encounter heavy anti-aircraft fire as the aircraft homed in from every direction on the 505th's DZ east of Gela. This was the American pilots' first experience of flak and they frantically maneuvered to avoid it. Those hit stood little chance of survival, as the C-47s were not armored and had no self-sealing fuel tanks. As the aircraft turned inland, they were greeted by small-arms fire but when the green light over the jump door went on and the paratroopers made their descents they landed to a mixed reception. Some met heavy fighting at once, others were unopposed for a while, but all were shaken up by the heavy landings on trees, buildings and rocky hillsides.

The defense of Sicily was in the hands of General Alfredo Guzzoni and the Italian 6th Army, which consisted of 12 divisions (six

Left: Glider troops emplane in a Waco CG-4A for a landing rehearsal.

in fixed coastal defense positions and six mobile divisions). Of the latter, the Livorno and Napoli Divisions were in the area of the Allied assault landings. Only two German divisions were on Sicily at the time of the invasion: the 15th Panzer Grenadier Division located in the western part of the island, and the Hermann Göring *Fallschirmjäger* Panzer Division (a strong armored, parachute division), which was stationed on the high ground at Caltagirone overlooking Gela.

The American paratroopers who had arrived in the night sky over Sicily were in fact spread over hundreds of square miles of the island, and their experiences ranged from engaging small parties of Italians and Germans with automatic fire to taking on 75mm and 155mm howitzers, and there were even encounters with German PzKpfw VI Tiger tanks. When facing tanks, the bazooka gunners knelt down, took aim, fired and then watched in amazement as their rockets bounced harmlessly off the thick armor of the Panzers. Gavin himself had managed to collect 20 "All Americans" and thence according to military tradition headed in the direction of the sound of guns, meeting with several adventures on the way. Many Americans had in fact dropped ahead of the British sector and this led to complications, as the two Allies did not share the same passwords.

Ridgway, who arrived on Patton's command ship on D-day morning, landed in Sicily soon after daylight. He immediately set out to find the command post which had been set up to await his arrival. Soon realizing how scattered the 505th was on the ground, Ridgway at the first opportunity made contact with his division's rear headquarters in Tunisia to order the 504th Airborne to emplane that evening, as already planned. The pre-arranged coded message read: "Mackall tonight. Wear white pajamas." Due to communications difficulties, Ridgway's deputy in Kairouan, Brigadier General Keerans, did not get the coded message until late morning. Word was immediately flashed to Tucker that his combat team would be jumping that night as expected. The drop zone was to be the Farello airstrip near Gela. Since the DZ was already in friendly hands, Tucker felt sure that the drop would amount to little more than a night training drop.

Ridgway had already anticipated the dangers of the 504th flying over the invasion fleet bristling with anti-aircraft weapons to repel attacks by German and Italian aircraft both on the ships and on the beach-heads. Ridgway's plan was that Tucker's combat team would fly in their C-47s wide around shipping lanes to the far right-hand end of the Allied beach-heads. There the aircraft

Right: Command party in Sicily. General Ridgway is on the left and the one-star general seated in the jeep with his map board is Maxwell D. Taylor.

were to proceed 3.2km (2 miles) inland, make a left turn, and fly the remaining 56km (35 miles) to the DZ directly above the beach-heads already secured by friendly troops. If the aircraft stuck to this course, the navy command said that it would guarantee that there would be no accidental firing by their ships just offshore. After confirming the go-ahead to Ridgway for "Husky Number Two," Patton instructed all his unit commanders to inform their troops of the jump with special emphasis given to notifying all anti-aircraft artillery units.

Having failed the previous day to halt the invading allies, Guzzoni ordered all available Italian and German bombers to hit the Allied forces on the ground as well as the ships lying offshore. The 504th arrived over the Sicilian coastline just as these attacks were dying down, the consequences of which amounted to a tragedy of great proportions. At 10.40 p.m. the paratroopers jumped from the lead

aircraft "according to the book." But when the second formation was approaching the DZ, an American machine-gunner opened up on the aircraft. It was night-time, of course, and thinking that enemy bombers had been identified, the anti-aircraft gunners greeted all their comrades in the sky with a murderous barrage of fire which in turn was joined by the gunners on the ships offshore. Six C-47s were set on fire and plunged to earth with the paratroopers trapped inside, two crash-landed in a field saving some of the men, others fell into the sea before they reached the coastline, and 37 limped back badly damaged to Kairouan. Tucker's aeroplane did manage to reach the DZ, however, and when he came to earth, he landed among American tanks still firing machine-guns at the C-47s overhead.

"Husky Number Two" had already cost the 504th 318 paratroopers and airmen killed or wounded.

Above: U.S. forces of General Patton's Seventh Army in Sicily advance on the road to Messina. Patton's spectacular progress brought a speedy conclusion to the Allied campaign in Sicily.

Right: American airborne dead in Sicily.

Below: Moving forward in files in Sicily.

In Tunisia, the British 1st and 2nd Parachute Brigades were awaiting their orders to jump in Sicily. Syracuse quickly fell to the 8th Army, but the 1st Air Landing Brigade had achieved a costly success at the Ponte Grande Bridge. In the event only the 1st Brigade, commanded by Brigadier Gerald Lathbury, took off. Lathbury's plan, code-named "Fustian" was to land on four DZs and two LZs all west of the main road from Syracuse to Catania. The principal objective was the Primasole Bridge, spanning the Simeto River, a few miles south of Catania. The 1st Brigade (consisting of the 1st, 2nd and 3rd Battalions, the Parachute Regiment) took off in 105 C-47s and 11 Albemarles (in which the men jumped through a hole in the fuselage) on the evening of 13 July. In addition, Halifaxes and Stirlings towed eight Waco and 11 Horsa gliders carrying gunners, anti-tank guns, sappers and field ambulancemen.

Flying in V-formation, the aircraft also took the Sicily route via Malta and, as with the 504th, soon hit trouble with "own forces." Anti-aircraft gunners aboard the invasion ships opened fire, mistaking the C-47s for torpedo-carrying enemy aircraft. Two of the C-47s were shot down and nine – after sustaining heavy damage – were forced to turn back. The close formations were broken up and it was now the German and Italian anti-aircraft gunners who brought fire to bear on the low-flying aircraft. Ten more turned back and 37 crashed into the sea and onto the beaches.

The pilots of the surviving aircraft dropped their paratroopers or advised their glider colleagues to cast-off whenever and wherever they could. Of the 1,900 men of the 1st Parachute Brigade that had taken off from North Africa, only about 250 men from the 1st and 3rd Battalions actually reached the Primasole Bridge, which was taken.

The battle for Sicily was a triumph for Patton. The U.S. 7th Army had made an amphibious landing on beach-heads secured by airborne troops, and although attacked by the Panzer division raced westward around the island seizing Palermo and arriving in Messina on 16 August, just before the British arrived from Catania. Patton's actual mission had been to protect the 8th Army's left flank.

Below: Watching for enemy movement in an orange grove in Sicily.

A Time
For Prayer

With the fall of Messina, the 82nd Airborne Division returned to North Africa to ready itself for the next campaign: Italy. At that time the Allies were asking themselves: "Would the Italians fight on?" The Italians had not fought particularly hard in Sicily, but the bulk of the Germans escaped to the Italian mainland. Although the 82nd had come across some sharp encounters during the Sicily campaign, the battle for the paratroopers was little more than a "shooting match." Valuable lessons were nonetheless gained from the experience. The most important lesson was that pilots and navigators needed much more training in locating DZs and LZs by day and night. Another lesson learned by the Americans was that weapon containers dropped from aircraft at night could be difficult to find on the ground. Henceforward the American paratrooper would jump with his equipment on his person. For example, a knife and pistol, entrenching tool, grenades, first-aid packet, map and some food. He also carried his M1 rifle of course, as well as a musette bag containing a raincoat, the main ration allocation and ammunition.

On 19 August, Marshal Badoglio who headed the Italian government after the deposition of Mussolini, established contact with General Dwight D. Eisenhower to negotiate an Italian surrender without the knowledge of the Germans. The Italian unconditional surrender was signed at Cassibile in Sicily on 3 September and announced five days later. At that time the bulk of the German forces in Italy were stationed in northern Italy. The hope that was immediately formed in the Allied commanders' minds was the availability of a number of Italian armored divisions in southern Italy, which would guide the Allied columns to Rome in a matter of days. All they had to do was to drop an airborne division on Rome to secure the city for the impending arrival of the heterogenous forces at the overall Allied commander's disposal. Orders were accordingly issued to mobilize the U.S. 82nd Airborne Division for the task. General Ridgway in his autobiography *Soldier: The Memoirs of Matthew B. Ridgway* has this to say of the scheme:

"I took an extremely dim view of this plan for it seemed to me to be exceptionally unsound. In the first place, Rome was completely out of range of escorting fighters, flying either from Africa or from take-off fields in Sicily, and we would have to go in without fighter support. It also meant that we'd have to depend entirely on our own light, parachute artillery and on bomber support, but would not have the help of the dive-bombers who could pinpoint a target and serve as our heavy artillery. Also I knew, as did everybody else, that the Germans had about six good divisions in the Rome area, and I felt sure that the ground forces couldn't get to us in time to save us from being chewed up by these divisions. Nor did I have any confidence at all that the Italians would be able to furnish us the trucks, the gas and oil and the ammunition and supplies... while help was fighting its way to us."

Above: September 1943. The Allies gain a toehold at Salerno in Italy. The wheeled, amphibious vehicle in the center of the photographers is one of the new DUKEs ("Ducks"), a 2 1/2-ton short-truck with a six-wheel drive and a boat's hull, rudder and propeller.

Far left: The amphibious invasion fleet sails into the Anzio beach-head, Italy, January 1944. The opposition to the landings was slight but once ashore the Allied forces were in for a long, bitter four-month campaign before the breakthrough to Rome.

Ridgway was in fact so deeply concerned about the proposal that he sought an interview with the Allied Deputy Supreme Commander in the Mediterranean, General Sir Harold Alexander, who said: "Don't give this another thought, Ridgway. Contact will be made with your division in three days – five at the most." (The Allies actually liberated Rome on 6 June 1944 after a long hard, winter campaign.) Ridgway was despondent, but hit on the idea to send his artillery commander, Brigadier General Maxwell D. Taylor, secretly into Rome to visit with Badoglio and learn from his own lips whether or not the Italians were willing and able to give the help they promised. Taylor was willing to go, but Ridgway's proposal was dismissed out-of-hand by Alexander as "too dangerous, too risky." While preparations were stepped up for the drop by the 82nd, Ridgway went to Lieutenant General Walter Bedell Smith, Eisenhower's chief-of-staff, whose strong argument persuaded Alexander to change his mind.

Taylor made the flight to Rome in the back of a North American P-51 Mustang. In the guise of a captured airman, he was taken to a secret rendezvous with Badoglio and there obtained a first-hand account of the situation. From the information he received it was clear to Taylor that the operation could not succeed, so he notified higher authority with the agreed code-word "Innocuous," before leaving Italy in a submarine. The loaded aircraft were already on the runway on the take-off airfields in Sicily when the 82nd received first word that the operation had been canceled, and was then called off entirely. Ridgway also wrote in his book:

"And when the time comes that I must meet my Maker, the source of most humble pride to me will not be accomplishments in battle, but the fact that I was guided to make the decision to oppose this thing, at the risk of my career, right up to the top. There were other operations which I opposed on similar grounds, but this was the one of the greatest magnitude, and I deeply and sincerely believe that by taking the stand I took we saved the lives of thousands of brave men."

The final plan for the amphibious invasion of Italy contained the following elements: 1) the main assault (Operation "Avalanche") by the U.S. 5th Army with the mission of landing in Salerno and moving north-west and capturing Naples; 2) two attacks by the British 8th Army, one against Calabria and another against Taranto; and 3) a naval diversionary attack against the Gulf of Gaeta. The 82nd Airborne Division was made available to the U.S. 5th Army for "Avalanche." The senior officers of the 82nd were promptly swamped with paperwork as they hastened to make plans for several operations which never in fact, took place. The first aborted mission called for the seizure by an airborne task force of the towns of Nocera and Sarno at the exits to the passes leading north-west from Salerno. On 18 August, Ridgway was told that a new decision had been reached to conduct an airborne operation farther inland on the Volturno River, north-west of Naples, and some 64km (40 miles) from the nearest beach landings in Salerno. On 31 August, Eisenhower himself decided to cancel the Volturno River plan and the Rome project, Operation "Giant II," was mooted a few days later.

On 3 September, the Canadian 1st and British 5th Divisions landed in the "toe" of Italy around Reggio; on 9 September, the U.S. 5th Army, comprising the U.S. VI Corps and the British X Corps, went ashore at two points in the Gulf of Salerno; and on the same day, the British 1st Airborne Division, sailing from Bizerta, arrived in Taranto harbor. The U.S. VI Corps had for the assault the 36th Division (Texas National Guard) with the 45th Division in reserve. Lieutenant General Sir Richard L. McCreery's British X Corps consisted of the 46th and 56th Divisions. In addition there were American Rangers and British Commandos involved in the operation. At the time of the first assaults, the bulk of the German armor in Italy was still north of Rome, but the reaction which came from Generalfeldmarschall (Field Marshal) Albert Kesselring, the overall German commander, and his subordinates was swift. The untried U.S. 36th Division, in particular, did well in seizing the high hills at Altavilla, Abanella and Rocco d'Aspide, but when Generaloberst (Colonel General) Heinrich von Vietinghoff-Scheel's experienced Panzers hit them the Texans could not hold their positions.

About mid-day of 13 September, the exhausted pilot of a fighter arriving from the Salerno beach-head landed at Licata Field in Sicily with a personal letter from Clark to Ridgway. It contained an appeal for immediate help. In essence the army commander wanted one regimental combat team dropped inside the beach-head south of the Sele River that night, and another on the mountain village of Avellino, far behind the German lines. Clark's messenger also delivered a plan to mark the drop zone. The troops already inside the area would use cans of sand soaked with gasoline, laid out in the form of a letter "T." They would light these on the approach of the first flight of transports over the DZs and douse them with dirt after

the aircraft had gone. In addition, special pathfinder homing equipment was to be dropped on the Sele River beach-head drop zone with the stick from the first aircraft. Such marking techniques were not feasible for the Avellino drop, which was well behind the enemy lines.

All plans were complete eight hours after the request for reinforcements and shortly after midnight, the 504th Parachute Infantry Regiment (with Company "C" of the 307th Airborne Engineers attached) dropped from Douglas C-47s near Paestum and immediately went into action. That same night the 509th Parachute Infantry Regiment landed at Avellino. The following night the 505th Parachute Infantry Regiment landed at Paestum. Gavin had this to to say about the flight and the drop into the American beach-head:

"After the Sicilian experience we were all quite apprehensive. However, we were in such a rush to get our proper orders out and assemble the necessary arms, equipment and ammunition that we had little time to think about what was going to happen to us. We took off on schedule. It was a beautiful clear night with considerable moonlight. Soon after we left the northwest corner of Sicily, the Italian mainland came into view to the east. We crossed a peninsula jutting out into the Tyrrhenian Sea. In the plane the red warning light came on to tell us that we were approximately four minutes out from the drop zone. We seemed to have been flying over the peninsula forever when a white beach and a river mouth appeared. The green light flashed on. There was no burning T as we had been told there would be, but the area appeared to be correct in every way, so we went.

The first parachutes had barely opened when the great T did light up directly underneath us. To the Germans who occupied the hills, the operation must have appeared bizarre. Units began to reorganize; they assembled without any interference. A combat team was in action by daylight."

(James M. Gavin. *On to Berlin – Battles of an Airborne Commander 1943–1946.*)

The mission of the regiment that dropped the previous night – the 504th commanded by Colonel Reuben Tucker – was to seize Altavilla situated on a hill top surrounded by hills. Tucker, who has been described as a "little colonel," was nonetheless one of the toughest regimental combat commanders of the war. While still dark, he deployed his two battalions and moved out against the German positions. Scouts soon learned that Altavilla was crammed with tanks and half-tracks, but the 504th moved in and held its positions in spite of four vigorous German counterattacks. Tucker's successful seizure and defense of Altavilla somehow turned the tide, and shortly after, the Germans in that sector began pulling out.

Colonel Edson Raff's 2nd Battalion of the 509th, which was on attachment to the 82nd Airborne, took off from Licata Field, Sicily, on the evening of 13 September. Avellino may be described as typical in that the pilots found it difficult to find with any certainty in the darkness. There were, moreover, no suitable drop zones in the area; the few flat areas with no obstacles to be found on pre-combat photographs were too small. Furthermore, the mountains were so high that it was impossible to jump at the usual low altitudes. Avellino was nevertheless an important objective, and had several good roads, along which the Germans were withdrawing. Due to the navigation problems, the assault on Avellino was a disaster. The 509th was scattered over a very wide area but Raff's men gave a good account of themselves in the guerrilla role with small units mining roads, destroying bridges and German lines of communication.

After the battles for the Salerno beach-heads were over, the 82nd Airborne Division was moved to Amalfi, and the 505th Parachute Infantry moved up the mountain road from Amalfi to the top of the Sorrento peninsula. The onward route lay to Naples and when the city fell, badly damaged by bombing and shellfire, the "All Americans" were given the task of cleaning up the place and restoring law and order. The 505th continued in the attack northward to the Volturno River. On 10 October, Ridgway appointed Gavin assistant division commander with the rank of brigadier general. The 504th was now chosen to plug the gap that had somehow arisen between the U.S. 5th Army to the west and the British 8th Army working its way up the eastern coastline. The 504th found itself in rocky, mountainous terrain, generally devoid of trees or cover. The weather turned very cold and the first snow began to fall. Fighting became more and more difficult, and as Christmas approached a measure of stalemate occurred along the entire front.

The Germans used the chain of mountains stretching across the Italian peninsula not far to the south of Rome to build a series of

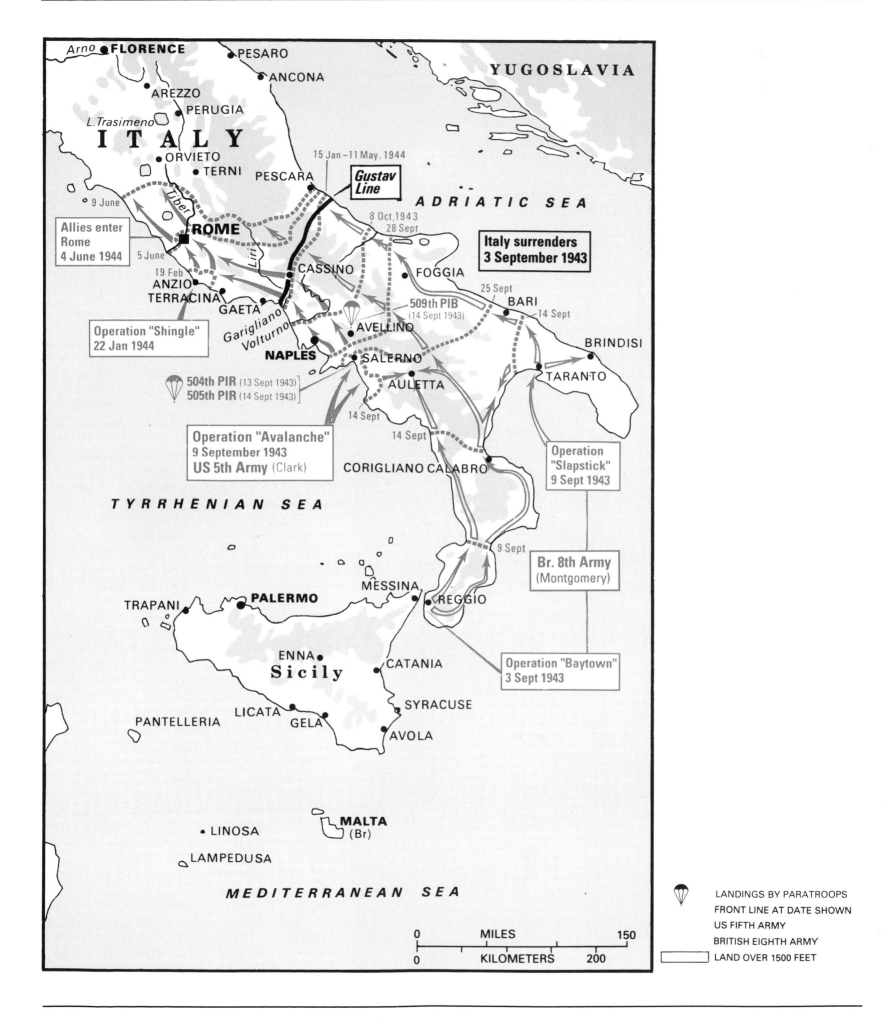

Arno *FLORENCE*
PESARO
ANCONA
AREZZO
PERUGIA
L. Trasimeno

ITALY

YUGOSLAVIA

ORVIETO
TERNI
PESCARA

15 Jan–11 May, 1944

Gustav Line

ADRIATIC SEA

Tiber

9 June

Allies enter Rome 4 June 1944

ROME

5 June

8 Oct,1943
28 Sept

Italy surrenders 3 September 1943

Liri

19 Feb
CASSINO
FOGGIA

ANZIO
TERRACINA

25 Sept
BARI
14 Sept

GAETA

Garigliano
Volturno

509th PIB (14 Sept 1943)

AVELLINO

BRINDISI

Operation "Shingle" 22 Jan 1944

NAPLES
SALERNO
TARANTO

504th PIR (13 Sept 1943)
505th PIR (14 Sept 1943)

AULETTA

14 Sept

Operation "Avalanche" 9 September 1943 US 5th Army (Clark)

14 Sept

CORIGLIANO CALABRO

Operation "Slapstick" 9 Sept 1943

TYRRHENIAN SEA

9 Sept

Br. 8th Army (Montgomery)

MESSINA

REGGIO

TRAPANI
PALERMO

ENNA
Sicily
CATANIA

Operation "Baytown" 3 Sept 1943

PANTELLERIA
LICATA
GELA
SYRACUSE

AVOLA

MEDITERRANEAN SEA

LINOSA
MALTA (Br)

LAMPEDUSA

LANDINGS BY PARATROOPS
FRONT LINE AT DATE SHOWN
US FIFTH ARMY
BRITISH EIGHTH ARMY
LAND OVER 1500 FEET

0   MILES   150
0   KILOMETERS   200

fortified positions known as the Gustav or Winter Line. The bastion of this position was Monte Cassino, which overlooked Highway 6, the only direct route available to the Allies in the advance on Rome. An urgent means was sought to break the winter deadlock. General Sir Harold Alexander, the Allied supremo in the Italian theater, was put under considerable pressure by Winston Churchill and the British chiefs-of-staff to make plans and preparations for an amphibious assault on the coast of Italy. Alexander accordingly selected a spot to the west at the coastal resort of Anzio, located only 48km (30 miles) south of Rome. Directly behind and around Anzio stretched a large coastal plain that gently sloped upward to the Alban Hills nearly 32km (20 miles) inland. Alexander's idea was that if Major General John P. Lucas's U.S. VI Corps, chosen for the initial assault, was to rapidly push inland to capture the Alban Hills then Kesselring would be obliged to pull back rapidly for the defense of Rome, thereby letting loose the bulk of the U.S. 5th Army. How wrong Alexander was remained to be seen over the first six months of 1944 until the Germans evacuated the Holy City without a fight on 6 June.

The Anzio landing on 22 January 1944 was virtually unopposed. The 509th did not take their parachutes this time. Scheduled to act as part of the floating reserve, the troopers (the first American troops to go into action in North Africa) in the event found themselves alongside the U.S. 3rd Division in the beach-head on the first day. Alexander declared the landing a great success, which it was as a huge amphibious exercise, but Kesselring quickly built up his forces and the Allies were to suffer over four months of aerial bombardment and straffing, continuous artillery and mortar fire, and heavy infantry attacks. The failure of the Allies to break out of the Anzio hell spot was attributed to Lucas, who was sacked. Churchill, the prime mover of the project, declared: "I expected to land a tiger and instead I have landed a whale." However, Kesselring somehow found enough forces to hold the Winter Line, which was not breached until after the fourth battle for Cassino and the breakout in mid-May, and also to attack the Anzio beach-head. The final debouchment from Anzio occurred virtually simultaneously with the race up Highway 6 from Cassino. If any blame was to be laid out for Anzio, on the principle that soldiers go where they are told to go, the fault must be with the paper tiger at the top.

In Italy, the 82nd Airborne Division lost no

time in making analyses of its two airborne operations and continued to conduct experiments in both parachute and glider landings. Parachute pathfinders were trained to drop carrying lights, which were used on landing to mark drop zones and landing strips for the glider pilots. Again there emerged the very real need to give both the tug and the glider pilots adequate training in airborne methods before embarking on operations, by day and by night. On take-off a glider was drawn forward by the tug until the towrope was taut and the two aircraft climbed steadily into the air. The glider pilots were apprised by the tug captains of the height and bearing of their course to the landing zone and at the briefing beforehand had already made a careful study of landmarks en route and aerial

photographs of the destination area. During the flight, the normal position for the glider was just above or just below the prop wash of the tug.

The precise moment of departure from the tug was chosen by the glider pilot and the release mechanism for the towrope was operated from the glider cockpit. Intercommunication was possible by means of a line wound round the towrope. On landing in favorable conditions, the glider came quickly to rest within a distance of 18m (60 ft) from the point of impact. Thus after gliding at anything from 97 to 161km/h (60 to 100 mph), the occupants of the glider were in for a rough jolt, or worse. The "All Americans" studied hard: they were in for a test in a big way in the summer of 1944.

Above: Tank landing ship unloading at Anzio, Italy, April 1944.

Facing page, above: Paratroopers of the 82nd Airborne Division in Naples, early October 1943. Naples was shattered by Allied bombers but, apart from broken windows, this building has remained intact.

Facing page, below: Pressing on into the mountains on the Venafro sector in Italy. Soon the winter will set in and the hills and mountainsides will be covered in thick snow.

The Invasion of France

In the late summer and fall of 1943, Major General William C. Lee's 101st Airborne Division arrived in the U.K. to begin preparations for the airborne invasion of France tentatively scheduled for the following spring. On paper, the division included two glider infantry regiments (the 327th and 401st) and one parachute regiment (the 502nd). However, the 506th Parachute Infantry had been attached since June 1943, and then in January 1944 a third parachute regiment (the 501st) arrived in the U.K. to be attached to the "Screaming Eagles." The 101st was joined by the now veteran, battle-tested 82nd Airborne Division not long afterward in December 1943. Arriving in Belfast, Northern Ireland, the "All Americans" took the 507th Parachute Infantry on strength to replace the 504th, which after a severe mauling in the Anzio beach-head was left behind in Italy. In January 1944, the 508th Parachute Infantry arrived in Belfast from the U.S.A. and was also attached to the 82nd.

Troop carrier units likewise were moving into the U.K. The IX Troop Carrier Command was set up in the U.S. 9th Air Force with Brigadier General Benjamin F. Giles in command. By the end of February 1944, three wings (the 50th, 52nd and 53rd) had been assigned to the new command. A survey on 22 May revealed that 1,176 transport aircraft were available but only 1,004 crews. The 82nd Airborne Division, still commanded by Major General Matthew B. Ridgway, moved to England from Northern Ireland in March and participated with the British 1st and 6th Airborne Divisions as well as the 101st in joint parachute and glider maneuvers. Between 15 March and 27 March, the various units participated in 38 exercises jointly with IX Troop Carrier Command. The exercises were in fact mounted mainly for the benefit of the transport pilots, most of whom were unused to flying in formation, by day and by night.

Instructions were given in March 1944 that each airborne division would organize 18 parachute pathfinder teams – each including one officer and nine men as the technical party – and train them to mark DZs and LZs for the incoming aircraft and gliders. The specially trained crew of the pathfinder aircraft was to find the designated zone by accurate dead reckoning and map reading, with close checking by radar aids, and the use of special drop zone maps. The main aircraft serials would find the areas by their own dead reckoning and radar aids, and then get to the DZs and LZs by use of "Rebecca-Eureka" radar equipment. Effectively a "Eureka" beacon placed by the pathfinders on the ground was monitored by "Rebecca" in the aircraft. The pathfinders also marked the drop zone with a series of five lights placed to form a "T." The jump signal was to be given when the leader of a group was over the head of the "T." For marking a glider LZ, a line of seven lights (in the order, going down-wind, one red, five amber and one green) was to be set up. The lights were to be placed through the main axis of the landing area, and a "Eureka" installation was to be set up off the down-wind end of the light.

In February 1944 Lee suffered a severe

Above: 101st Airborne Division paratroopers line up in stick order in preparation for emplaning in a C-47 bound for the Contentin peninsula in Normandy, 5 June 1944. The officer on the left is checking out his flight manifest, which lists the men's names in jump order.

Far left: A glider assembly point "somewhere in England," May 1944. American glider troops were lifted in both Waco CG-4As and British Horsas for Normandy.

Above: A line-up of C-47 tugs, Wacos and Horsas on an English airfield prior to D-Day.

Right: Winston Churchill addresses the 101st Airborne Division at a camp in southern England shortly before D-Day. It is just four years since the prime minister reviewed the first British airborne troops at R.A.F. Ringway. The Allies now have three airborne divisions to spearhead the invasion of continental Europe.

heart attack and was returned to the U.S.A. for urgent treatment. His life was saved, but Lee was retired from the U.S. Army. His place as commander of the 101st was taken by Major General Maxwell D. Taylor. The 101st was stationed in the south of England, and after some hard training in Northern Ireland the 82nd was based in the English midland counties, where there was friction between the paratroopers and some of the American units already in the area. The veteran incumbents were anxious that the "All Americans" did not get to work on the English girls with whom the former had established friendly relations. The paratroopers' jump boots, which were worn on and off duty, were also an unwelcome demonstration of elitism to the "ground-borne" G.I.s. Near the end of April the entire 101st Airborne Division, along with a token force from the 82nd, was lifted by the U.S. 50th and 53rd Troop Carrier Wings to

189986

participate in a huge airborne exercise on Salisbury Plain. With the aircraft achieving tight formation drills and over 6,000 paratroopers making their jumps, the maneuver was generally adjudged to be a success.

On 8 May the Supreme Commander Allied Forces Europe, General Dwight D. Eisenhower, designated D-day as 5 June, but as the day for the invasion of France drew near, a bad weather forecast caused the assault on the Normandy coastline to be postponed until the following day. Some 2,876,000 men were ready to cross the English Channel for the greatest seaborne military operation in history, over 20,000 invasion troops being scheduled to go ashore from ships and craft on D-day. Starting at 6.30 a.m. on 6 June the U.S. 1st Army was due to land on the right of the line on the Cotentin peninsula south-east of Cherbourg on "Utah" and further east on "Omaha" beaches, and the

British 2nd Army (including the Canadian 3rd Division) 50 minutes later on the left on "Gold," "Juno" and "Sword" beaches. Some 5,000 vessels made up the cross-channel fleet, and Allied bombers and fighters were poised to strike along the entire invasion coast.

The American attack was to be spearheaded by the U.S. 82nd and 101st Airborne Divisions, which landed shortly after midnight astride the Merderet River in the vicinity of Ste. Mère-Eglise to facilitate the advance of the U.S. VII Corps. At the same time the British 6th Airborne Division, landing 64km (40 miles) to the east, was to secure the Allied left flank between the Orne and Dives Rivers. The 3rd and 5th Parachute Brigades were to drop in the early hours of D-day on the high ground north-east of Caen and, together with the 6th Air Landing Brigade arriving mostly in the afternoon, were to consolidate in the area and both capture and destroy road and railway bridges over the Caen Canal as well

Above: G.I.s approach Omaha Beach on the second day of the invasion, 7 June. The Germans are still firmly entrenched on the high ground in the background and the American infantry ashore is having a tough time holding its own, in the face of artillery, mortar, machine-gun and sniper fire.

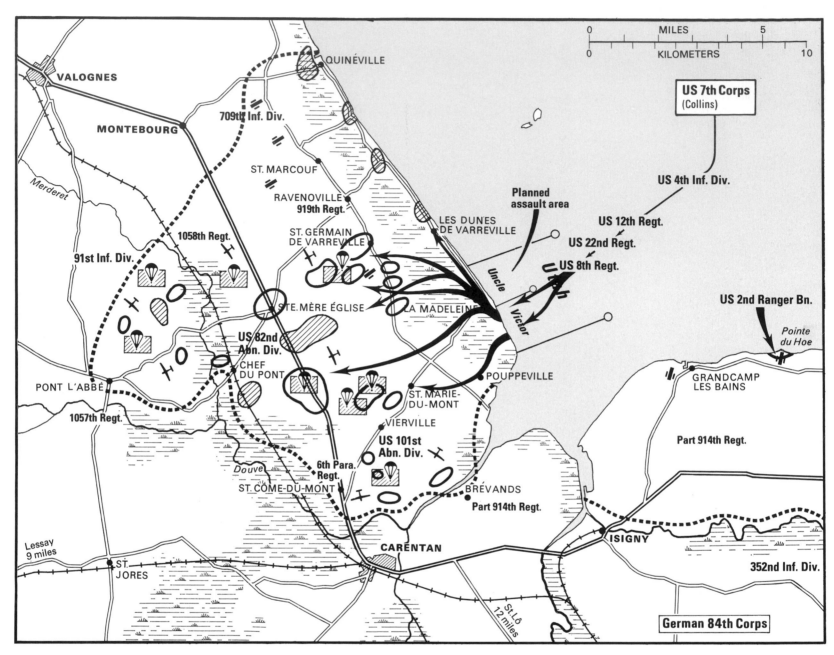

The map labels, clockwise and within:

US 7th Corps (Collins)

MILES 0 — 5
KILOMETERS 0 — 10

QUINÉVILLE
VALOGNES
709th Inf. Div.
MONTEBOURG
ST. MARCOUF
Merderet
RAVENOVILLE 919th Regt.
1058th Regt.
ST. GERMAIN DE VARREVILLE
91st Inf. Div.
LES DUNES DE VARREVILLE
Planned assault area
US 4th Inf. Div.
US 12th Regt.
US 22nd Regt.
US 8th Regt.
Uncle
Utah
Victor
STE. MÈRE ÉGLISE
LA MADELEINE
US 82nd Abn. Div.
CHEF DU PONT
PONT L'ABBÉ
1057th Regt.
ST. MARIE-DU-MONT
POUPPEVILLE
US 2nd Ranger Bn.
Pointe du Hoe
GRANDCAMP LES BAINS
VIERVILLE
US 101st Abn. Div.
Part 914th Regt.
Douve
6th Para. Regt.
ST. CÔME-DU-MONT
BRÉVANDS
Part 914th Regt.
Lessay 9 miles
ST. JORES
CARENTAN
ISIGNY
352nd Inf. Div.
St-Lô 12 miles
German 84th Corps

Legend:
PLANNED AIRBORNE DROPPING AND LANDING ZONES
Utah ASSAULT AREAS GLIDER LANDINGS
FIRST ASSAULT WAVES
HELD BY US 5th CORPS AT 2400 HRS ON D-DAY
US OBJECTIVE AT 2400 HRS ON D-DAY
709th Inf. Div. SITUATION OF GERMAN UNITS AT DAWN ON D-DAY
HELD BY GERMAN TROOPS AT 2400 HRS ON D-DAY
MAJOR GERMAN GUN BATTERIES
FLOODED AREAS (PRAIRIES MARECAGEUSES)

as over the Orne and Dives Rivers.

The U.S. 1st Army commander, Lieutenant General Omar N. Bradley, planned to use the 82nd and 101st Airborne Divisions to ensure success of the "Utah" beach landings and to seal off the main roads leading in and out of the Cotentin peninsula. His plan was to drop both divisions along the base (or neck) of the peninsula where they were to key into the Douve River, which slices across two-thirds of the neck. The American airborne troops were to put a stranglehold on the huge peninsula, cutting off routes of supply and escape to thousands of German troops inside it. Bradley assigned to the 101st Airborne Division the mission of landing by parachute and glider behind "Utah" beach. A small patrol (one officer and six men of the British 1st S.A.S. Regiment) was also to be dropped south of Carentan to assist the 101st by creating diversions with pyrotechnics.

"Utah" beach was 8km (5 miles) long, so the airborne assault and sea-landing were focused on the small town of Ste. Mère-Eglise. The initial objectives for the airborne division were to attack German coastal defenses from the rear, secure crossings over the Merderet River, and seize control of four vital "causeways" leading inland from the beach. These "causeways" were actually country lanes which had been built sufficiently high off the ground to remain unaffected by the deliberate flooding of the adjoining fields. Apart from the flooding, in which many American and British paratroopers drowned, Generalfeldmarschall (Field Marshal) Erwin

Left: A heavily-laden American paratrooper climbs aboard a C-47, which will shortly take off for Normandy. The time is around 10·30 p.m., 5 June. Note the knife attached to the right lower leg.

Left: Night flight to Normandy. Lights have been extinguished in the fuselage except for the trooper on the right puffing at a PX cigar. All quiet so far but soon the enemy flak will open up with deadly fire.

Rommel, who was in command of all German forces from the Zuider Zee to the Loire, had ordered long poles to be placed and linked by barbed wire in areas where the ground was sufficiently flat to be used as LZs by the gliders. The linked poles "sewn" in the ground came to be known as *Rommelspargel* (Rommel's asparagus). Link-up between seaborne and airborne forces was almost entirely dependent on the 101st Airborne's ability to gain control of the four causeways. The main invasion force on this flank would then push north to capture the port of Cherbourg.

Minutes behind the 101st Airborne Division, a three-regiment parachute infantry, artillery and engineer task force from the 82nd Airborne Division was to be dropped 32km (20 miles) inland behind "Utah" beach near St. Sauveur-le-Vicomte. This unit, designated Task Force A, would be led by Brigadier General James M. Gavin, the assistant division commander of the 82nd Airborne. Of the two American airborne divisions, Gavin's Task Force A was to jump into the middle of a heavily fortified area and faced the toughest task. However, some "last minute" thinking averted what might have been a dangerous situation for the 82nd when it was decided to land both divisions into one large airhead centering on Ste. Mère-Eglise.

Shortly after dark on the night of 5 June, the pathfinder aircraft of the IX Troop Carrier Command roared down the runways of the airfield at North Witham. The troop carrier flight plan from numerous airfields was the most complex that had ever been attempted, and involved several thousand aircraft. It had been carefully co-ordinated with the operations of the amphibious force. The first flights of the American airborne divisions flew to the west of the ships sailing in the English Channel and passed around the Cotentin peninsula, carefully staying out of range of the flak from the guns known to be on the Channel Islands to the west of the peninsula. They kept this course until they reached the coast. Then the aircraft made a straight run to the drop and landing areas. The first airborne men to touch down on French soil were the pathfinder personnel who landed between 0.10 and 0.20 a.m. on D-day. (Visitors to Ste. Mère-Eglise today will find a tree now marking the spot where the first man – a Sergeant Tucker – "hit the deck" that morning, only minutes ahead maybe of the British pathfinder team to the east.)

The 82nd's operation launched after the take-off of the pathfinder teams was headed by the 505th Parachute Infantry. It had the farthest to go and had as its objective the seizing of the town of Ste. Mère-Eglise. Gavin himself flew in the lead aircraft of the 508th Parachute Infantry. The 507th followed the 508th. Altogether, it took 378 C-47s to lift the parachutists. They were to be followed by 375 gliders a day later. Fifty-two gliders carrying anti-tank weapons and heavy communications and other equipment were to land with the parachute echelon during the first lift. Ridgway was to take part in the parachute assault.

In the words of Gavin, taken from his book mentioned earlier:

"About seven minutes after we crossed the coast, the clouds began to clear. As they did, I could see a great deal of heavy flak coming up off the right of our flight. I had studied the anti-aircraft gun dispositions, and the only town in that part of the peninsula that had any heavy anti-aircraft guns was Etienville. That should be about where we were in terms of time. I had quickly scanned the skies for other airplanes; none could be seen. Directly ahead of us in the distance I could see the moonlight reflecting off a wide river that made a sharp right-angle turn to the north. For a moment I thought we were south of the Douve River, but that did not check with Etienville and its flak. Very likely, therefore, we were farther north, farther to the left by a number of miles than we should have been.

"We began to receive small arms fire from the ground. It seemed harmless enough; it sounded like pebbles landing on a tin roof. I had experienced it before and knew what it was. So far none of our aircraft had been hit. Directly ahead of us there was a tremendous amount of small-arms fire, and apparently buildings were burning. That almost certainly had to be Ste. Mère-Eglise. The 505th by now should have landed and should be attacking the Germans in the town.

"We were at about 600 feet, the green light went on, and I took one last precious look at the land below. We were about 30 seconds overtime. A wide river was just ahead of us, plainly visible in the moonlight. Small-arms fire was increasing. About three seconds after the green light went on, I yelled, 'Let's go,' and went out of the door, with everyone following. I landed with what seemed to be a pretty loud thud in an orchard. Among the trees were some grazing cows which kept munching quite contentedly – entirely unconcerned about what to me was a most momentous occasion."

Facing page: A somewhat macaber tribute to the Allied airborne lands, draped from a Normandy church on the 45th Anniversary of D-day.

It was a moonlight night and most of the townspeople of Ste. Mère-Eglise were in bed only to be awakened by the roar of aircraft engines as the C-47s flew in fast and low, instantly attracting thunderous anti-aircraft fire. There was an albeit deadly air of the Fourth of July, as the pathfinders descended to earth through a weaving mass of "firecrackers." One trooper of the 82nd, whose face was daubed with Red Indian war paint, tumbled into the yard of a French school mistress. The time was midnight. So intense was the flak fire that many of the aircraft were forced off course. The pathfinders were spread out all over the place. They dropped into fields, gardens, streams and swamps; two of the troopers landed by the entrance of a German company headquarters. The cry of "Fallschirmjäger! Fallschirmjäger!" echoed through the night air as the Germans wildly sprayed the shadowy figures of the paratroopers with machine-gun fire. Only 38 of the 120 pathfinders actually landed on target; the remainder of those who survived the drop groped from hedgerow to hedgerow to find their bearings.

Now came a steadily mounting roar of aircraft engines, and with it a chain of anti-aircraft fire as battery after battery on the Cotentin peninsula picked up the main personnel lift on its way to six drop zones near Ste. Mère-Eglise. The C-47s were flying so low that when many of the local people rushed to the town square, they raced through shadows cast by the aircraft on the cobblestones, and could clearly see the green "go" lights in the aircraft. One trooper of the 505th Parachute Infantry, Private John Steel, realized as soon as he left his aircraft that he was not jumping into a lighted DZ but heading instead for the town center, which appeared to be on fire. Steel was hit in the boot by a bullet but was even more alarmed when he saw he was floating helplessly toward the church steeple at the edge of the square.

Amid the wholesale slaughter of the Americans who dropped into the town, Steel clung tenaciously to life, his parachute draped over the steeple of the church, he himself suspended just under the eaves. The young paratrooper, paralyzed with fear, later did not recall the church bell tolling only a few feet from his head. He decided that with all the random shooting going on that his only chance of survival was to "play dead," so he hung inertly in his parachute harness. He performed the role so realistically that he got away with it until the Germans cut down his "dead" body and took his "corpse" prisoner!

From the beginning the two American airborne divisions worked against staggering odds. Only one regiment, the 505th, was dropped more or less accurately. Sixty per cent of all equipment was lost, including most of the radios, mortars and ammunition. Worse still, the casualties were already heavy. At least five Americans were killed on landing in the town square of Ste. Mère-Eglise, and a 505th padre in the same place was captured and executed by the Germans. Hundreds of men, heavily weighted with equipment, fell into the treacherous swamps of the Merderet and Douve Rivers. Many drowned, some in less than 0·6m (2 ft) of water. Others, jumping too late, fell into the darkness over what they thought was Normandy and were lost in the Channel. A great many of the paratroopers had come to earth on the western side of the peninsula, making their way in the darkness toward their objective areas with extreme caution. Each man had been issued with a tin instrument fashioned in the shape of a child's snapper which when used emitted the sound of a cricket. When challenged with one snap of the cricket, the password was two snaps.

All over Normandy this night paratroopers and German soldiers met unexpectedly. In those encounters men's lives depended on their keeping their wits and often on the fraction of a second it took to pull the trigger. Ridgway had a good landing in a "nice, soft, grassy field." On hitting the ground he grabbed his .45 caliber pistol, which he temporarily lost in the tussle to get out of his harness. As he groped around on the grass to find it, he heard a movement nearby. The 82nd also had a password, "Flash" to which the response was "Thunder." Ridgway got no reply to his challenge, shortly discerning the bulky outline of a cow in the dim moonlight.

One trooper of the 101st, Private Donald Burgett, also pulled out his .45 on hearing the movement of a cow while struggling to free himself of his harness. Troopers were not allowed to carry pistols but his father had bought this one from a gun collector in Detroit and sent it to him in a package containing a date and nut cake. He was horrified when he saw the shadowy figures of troopers plunging downward. Seventeen men hit the ground before their 'chutes had time to open.

Unlike the paratroopers' aircraft, the tug aircraft and gliders came in from the English channel and approached the peninsula from the east. They were only seconds past the coast when the 101st Airborne Division's glider train saw the lights of the landing zone at Hiersville, 6·4km (4 miles) from Ste. Mère-Eglise. One by one the nylon tow ropes were released and the gliders came soughing down. Wings were shorn off those CG-4As and Horsas that were unfortunate to encounter "Rommel's Asparagus" as they whizzed past the poles. Others were broken in two or shattered. One trooper was able to drive his jeep out of the gaping hole in the fuselage of his CG-4A. The 101st's assistant division commander, Brigadier General Don Pratt, who was gliderborne, was killed instantly on landing. Although most of the 101st's gliders were totally wrecked, most of their equipment in fact arrived largely intact.

The 82nd's 50-glider train was not so lucky. Fewer than half their formations found the right LZ north-west of Ste. Mère-Eglise; the remainder plowed into hedgerows and buildings and dove into rivers or came down in the marshes of the Merderet. Equipment and vehicles so urgently needed were strewn everywhere and casualties were high. Eighteen pilots alone were killed within the first few minutes. For the hard-pressed 82nd, the wide dispersion of the gliders was calamitous. It would take hours to salvage and collect the few guns and supplies that had arrived safely. In the meantime, troopers would have to fight on with the weapons they carried with them. Gavin collected a bunch of his troopers and organized a hunt for equipment in a swampy area. He was not too happy as he was not sure where he was, but he was able to pinpoint his position when one of his officers, wading waist-deep in water, came across the Carentan–Cherbourg railway, which was built on an embankment.

Other glider serials were scheduled for the evening of D-day, though the main glider elements were to come in the next morning. Late in the afternoon of 6 June Colonel Edson Raff arrived by sea with a company of tanks and 90 riflemen of the 325th Glider Infantry for the 82nd Airborne Division. Raff found the glider LZs in German hands and tried to get them cleared before the arrival of the gliders, scheduled for 9.00 p.m. The gliders arrived on schedule while the Germans yet held the landing zones. Coming under intense fire, many of the gliders crashed with heavy casualties; many swooped in way off their LZs. But the next morning most of the 325th Glider Infantry was able to land and assemble. Glider serials also had arrived for the 101st Airborne Division at 4.00 a.m. and 9.00 p.m. on D-day and with somewhat similar results. (The 327th Glider Infantry arrived by sea on D-day and D-day plus 1.) Damage to the

Facing page, above: A Horsa glider has crashed through a hedgerow in the Normandy countryside. These hedgerows, known in Normandy as the *bocage*, are so thick that the infantry found them virtually impossible to break through. The British used a special attachment on the front of Sherman tanks to surmount these otherwise impenetrable barriers.

Facing page, below: Airborne troops turned cavalry ride through Ste. Mère-Eglise. Visitors to this small French town today will find a road named after General Gavin and a museum dedicated to U.S. airborne forces. In the grounds of the museum grows a tree bearing a plaque denoting the spot where a certain Sergeant Tucker hit the ground – the first Allied paratrooper to land in Normandy on D-Day, 6 June 1944.

bigger Horsa gliders was generally greater than for the CG-4As because of their greater landing speed and size in tall hedge-rowed, small fields, known in Normandy as the *bocage*.

In a way the widespread American landings may have actually contributed to airborne success. German patrols despatched to destroy the sky invaders became involved in fighting in every direction. There were no battalion concentrations against which an effective counter-attack might be launched. The Germans nevertheless fought tenaciously from the time the first shot was fired in the Normandy campaign. Having seized Ste. Mère-Eglise, the 505th Parachute Infantry set up its position to defend the town. The stunned townspeople watched from behind their shuttered windows as the troopers slipped cautiously through the streets. When other paratroopers came into the square for the first time and saw hanging from the trees the bodies of shot Americans, they were deeply

Right: An 82nd trooper helps a mother and daughter move home in Ste. Mère-Eglise, D-Day plus two.

Below: A French villager is happy to meet two 82nd troopers by the wayside, D+2.

shocked. Lieutenant Colonel Edward Krause pulled an American flag from his pocket. It was old and worn — the same flag that the 505th had raised over Naples. He walked to the town hall and, on a flagpole by the side of the door, ran up the colors. The Stars and Stripes flew over the first town to be liberated by the Americans in France.

Bradley concluded after the first day of fighting in the Cotentin peninsula, and with American troops pouring ashore at "Utah" beach, that the risk of striking hard and fast for Cherbourg, as was originally intended, would be intolerable unless the peninsula was first cut to isolate the port from German reinforcements. In the first few days after 6 June, the American airborne divisions fought their way forward inch by inch to consolidate the tenuous footholds they had gained and to defeat dangerous German counter-attacks such as that on 7 June against Ste. Mère-Eglise. Then, led by the 9th and 90th Infantry Divisions and elements of the 82nd Airborne, Lieutenant General Lawton Collins's U.S. V Corps launched its drive westward, completed at the little coastal resort of Barneville-Carteret on 18 June.

Left: American paratroopers take the Nazi flag after capturing a German headquarters unit in the Carentan area. This sharp-fought action took place on D+2.

Below: An American airborne patrol moves cautiously through a churchyard taking cover from a stone wall in Ste. Marcouf, near Utah Beach.

Carentan fell to the 101st Airborne Division on 12 June. Shortly after that the division had to fight hard against a heavy German counter-attack mounted by S.S. troops and *Fallschirmjäger* supported by tanks and artillery. But Taylor's paratroopers and glidermen were able to beat off the Germans and retain their grip on the town. Except for a few small-scale assaults, the battle for Carentan marked the end of the Normandy fighting for the 101st Airborne. During the second week in July, with the Normandy beach-head firmly secured and Cherbourg captured, both the 82nd and the 101st Airborne Divisions were returned to England aboard tank landing ships. The two U.S. airborne divisions had suffered high casualty rates. Taylor's 101st Airborne left France with 4,670 troopers either killed, wounded or missing in action. Ridgway's 82nd Airborne was worse off, for 5,245 of its troopers were listed as casualties.

Left: An airborne medical officer from the 82nd hands a lighted cigarette to a trooper who made a rough landing in the Ste. Mère-Eglise area. Allied airborne surgeons had the equipment, including blood plasma and other essential medical supplies, to carry out operations in the field from the first day of the invasion.

Far left: Two weeks have now elapsed since D-Day and this landing strip has been prepared to take re-supply gliders. The gliders that landed intact could be snapped up by a rope and hook suspended from a C-47 flying almost at ground level.

Left: An American bugler sounds "taps" at the end of the day for his fallen comrades at rest in their ranks in the U.S. cemetery in Ste. Mère-Eglise.

Far left: These American glider pilots have returned from Normandy to England and are waiting to fly another mission to the battle zone.

On 20 June, with the invasion of France now well under way, Eisenhower approved the organization of the 1st Allied Airborne Army. This was to comprise the U.S. XVIII Airborne Corps, made up of the 17th, 82nd, and 101st Airborne Divisions (and later the 13th) and several Airborne Aviation Battalions; the British I Airborne Corps, consisting of the 1st and 6th Airborne Divisions and the S.A.S. Brigade; the 1st Polish Independent Parachute Brigade Group; the British 52nd (Lowland) Division re-assigned from a mountain role to fly in transport aircraft; the U.S. IX Troop Carrier Command; and Nos. 38 and 46 Groups of the R.A.F. Lieutenant General Lewis H. Brereton, U.S.A.A.F., was selected to lead the new army, with Lieutenant General Ridgway as the American corps commander and Lieutenant General F.A.M. "Boy" Browning in command of the British corps. Browning was also deputy army commander.

The appointment of Brereton as overall commander was timely recognition of the fact that airborne forces are an instrument of air power, and as it happened Brereton had a long-standing interest in parachute forces. During World War I, he had in 1918 concocted a plan with Brigadier General "Billy" Mitchell, then commanding the American Expeditionary Force's air wing, to airdrop part of the U.S. 1st Army, then fighting in the Argonne, from British bombers to capture Metz, a vital rail center. As deputy army commander, Browning was *ipso facto* the "man at the top" so far as ground operations were concerned. Browning, who had his uniforms cut by his own tailor, and whose wife, the authoress Daphne du Maurier (it is said) chose the red beret for the British paratroopers, had at last realized his ambition since the North African campaign to take command of the Allied airborne forces. The American airborne commanders still regarded Browning's manner as patronizing; it remained to be seen how he would acquit himself in action when another massive Allied airborne assault was launched, Operation "Market Garden," to be launched in the Netherlands on 17 September 1944.

Even as Allied troops debouched victoriously out of Normandy in the late summer of 1944, another Allied force staged a second amphibious invasion, this time on the south coast of France between Cannes and Toulon. The overall objective of this force was to form the extreme right flank for the Allied advance into Germany. The planning for Operation "Dragoon" first took shape in the headquarters of the U.S. 7th Army in February 1944. Three U.S. divisions (the 3rd, 36th and 45th) and an attached French armored force would begin landing early in the morning of 15 August on either side of St. Tropez. Meanwhile an airborne task force consisting of American, British and Canadian airborne troops would land behind the invasion beaches to cut roads and isolate the German defenders. The 7th Army was commanded by Major General Alexander M. Patch, and the 1st Airborne Task Force by Major General R.T. Frederick, U.S. Army, who had led the Devil's Brigade (1st Special Service Force) in some spectacular mountain operations in the Winter Line in Italy. The Devil's Brigade was a unit in the U.S. Army recruited largely from penal offenders lodged in the stockades, and from Canadian volunteers. They were trained at Helena, Montana, to fight in snow conditions which is why, after a hair-raising plan to fight in Norway with Snowcats (tracked vehicles) had been abandoned, they were posted to the Apennine mountains in Italy in the winter of 1943–44. The Devil's Brigade were also parachute-trained at Helena – one jump after 15 minutes of ground training – but the mountain men were never used in action in that role.

Below: Lieutenant General Lewis H. Brereton presents the Distinguished Flying Cross to a C-47 pilot at a base in England.

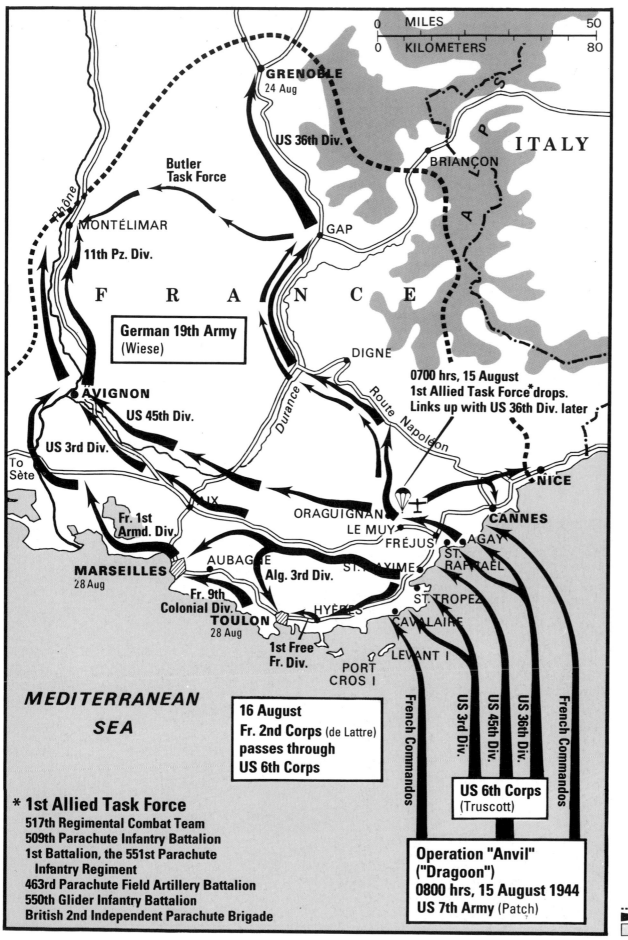

MILES
0   50
KILOMETERS
0   80

GRENOBLE
24 Aug

US 36th Div.

ITALY

BRIANÇON

Butler
Task Force

A L P S

Rhône

MONTÉLIMAR

11th Pz. Div.

F R A N C E

German 19th Army
(Wiese)

DIGNE

Durance

Route Napoléon

0700 hrs, 15 August
1st Allied Task Force drops.*
Links up with US 36th Div. later

AVIGNON

US 45th Div.

US 3rd Div.

To
Sète

NICE

AIX

Fr. 1st
Armd. Div.

ORAGUIGNAN

CANNES

LE MUY

AGAY

FRÉJUS

ST.
RAPHAËL

MARSEILLES
28 Aug

AUBAGNE

Alg. 3rd Div.

ST. MAXIME

ST. TROPEZ

Fr. 9th
Colonial Div.

HYÈRES

CAVALAIRE

TOULON
28 Aug

1st Free
Fr. Div.

LEVANT I

PORT
CROS I

MEDITERRANEAN
SEA

French Commandos

US 3rd Div.

US 45th Div.

US 36th Div.

French Commandos

16 August
Fr. 2nd Corps (de Lattre)
passes through
US 6th Corps

US 6th Corps
(Truscott)

* **1st Allied Task Force**
517th Regimental Combat Team
509th Parachute Infantry Battalion
1st Battalion, the 551st Parachute
    Infantry Regiment
463rd Parachute Field Artillery Battalion
550th Glider Infantry Battalion
British 2nd Independent Parachute Brigade

**Operation "Anvil"
("Dragoon")
0800 hrs, 15 August 1944
US 7th Army (Patch)**

AIRBORNE LANDINGS BY
PARATROOPS AND GLIDERS
FRONT LINE 28 AUGUST 1944
GERMAN COUNTERATTACKS
LAND OVER 6000 FEET

Parachute units of the 1st Allied Task Force included the 517th Regimental Combat Team, the 509th Battalion, the 1st Battalion of the 551st Parachute Infantry, and the 463rd Parachute Field Artillery Battalion. One glider infantry battalion, the 550th, and a number of special units made up the remainder of the American element. The Anglo-Canadian element was represented by the British 2nd Independent Parachute Brigade Group. The fly-in from an airfield in Italy was to be handled by the U.S. 51st Troop Carrier Wing, a glider force numbering 61 CG-4As and Horsas following on with the support weapons. An Airborne Training Center was set up near Rome, mainly for the benefit of the air crews and the newly formed glider unit. The pathfinders were also able to complete a period of joint training, and all troop carrier serials flew a practise flight over a course set up to resemble the one to be used for the operation.

Operation "Anvil" – the airborne arm of "Dragoon" – began before the main assault early on 15 August when, by way of a diversionary mission, six aircraft dropped "window" (masses of aluminum foil strips) to create the impression on enemy radar that a massive force was on the way. These aircraft also dropped 600 parachute dummies and rifle simulators and battle noise effects on a false drop zone north and west of Toulon.

(According to German radio reports, the ruse was a success.) The pathfinders dropped at 3.30 a.m., at which time the main parachute lift of 396 aircraft in nine serials took off to make V of Vs formation for the two-hour flight on a clear night to the Côte d'Azur.

Only one of the pathfinder teams jumped onto its assigned drop zone. One team jumped prematurely east of Le Muy, and found its way to the drop zone only just in time to help guide in one afternoon glider serial. A third aeroplane became completely lost and the men jumped about 24km (15 miles) from the assigned spot. However, relying on the beacons of the "Eureka-Rebecca" equipment the pathfinders did manage to set up and use their radio compass homing devices (MF beacons), the pilots and the navigators bringing in the main parachute assault force.

Approximately 60 per cent of the paratroopers landed on the three assigned drop zones or in the immediate vicinity of them. About 120 aircraft missed the DZs altogether. Fortunately the 1st Airborne Task Force was organized in a way that permitted small groups to act independently, and the Allied paratroopers were soon in action co-operating with the French Forces of the Interior (FFI) in seizing towns, undertaking local missions and intelligence work generally. By the end of D-day the villages of La Mitan, La Motte, Castron and Les Serres had been

Right: American paratroopers of the 1st Allied Airborne Task Force are briefed at an Italian aerodrome for Operation "Anvil-Dragoon," the invasion of the South of France, 15 August 1944. This was to be a combined parachute and glider assault mounted by American, British and Canadian airborne troops in support of the main amphibious forces.

Left: An aerial view of the DZs and LZs on the Côte d'Azur between Hyères and Cannes, southern France.

Below: American paratroopers are in charge of German prisoners on a dusty road at the height of summer in the South of France.

Below: British glider troops land in the Fréjus area, South of France. A shirt-sleeved "red beret" watches a Waco sailing in to land nearby.

captured, and the British 2nd Brigade was holding three vital road junctions, including the one at Le Muy, which was its principal objective.

Glider landings began in daylight at 9.00 a.m. after heavy overcast had delayed the first serial for an hour. Nine gliders were released too soon, four of them going down in the sea. Fortunately most of the men clinging to the wreckages of their gliders were picked up by ships of the invasion fleet heading for the French coastline. "Rommel's Asparagus" had also found its way to the soil of the south of France, but fortunately the poles that were found on the chosen LZs did little damage to the gliders as they sailed in. Resupply

missions were carried out but the cargoes were scattered over a wide area on the ground. Altogether the troop carriers flew 987 sorties and brought in 407 gliders. They carried 9,000 troops plus 221 jeeps and 213 artillery pieces. In some parachute resupply missions for ground troops on Cape Negre and near Vidauban, Douglas A-20 aircraft were found to be more suitable in this role than the C-47. The fighting in what has popularly been described as the "champagne" invasion was over for the airborne troops on the second day. The U.S. 7th Army and the French 1st Army made contact with the U.S. 3rd Army north-west of Dijon on 11 September.

Above left: American "glider riders" dismount through the nose of a Waco near La Motte, South of France.

Above: American paratroopers rest in a roadside position near La Motte. The objective of the 1st Allied Airborne Task Force was to capture bridges and road junctions to facilitate the advance of the U.S. Seventh Army, which consisted of the U.S. VI and French II Corps, through southern France to link with the U.S. and French armies advancing across the country to the north. Operation Anvil-Dragoon is also aptly known as the "champagne invasion." The airborne objectives were taken in 48 hours.

Bridges Galore

After General Sir Bernard Montgomery's 21st Army Group finally broke out of the Normandy beach-head in August and rapidly pursued the fleeing German army north-eastward, the British and Canadian forces surged through Belgium, arriving at the Dutch frontier by the end of the month. General Dwight D. Eisenhower had allowed Montgomery the fullest logistic support, as the former believed that the capture of the port of Antwerp was vital for the landing of supplies for the advance into Germany. Now the drive of the British 2nd Army stalled, partly because its existing lines of communication from Normandy were already strained to the limit, but partly also because Montgomery was strongly of the opinion that if he was given sufficient supplies of gasoline and ammunition his forces led by the tanks of XXX Corps could speed through the Netherlands, swing right to the north of the Reichswald, sweep across the North German Plain and be in Berlin by Christmas.

Although aware that Montgomery's forces had captured the port of Antwerp but left 86km (54 miles) of the estuary under German control, Eisenhower surprisingly agreed to Montgomery's demands. The American commanders were furious to say the least. Between 27 August and 4 September, the advance of Lieutenant General Omar N. Bradley's 12th Army Group faltered as gasoline supplies were switched to XXX Corps. Lieutenant General George S. Patton's U.S. 3rd Army crossed the Meuse (30 October) only to be halted there with empty fuel tanks. Lieutenant General Courtney Hodges's U.S. 1st Army, after bagging 25,000 prisoners at Mons on 3 September, was also reduced to inchworm progress. Patton was certain that if he had the gasoline he could be in Berlin long before the British general.

In *On to Berlin – Battles of an Airborne Commander 1943–1946*, General James M. Gavin writes:

"To add to the difficulty that Montgomery was unwittingly getting himself into in Europe, the impression that he was making in America was far from favorable. Aware of Patton's spectacular break-out and overrunning of Brittany, the Americans were at last beginning to see Montgomery as the 'do-nothing' general. They were beginning to tire of the publicity he was receiving for battles fought and won by the Americans. American wounded were returning in large numbers...

"The problem of public opinion in America seemed to escape Montgomery entirely. At one time in late August he recommended to Eisenhower that Patton be brought to a full stop and that he, Montgomery, 'be given all the resources to go ahead and win the war.' 'The American public would never stand for stopping Patton in full cry, and public opinion wins wars,' Eisenhower told him. 'Nonsense,' Montgomery shot back angrily. 'Victories win wars. Give people victory and they won't care who won it.' "

As it happened, Eisenhower did give Montgomery the supplies but he also reduced

Far left: General Dwight D. Eisenhower talks to men of the 101st Airborne Division in southern England.

Above: Lieutenant General Brian Horrocks, commander of British XXX Corps, and Field Marshal Montgomery, supremo of 21st Army Group in Holland, September 1944.

FRONT LINE 17 SEPT. 1944

PLANNED ALLIED AIRBORNE
DROPPING ZONES

PLANNED MAIN AXIS
OF ALLIED ADVANCE

7th Div. MAIN GERMAN DISPOSITIONS
17 SEPT 1944

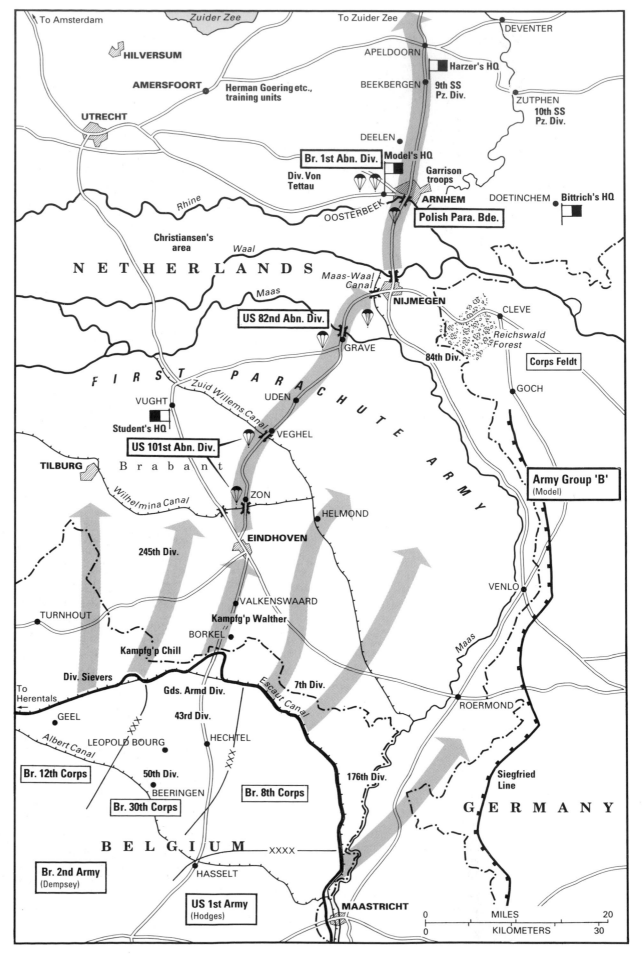

Facing page, above: After the breakout from Normandy in August 1944, the Anglo-Canadian 21st Army Group swept across France and Belgium to the Dutch border. Here the newly promoted Field Marshal Montgomery conceived a plan to deploy three airborne divisions to seize a corridor through Holland for his armor to advance beyond the Lower Rhine into Germany. (Left to right) Major General Allan Adair, G.O.C. the Guards Armoured Division, Field Marshal Montgomery, Lieutenant General Brian Horrocks, G.O.C. XXX Corps and Major General G.P.B. Roberts, G.O.C. 11th Armoured Division, discuss their chances of success in the impending Operation "Market-Garden."

Facing page, below: General James M. Gavin, at 37 years of age the youngest general in the Allied armies, points out the 82nd Airborne Division's dispositions in the Nijmegen area to General Sir Miles Dempsey, commanding the British Second Army. Dempsey described the 82nd as the finest division in the Allied services.

the British Commander's demands considerably. Montgomery was nevertheless all ready to go. General Sir Miles Dempsey's British 2nd Army, with Lieutenant General Sir Brian Horrocks's XXX Corps in the center, was then positioned on the line of the Albert Canal with a bridgehead over the Meuse–Escaut Canal. In this bridgehead the Guards Armoured Division stood astride the main highway leading northward from the Dutch frontier through Eindhoven, Nijmegen, Arnhem and Apeldoorn to the Zuider Zee. The road to Arnhem on the Lower Rhine offered a means of creating a corridor through the enemy defenses into Germany. The West Wall that protected the German homeland lay less than 64km (40 miles) to the east and ended at Goch a few miles south of the Reichswald.

Montgomery's idea was to turn the flank of the frontier defenses by advancing across the Lower Rhine at Arnhem and then to wheel eastwards. Masses of airborne troops would be required to seize road and rail bridges over the waterways straddling the highway from the Dutch frontier to the bridge at Arnhem. In the early evening of 10 September, within hours of a meeting between Lieutenant General F.A.M. Browning and Montgomery, who had now been promoted to field marshal, Browning attended a meeting convened by Lieutenant General Lewis H. Brereton for the first basic planning conference for Operation "Market." Brereton told the assembled senior officers that the objective was to "grab the bridges with thunderclap surprise" to provide the one-highway corridor for the advance of the British tanks in Operation "Garden." To invade the Netherlands, which had first been invaded by German paratroopers in 1940, Brereton planned to land almost 35,000 men. The U.S. 101st Airborne Division, under Major General Maxwell D. Taylor, was ordered to drop north of Eindhoven to capture the bridge over the Wilhelmina Canal at Veghel. The U.S. 82nd Airborne Division, under Major General James M. Gavin, was to land south of Nijmegen on both sides of the highway near Grave. In this locality Gavin's objectives were the bridge over the Maas River at Grave, and the road and the rail bridges over the Waal River at Nijmegen. Farthest away from the land advance's start line, Major General Robert Urquhart's 1st Airborne Division (with Major General's Stanislaw Sosabowski's Polish Parachute Brigade under command) was to seize the road bridge at Arnhem. The British 52nd (Lowland) Division was

Some 1,543 parachute and tug aircraft were available to Browning's I Airborne Corps. The British share of 519 aircraft was equitable, but insufficient to transport three British and one Polish brigades to Arnhem in one operation. While the American assault troops could be carried to their DZs in one lift, the British and Polish brigades would therefore require several lifts to take them to Arnhem. This meant that as on 6 June in Normandy, the British airborne troops would again be denied the tactical benefit of concentration in strength. The U.S. IX Troop Carrier Command did, however, lay on 279 C-47s for the parachutists to supplement the Royal Air Force's 240 converted bombers. Most of the latter were Short Stirlings but there were 40 Handley Page Halifaxes and a few Armstrong Whitworth Albemarles.

When Taylor looked closely at the map, he quickly noted that over the 24km (15 mile) stretch of highway his troops must capture two major canal crossings and no less than nine highway and railroad bridges. At Veghel (over the Aa River and Zuit Willemsvaart Canal) there were four bridges, one a major canal crossing. A few miles south in St. Oedenrode, a bridge over the Lower Dommel had to be taken; 6·14km (4 miles) from there was the second major bridge over the Wilhelmina Canal near the village of Zon, and to the west a bridge near the hamlet of Best. Some 8km (5 miles) farther south in Eindhoven, four bridges over the Upper Dommel had to be taken. The DZ terrain was generally speaking flat, but a maze of waterways, dikes, ditches and trees lined the roads, and all constituted serious obstacles for the parachute and glider men. Taylor decided to pinpoint his main landing areas for the "Screaming Eagles" on the edge of a forest near Zon, roughly equidistant between Eindoven and Veghel.

The task of the 82nd Airborne was more daunting. Its 16km (10 mile) sector was wider than that of the 101st and it would be farther away from the advancing ground forces. In this central segment of the corridor, the huge, nine-span, 450m (1,475 ft) long bridge over the Maas River at Grave and at least one of four smaller railway and road crossings over the Maas-Waal Canal had to be taken. The huge 550m (1,805 ft) long bridge over the Waal River at Nijmegen, placed almost in the center of this city of 90,000 inhabitants, was a prime objective. Once captured, none of these objectives could be made secure without seizing the Grosbeek Heights, dominating the area a few miles south of

Above: Lieutenant General F.A.M. "Boy" Browning (left) and Air Chief Marshal Sir Arthur Tedder confer with an American troop carrier officer at an airfield in England prior to "Market Garden."

scheduled to fly into Deelen airfield after consolidation in the Arnhem area. Browning, whose headquarters was to be located in the neighborhood of Nijmegen, was chosen to command I Allied Airborne Corps. Although there was little time to obtain intelligence reports on the dispositions of the German troops in the Netherlands, Browning predicted a brilliant victory with minimal resistance – but he did add reflectively after one conference before take-off: "We may be going one bridge too far."

Nijmegen. Gavin's troops also had to contend with Panzers advancing from the cover of the Reichswald and a regiment of troops in barracks in the city. Nijmegen was also heavily defended by anti-aircraft batteries.

Gavin noted especially at a conference in Sunningdale that the Grave bridge was a "huge affair," several stories high, and he was later to learn that when the bridge had originally been built, cavities for demolitions had been constructed into the bridge structure and explosives put in place. On Tuesday morning, 14 September, the division commanders, each with some of their staff officers, assembled for a meeting at Browning's headquarters at Moor Park, Hertfordshire. Taylor obtained approval to use three major landing zones, for the 101st. Gavin was in full agreement with Browning's directive to capture all other objectives before tackling the Nijmegen bridge. Urquhart caused concern among his American colleagues when he announced he would use DZs and LZs 9·15 to 12·75km (6 to 8 miles) west of Arnhem. Urquhart's reasons were that the Royal Air Force was anxious to avoid the anti-aircraft batteries defending Arnhem and nearby Deelen airfield and in any case the soggy polder abutting the Lower Rhine was thought to be unsuitable for parachute and glider landings.

(As it happened, the polder-reclaimed floodland on the river banks would certainly have been firm enough to take the landings, but although Urquhart was later strongly criticized for his choice of landing areas, the fact remains that the R.A.F. refused to drop the 1st Airborne Division any nearer to the Arnhem bridge.)

On the evening of 16 September, 282 Royal Air Force bombers took off from their bases in the eastern counties to drop 890 tons of bombs on German airfields within range of the Dutch target areas. Early on the morning of Sunday 17 September, finally designated as D-day, 200 Avro Lancaster and 23 de Havilland Mosquito bombers of the R.A.F. began attacking flak batteries along the coast of the Netherlands. Then, following closely on the heels of the British bomber force, 852 Boeing B-17 Flying Fortresses, with an escort of 153 fighters, flew out over the North Sea before splitting into two streams, one to beat up opposition on the northern paratroop and gliderborne flight route in the Netherlands, and the other to perform the same tasks on the southern route. It must now have been clear to the Germans that the Netherlands was the target for an invasion; the immense scale of which they were to learn before the day was out.

Altogether, on that warm, sunny, Sunday

Above: This B-17 "Flying Fortress" forms part of waves of bombers which for four days hammered enemy targets in Holland in preparation for the Allied airborne invasion of Holland.

morning, the airborne troops having donned their parachutes and humping their weapons and heavy kitbags descended from their trucks at 24 airfields and made their way in files to the waiting aircraft, the gliders carrying cargo having already been loaded the previous day. Soon a total of 1,543 troop transports and 478 tugs with gliders in tow were airborne heading for the English coast. The roar of the aircraft engines overhead was deafening, as can be confirmed by the present writer who, as a small boy, was cycling along a country lane near Hatfield, Hertfordshire, that morning so long ago. The lone cyclist was not aware that the sky over Hatfield had been chosen as the rendezvous for the entire 82nd Airborne Division, the British pathfinders and the 1st Air Landing Brigade taking off from airfields as far west and south as Fairford in Gloucestershire and Tarrant Rushton in Dorset, converging over Hatfield before flying north-east to Aldeburgh on the Suffolk coast. From Aldeburgh the skytrain then proceeded to cross the Dutch coast over Schouwen Island before the British element wheeled left for Arnhem and the American element right for Nijmegen.

The 101st Airborne Division, on the other hand, took off from airfields in the East Midlands and set a south-east course for the North Foreland in Kent before crossing the Channel to the Belgian coast; the "Screaming Eagles" then turned north over Ghent for Eindhoven. The 1st Parachute Brigade, forming the first British paratroop lift stationed in the Lincolnshire area, joined forces with 1st Airborne Division's glider brigade over Aldeburgh. In addition to the airborne force flying in the slow-moving transport aircraft and gliders, 1,130 Allied fighters flew in support of the greatest air armada to date of the war. Along the northern flight route the 82nd Airborne managed to get all the way to its DZs and LZs without losing a single aircraft but, flying in its C-47s at only 120m (400 ft) as it crossed over Schouwen, took hits from a combination of flak and rifle fire as it progressed inland.

Below: American paratroopers emplane in a C-47 for Holland.

The 101st Airborne, flying on the southern route, was not so lucky. All went well until Ghent was reached and the skytrain turned north. On the way to Eindhoven, the C-47s and the CG-4As were subjected to devastating anti-aircraft fire. Farther back in the air column, the pilots of IX Troop Carrier Command knew what they were flying into but there was no question of turning back. It was mid-day when the 82nd approached Nijmegen. As usual Gavin was scanning the terrain below for features that would confirm beyond doubt that the division was heading in the right direction. Suddenly he was almost relieved to see the Groesbeek high ground looming up ahead of them. As they jumped, the men of the "All American" were so low down that they hit the ground almost at once. Gavin, heavily laden with ammunition, weapons and grenades, landed with his parachute canopy still swinging violently.

The Germans stationed in the Nijmegen area, although taken completely by surprise in spite of the pre-drop aerial bombardment, responded swiftly to the assault from the sky and the men of the 82nd were subjected to murderous rifle and machine-gun fire.

The fly-in 9·75km (6 miles) to the south of the 101st Airborne was watched through binoculars with admiration by at least two important generals that morning, one British and one German. Even as Taylor's division crossed the Dutch coast, Horrocks was already standing on a slag heap by the Meuse–Escaut Canal with his field glasses trained northward for the first sight of the airborne armada. "We can hold the Arnhem Bridge for four days," Browning told him, "but I think we might be going a bridge too far." As soon as I Airborne Corps touched down, Horrocks's orders would send the Guards Armoured Division thundering down the road to Eindhoven heading the XXX Corps race through Eindhoven, up the road to Nijmegen, Arnhem, Apeldoorn and "on to Berlin." Some 20,000 corps vehicles were waiting for Horrocks's signal to move.

Below: C-47s and Wacos take the southern route to Eindhoven and Nijmegen, Sunday, 17 September 1944.

At Vaught, a small village situated only 11·2km (7 miles) west of one of the 101st's DZs, Generaloberst (Colonel General) Kurt Student, the commander of the German 1st Parachute Army, was sitting at his desk in his headquarters when he heard the unmistakable drone of parachute transport aircraft. Student rushed out onto his balcony where, as he was to say after the war, he saw an "endless stream of enemy transport and cargo planes as far the eye could see." While staring skyward, he knew that those aircraft must be full of paratroopers standing hooked up and ready to jump, and turning to one of his officers, he remarked breathlessly: "Oh, what I might have accomplished if only I had such a force at my disposal." It might indeed be truthfully said that if it had not been for Student's vision way back in 1935 in raising German airborne forces, Operation "Market" might never have taken place.

The 101st Division dropped 9·75km (6 miles) south of the 82nd's positions alongside the key main road, which quickly became known

as Hell's Highway. The regiment that dropped closest to Student's headquarters was the 501st Parachute Infantry. The 502nd and the 506th Parachute Infantry landed between St. Oedenrode and Best. The 1st Battalion of the 502nd immediately captured the road bridge over the Dommel River at St. Oedenrode. The 506th suffered the only setback to the "Screaming Eagles" on D-day. The 1st Battalion of the 506th was under orders to grab the main road bridge and two other small bridges over the Wilhelmina Canal

at Zon. Once the battalion had secured the Zon bridges, the objective was to race, followed by the other two battalions, into Eindhoven, where the Americans were due to link up with advancing British armor. Unhappily the main Zon bridge was blown up by the Germans in the faces of the 1st Battalion of the 506th, and at the end of D-day Eindhoven was not, as scheduled, in American hands.

Throughout the 40km (25 mile) perimeter of the 82nd Airborne's landing area, the division's three parachute infantry regiments

Above: Wacos find a perfect landing zone for the glider troops of the 101st Airborne Division near Zon. The bridge objectives in this area were the closest to the Dutch frontier.

Above: "Screaming Eagles" glider infantry are about to emplane in Wacos for Holland.

Above: A platoon of the 101st uses the cover of a hedgerow to attack isolated enemy positions near Zon.

Left: 101st paratroopers pause to regroup after a fire-fight on the Eindhoven sector.

Below: Men of the British 1st Airborne Division aboard a C-47 heading for Arnhem. Unlike the American paratroopers, the British did not carry reserve 'chutes at this time, and for a long time after the war. The "red devil" was not as heavily laden as his American counterpart, but he still carried a substantial load in an airborne kit-bag attached by straps to thigh and ankle, and released on the end of a rope in mid-air. Rifles and Bren guns were carried wrapped in green felt sleeves, also dropped on the end of a rope. Sten carbines were usually held between the upper straps of the parachute harness.

and the 376th Parachute Field Artillery Battalion were landing with great accuracy on their DZs. The 504th Parachute Infantry was able to seize the enormous nine-span bridge over the Maas River near Grave. The 504th's veteran paratroopers were able to capture the bridge swiftly as the men were dropped accurately on both sides of the bridge. The capture of the Maas bridge was the first major achievement of Operation "Market Garden." The 505th Parachute Infantry had been dropped on the other side of the Groesbeek Heights, capturing the small town of Groesbeek with little difficulty before occupying defensive positions along the southern edge of the heights of the Reichswald. The 508th Parachute Infantry having landed compactly, the 1st Battalion's commander sent a reinforced rifle platoon on a patrol into Nijmegen to find out how heavily the big bridge there was being guarded by the Germans, Gavin's orders to the 509th being to capture the bridge with the 1st Battalion.

The subject of this book is the U.S. airborne forces, and it is not therefore proposed to describe the ten-day Battle of Arnhem in any detail. An outline of the grim and tragic struggle to capture the Arnhem bridge over the Lower Rhine by the British 1st Airborne Division is nonetheless vital to understanding the outcome of Operation "Market Garden" as a whole. The taking of the Arnhem bridge in theory was not the toughest of the Allied assignments, but it was the farthest of XXX Corps' objectives to reach by road. It was not a case, as many historians aver, of how soon the 1st Airborne could take the bridge but rather how long the tanks of XXX Corps would take to relieve the encircled, lightly armed parachute and glider troops, who as it happened were soon fighting for their lives against an S.S. Panzer division.

The 1st Airborne's parachute and glider landings took place between 1.15 and 2.00 p.m. on 17 September, and were the most successful that had been achieved so far by

either side in the war. By that time the pathfinders were already on the ground and had marked the DZs and LZs. The bombers towing the glider pilots came in first, followed by the carrier aircraft. Handling their flimsy craft with considerable skill, the glider pilots came in on the pathfinders' smoke signals and orange and crimson markers with tremendous accuracy. Punctually came the Royal Air Force and the blue sky blossomed with over 2,000 parachutes of many colors floating gently to earth in the warm breeze. The landing was virtually unopposed.

After reaching its rendezvous on the ground, the 1st Parachute Brigade (with the 2nd Parachute Battalion leading) formed columns to move into Arnhem, which lay 8km (5 miles) as the crows fly to the east of the heathland forming the Renkumse DZ and LZ. Meanwhile the glider troops moved northward across the main railway line to guard the DZ at Ginkel Heath and the LZ at Reyerscamp for the arrival of the 4th

Parachute Brigade the following day. On the afternoon of 17 September after joyous greetings by the Dutch villagers, the 1st Parachute Brigade began to experience a foretaste of things to come.

While preparations were being made to secure the landing zones for the American glider reinforcements on D+1, the 101st's 506th Parachute Infantry fought its way south in the early morning, capturing four bridges on the road to Eindhoven. The Americans expected to see British tanks approaching, but the leading tanks of the Guards Armoured Division advancing along the highway in single file were at that time locked in a fierce battle 8km (5 miles) to the south and did not reach Eindhoven until the early evening. Having lost the bridge over the Wilhelmina Canal at Zon, the 502nd Parachute Infantry attempted to capture an alternative bridge situated nearby at Best, but that too was blown up in the faces of the leading platoon of Company "H." In the confusion that

Above: Glider troops of the 1st Airborne Division at an airfield in England destined for Arnhem. Stirling bombers to be used as tugs are seen lined up in the background.

Right: The first two Horsa gliders to touch down on the Arnhem landing zones, 17 November. They landed so close to each other that their wing tips interlocked. These gliders brought in the headquarters section of the Royal Artillery Support regiment; its commanding officer, Lieutenant Colonel "Sheriff" Thompson strides past the jeep on the left.

Below: The DZs and LZs for the Arnhem lift were located on heathland surrounded by thick wooded terrain 25km (15 miles) to the west of Arnhem. The first lift on 17 September was virtually unopposed; the Horsas of the 1st Air-Landing Brigade landed first but many of the gliders had been lost en route resulting in an acute shortage of jeeps on the ground; the paratroopers of the 1st Parachute Brigade came in next, hot in the wake of the glider troops. On a warm sunny morning, 2nd Parachute Battalion assembled at their rendezvous and set out to walk to the Arnhem bridge.

reigned the platoon knocked out a nearby 88mm (3·46 in) gun position. Throughout the day this platoon was engaged in random firefights which continued until the following morning in the thick mist.

The gliders came in punctually on the afternoon of D+1. All told, the CG-4As and Horsas brought in 2,575 men, 146 Jeeps, 109 trailers, two small bulldozers, and supplies of food and ammunition. For the most part the landing went smoothly. A few gliders were smashed but nobody was killed. However, Brigadier General Anthony C. McAuliffe, the 101st Division's artillery commander, who had travelled in a glider towed by a C-47 which had been badly shot up, did not enjoy the ride. He was firmly of the opinion, as were most of the wartime parachutists, it was safer to jump than sit helplessly in a glider!

Browning traveled to his corps HQ location in a Horsa glider piloted by the 1st Air Landing Brigade's commander, Brigadier George Chatterton. For the immaculate general dressed in a barathea battledress with knife-edge creases, and a gleaming Sam Browne belt and revolver holster, "Market Garden" was the crowning moment of his military career. But his optimism about the overall success of the operation was soon to be squelched. He was in a good position to view the progress of the two American airborne divisions but he had no news of what was going on in the Arnhem sector where, although a company of the 2nd Parachute Battalion had reached the bridge by dusk of the first day, the main body of the 1st Airborne Division over the next few days was brought to a standstill west of the village of Ooster-beek by the 9th SS Panzer Division "Hohenstaufen." The situation was made no easier by the fact that airborne signalers were having little or no luck in the closely-wooded sandy terrain with the voice radio sets, and contact was soon lost with the battalion at the bridge.

On the 82nd's front, the "All Americans" were holding on tightly to the Groesbeek heights. The 508th Parachute Infantry, which had been unsuccessful in its first approach to the Nijmegen bridge, was ordered by Gavin to make another attempt at capturing it. Company "G" of the 508th led the way but was recalled when it ran into a murderous blast of rifle and machine-gun fire from the bridge defenders. As early as D+2, 18 September, a fierce argument developed in the enemy camp between Gruppenführer (Lieutenant General) Willi Bittrich,

commander of II S.S. Panzer Corps, and Generalfeldmarschall (Field Marshal) Walter Model, in overall command of the German forces in the region, as to whether the Nijmegen bridge should or should not be destroyed. Bittrich argued that if the bridge over the Waal were destroyed the Allied offensive would be stopped in its tracks, and the British at Arnhem cut off and destroyed. Model, on the other hand, insisted that he had enough forces at his disposal to hold the bridge and ordered Student's parachute army, assisted by 10th SS Panzer Division "Frundsberg" to defend it at all costs.

Above: Dutch civilians turn out to greet American paratroopers on the southern sector.

Left: Pvt. Bernard M. Nakla of the 101st Airborne Division gives a Dutch girl chewing gum. The boy and the young Dutchman are dressed in battle garb.

Early on the morning of D+2, 19 September, the tanks of the Guards Armoured Division rolled into the 82nd Airborne's air-head and linked up with the 504th Parachute Infantry near Grave. At this point, the airborne mission of the "Screaming Eagles" came to an end, but during the next few days the division was engaged in a fierce struggle to keep the newly christened Hell's Highway open.

Horrocks reached Gavin's command post in the afternoon of D+2. The 82nd's focus was now on capturing the Nijmegen bridge, and Horrocks agreed to lend the Americans one company of British infantry and a battalion of tanks to help the 2nd Battalion of the 505th Parachute Infantry take the bridge from the south end. Gavin also announced that he had a plan to send another force across the Waal in small boats to converge on the north end of the bridge. Gavin had to admit, though, that he could find no civilian boats for the purpose. So Horrocks arranged for 33 engineer assaults boats to be brought up to the 82nd's zone of operations. Gavin immediately sent for Colonel Reuben Tucker, the commander of the 504th Parachute Infantry, and in a meeting after dark in the command post area told him to be ready to cross the river the following day.

Tucker had a tough assignment. The Waal was 365m (1,200 ft) wide and had a very fast current. The site chosen for the crossing was about 1·6km (1 mile) downstream from the bridge, and in the Netherlands the terrain along the banks of the rivers is usually very flat. This meant that the American paratroopers would be exposed to enemy fire even before they embarked in the boats.

But the British tanks were behind schedule and therefore eager to move, so there was no time to wait for the cover of the night when the boats were delivered the following day. Late that morning, 20 September, Tucker moved the 504th up to the river bank, the 1st and 2nd Battalions being heavily attacked on the way. Tucker planned to send Major Julian A. Cook's 3rd Battalion across first to be followed, once Cook had reached the other bank, by Major Willard E. Harrison's 1st Battalion. The amphibious force was in cover just behind the riverline a full hour before H-hour, but there were no boats to be found. When they did arrive shortly after this, Cook's boatmen had just 20 minutes to discuss the art of river craft.

The Irish Guards sent a force of 30 Sherman tanks under the command of Lieutenant Colonel J.O.E. ("Joe") Vandeleur up to the bridge to support this crossing, and the 82nd Artillery was alerted to give covering fire. At 2.30 p.m. fighters swooped in on schedule, machine-gunning and rocketing the far shore.

Right: A photograph of the Nijmegen bridge taken after its capture and the Shermans have passed over it in the direction of Arnhem. The hole has been caused by a German bombing raid.

Twenty-six boats (each expected to carry 13 paratroopers) were assembled, someone yelled "Go" and there was a frantic rush for the water's edge. The troopers had a hard time getting the boats into deep water while they climbed in over the sides with their weapons. Now German small-arms fire began to open up on the tiny flotilla. Engineers were assigned to the boats to paddle them but the troopers were forced to lend a hand to keep the boats on a steady course by grasping their rifles upside down, using the butt ends as paddles.

A smoke screen was laid to afford protection to the paratroopers, but as they crossed huge gaps appeared in the swirling smoke, which then virtually disappeared. Just as soon as the paratroopers left the south bank German heavy artillery and machine-gun fire opened up, automatic rifle fire whipping into the boats from a road running along the embankment 180m (600 ft) ahead of them. Some of the boats were kept afloat only when the men stuffed their handkerchiefs in the bullet holes. A party at the bridge with Vandeleur, which included Horrocks and Browning, was amazed to see Cook leading his men as they ran straight for the embankment, firing their automatics, as they scrambled up to come to grips with the Germans on the roadway. The observers were also astonished to see the boats turn swiftly back to pick up the next wave of 504th. The troopers charged forward, throwing grenades and winkling out the Germans in the fox holes on the other side of the road.

By now the 3rd Battalion was badly shot up, but two captains rounded up all the men they could find and led the race to the bridge through intense fire. The Germans began shortly to retreat, and the northern end of the bridge was in American hands two hours after the start of the assault. Meanwhile the other American paratroopers and tanks of the Grenadier Guards were engaged in a ding-dong battle on the far-side approaches to the bridge, but by 6.00 p.m. the tanks were closing in on the last fox holes at the southern entrance. It was nearly 7.00 p.m. when the tanks started to cross the bridge. The question now was would the Germans blow the explosives which were known to have been laid? The answer lay with Oberführer (Major General) Heinz Harmel, who already had the bridge under observation. At his side was an engineer with a detonator box connected to wires to the bridge. At the beginning of the afternoon he believed the Germans had the situation well in hand but now he was not so sure. The leading tank was halfway across

when, as Cornelius Ryan vividly described in *A Bridge Too Far*:

"He shouted, 'Let it blow!' The engineer jammed the plunger down. Nothing happened. The British tanks continued to advance. Harmel yelled, 'Again!' Once again the engineer slammed down the detonator handle, but again the huge explosions that Harmel had expected failed to occur. 'I was waiting to see the bridge collapse and the tanks plunge into the river,' he recalled. 'Instead, they moved forward relentlessly, getting bigger and bigger, closer and closer.' He yelled to his anxious staff, 'My God, they'll be here in two minutes!' Rapping out orders to his officers, Harmel told them 'to block the roads between Elst and Lent with every available anti-tank gun and artillery piece because if we don't, they'll roll straight on through to Arnhem.' "

While the American paratroopers were mopping up at the northern end of the bridge, they were amazed and angry to see the British tanks grind to a halt. Several hours went by and no move now looked likely as the dismounted crews brewed up and chatted on the road side. Tucker, in particular, was furious, being of the belief that his regiment had been wasted in the cross-river assault. The reason lay with Model's decision on 20 September to throw in the bulk of his forces to annihilate the 1st Airborne Division at Arnhem. As a result the situation was fast deteriorating on the British sector, and German armor in any case now straddled the

Below: Major General "Jumping Jim" Gavin introduces King George VI to his regimental and battalion commanders of the 82nd Airborne Division at XXX Corps headquarters. The corps commander, Lieutenant General Brian Horrocks is on the left.

road between Nijmegen and Arnhem, making an advance on a "one-tank" front impossible. The Shermans did move north again on the morning of 21 September but soon came to a halt again. A decision had been made to call off Operation "Market Garden;" the Red Berets at Arnhem were to be abandoned to their fate.

At the outset of the Battle of Arnhem, the Germans had two Panzer formations at their disposal, the 9th and 10th SS Panzer Divisions, but Model decided that one Panzer division was enough to smash an airborne division, ill-equipped to fight the latest Tiger tanks. The 10th SS Panzer Division was thus switched south to fight the Americans on the Nijmegen sector. Within two days the Battle of Arnhem assumed a definite pattern. The 4th Parachute Brigade had arrived on the afternoon of 18 September and when its commander, Brigadier J.W. Hackett, hit the ground he sensed that all was not well. Urquhart, the division commander, had set out to make personal contacts with the 1st and 3rd Parachute Battalions advancing with some other units already in Arnhem, and with the 2nd Battalion at the bridge, but was now sheltering in a house in Arnhem with a German tank parked outside. Effectively, for a few days, 1st Airborne had no commander.

The besieged battalion group at the bridge was engaged in a desperate stuggle with Panzer forces. The 1st, 3rd and 11th Battalions of the Parachute Regiment together with the South Staffords (a glider battalion) were fighting their way yard by yard into the town. These forces were followed by the 10th and 156th Parachute Battalions moving alongside the railway line to Arnhem, while the glider men of the 7th King's Own Scottish Borderers remained in the rear to secure a landing zone for the Polish glider troops. "Black Tuesday" (19 September) was really the day that set the seal on 1st Airborne's misfortunes. At Spanhoe and Cottesmore in England the Independent Polish Parachute Brigade Group was already emplaned when adverse weather conditions forced a postponement of its drop for 24 hours. But when the Polish paratroopers were finally airborne on 20 September they were routed to a DZ south of the Lower Rhine at Driel. The idea was that the Poles would first cross the river and then fight their way into the airhead. No boats were available, so the Polish paratroopers were lost to the fight.

The Polish gliders appeared over their LZ

north of the river on 20 September, but they flew in at all angles and from every direction to the landing ground near Joanna Hoeve to be smothered in flak from all types of German guns. Some were on fire before they landed; jeeps with punctured petrol tanks flooded the wooden fuselages of the Horsas and red-hot flak turned them into flaming infernos. The Polish troops who survived the landing formed a fast-moving column of jeeps, trailers and 6-pounder anti-tank guns, then raced headlong into the cauldron at Oosterbeek, just a few miles west of Arnhem. The fighting continued unabated until well into 25 September, by which time Urquhart had heard officially about the halt of the advance of the British 2nd Army. At this stage of the battle the paratroopers at the bridge were virtually without ammunition and there was no alternative but to surrender when the last round of ammunition had been expended. By that time Urquhart's command was compressed into a small pocket around Oosterbeek. The only route available for withdrawal was south over the Lower Rhine; the evacuation from the Oosterbeek perimeter commencing in pouring rain just before midnight on 25 – 26 September.

Some of the wounded were to be taken with the escaping parties but there was no alternative but to leave the majority of them behind. All the doctors volunteered to stay. The escapers blackened their faces and muffled their boots, and loose equipment was tied tightly to the body. The distance to be covered from the northern outposts was approximately 3·2km (2 miles). The men moved cautiously in single files, each man holding onto the smock of the man in front. Fortunately for the 1st Airborne, the Germans did not know they were going but even so desultory shell and mortar fire straddled their lines of retreat. The men were halted in their tracks by the occasional sounds of small arms and machine-gun fire. The engineers from the south bank had performed wonders in assembling the river craft but inevitably there were not enough to go round. When the last boat had gone about 500 men were left behind; some plunged into the river and swam and others went off in a hopeless search for other crossing points.

Urquhart brought out of the battle of Arnhem less than 3,000 of the original 10,005 men landed on 17-18 September. During the battle 5,000 men (including 3,000 wounded) went into captivity, including two brigadiers and four battalion commanders. Altogether, 2,050 men were killed. About 200 men were

at large on the north bank for several weeks before falling prisoner or crossing the river with the help of the Dutch resistance. Although the British 1st Airborne Division now ceased to exist, the Americans continued in the thick of the action on Horrocks's XXX Corps front. Casualties taken since 17 September by the U.S. airborne divisions amounted to 3,344 dead, wounded and missing in the 82nd zone of operations and 3,792 casualties of all types in the case of the 101st.

Facing page, above: A group of Germans shelter among trees and bushes in the Arnhem area.
Facing page, below: An aerial view of the Arnhem bridge held at the north end by a composite group based on Lieutenant Colonel John Frost's 2nd Parachute Battalion.
Above: Four British officers of 1st Airborne Division land in a rowing boat from the River Waal near the Nijmegen bridge.
Below: US paratroopers mop up in the XXX Corps sector.

Hitler's Last Bow

The fighting in the southern part of the Netherlands finally petered out early in November 1944, and by the end of the month the two American airborne divisions had been withdrawn by rail to base camps in the cathedral city of Reims in France. They were met there by members of the 517th Parachute Combat Team, the 509th and the 551st Parachute Infantry Battalions, and 463rd Parachute Field Artillery Battalion, all of whom had been in combat in southern France. Once they were grouped in the Reims area, all these airborne units came under the command of Lieutenant General Matthew B. Ridgway's XVIII Airborne Corps HQ. Reims was also the center of General Dwight D. Eisenhower's Supreme Headquarters Allied Expeditionary Forces. Ridgway's command also included Major General William M. Miley's 17th Airborne Division – originally raised at Camp Mackall, North Carolina – and which was now in England. In December, Major General Maxwell D. Taylor temporarily left the 101st Airborne Division on a posting to Washington to look after U.S. Airborne interests in high places.

A day before the start of Operation "Market Garden," a meeting of high-ranking German officers, which included Generalfeldmarschall (Field Marshal) Wilhelm Keitel, chief of the Armed Forces High Command, was taking place in the briefing room of Adolf Hitler's headquarters at Wolfschanze in East Prussia. The officers were stunned when the Führer announced his plan to launch a massive fast-moving offensive, using as much armor as could be mustered, from the Ardennes forest

heading directly for the port of Antwerp. Once this objective had been achieved, the Allied armies would be split in two parts with Field Marshal Montgomery's 21st Army Group in the Netherlands in an especially vulnerable position. Thus commenced the "Battle of the Bulge."

Two objectives were the keys to the successful outcome of Hitler's venture: 1) the quick seizure by German troops of St. Vith and Bastogne, both vital hubs for road and rail traffic through the rolling jumbled hills of the Ardennes forest; and 2) the rapid widening of the initial breaches in the Allied line so that follow-up armored units could thunder through racing for Antwerp, which is not actually situated on the Belgian coast but inland on the estuary of the Schelde River. Generalfeldmarschall (Field Marshal) Gerd von Rundstedt, the German army's most successful general, was appointed to lead the Ardennes offensive. The Allied front in that area which measured 136km (85 miles) in width, was defended by Major General Troy H. Middleton's U.S. VIII Corps, which consisted of three infantry divisions and assorted armor and support units.

The Germans struck at 5.30 a.m. on the morning of the 16 December under cover of a rolling barrage of artillery fire. The preparatory assault lasted nearly an hour and a half, and the American defenders were caught totally by surprise. Hard on the heels of the artillery barrage came the elite German infantry storm-trooper battalions, which opened the way for the Panzers. Plowing through a curtain of ground fog and a sea of mud and

Far left: On 16 December 1944, three German armies launched an all-out offensive in the Ardennes Forest area of Belgium. Hitler's objective was to drive across Belgium to Antwerp cutting off Field Marshal Montgomery's 21st Army Group north of a line between Antwerp, Brussels and Bastogne from American forces to the south.

The key to the door of the operation was centered at Bastogne and neighbouring St. Vith at the hub of highways leading to the west. Both the 82nd and 101st Airborne Divisions were committed to the ensuing battle from the SHAEF reserve at Reims, and in the absence of General Ridgway, Gavin took over temporary command of the U.S. Airborne Corps. The American airborne troops motored to the Ardennes in trucks in freezing cold conditions with deep snow on the ground.

The "Screaming Eagles" (now under Brigadier General Anthony C. McAuliffe) attached to U.S. VIII Corps took the main weight of attack of the Fifth Panzer Army at the town of Bastogne which was to become an immortal name in the history of the 101st Airborne Division.

In this photograph C-47s are seen dropping pathfinders to mark drop zones for airborne supplies for the besieged defenders of Bastogne.

Above: Troopers of the 101st Airborne march out of Bastogne to take up defensive positions.

Above: B Company, 325th Glider Regiment, 82nd Airborne Division bound for Herresbach, Belgium, January 1945.

snow, the German armored columns drove westward against light opposition. One novel feature of the German offensive at the onset was the use of small motorized parties of German commandos dressed in American uniforms and riding in captured jeeps. The Americans quickly cottoned on to the ruse and the commandos who were captured were executed.

The XVIII Airborne Corps was alerted at Reims on the evening of 17 December. Ridgway was in England when the alarm call came, Major General James Gavin assuming temporary command of the corps. The two airborne divisions immediately moved off in trucks: the 82nd to St. Vith and the 101st,

in Maxwell Taylor's absence commanded by Brigadier General Anthony C. McAuliffe, to Bastogne. The weather was bitterly cold and the convoys were routed through the snow-covered countryside from France to Belgium. The 82nd took station at Werbomont on the Amblève River, but it was soon obvious to Gavin that the German tanks and infantry were concentrating their main forces for the breakthrough at Bastogne, the key to the southern flank. Gavin consequently ordered McAuliffe to organize the town for all-round defense and stay there till he received further orders. On 19 December Middleton, the VIII Corps commander, visited Bastogne and ordered McAuliffe to "Hold Bastogne."

Above: Paratroopers of the 101st move out of Bastogne on the road to Haufelize, 19 December. Bastogne was still under siege at the time.

Left: Together since sunny Sicily, Generals Ridgway and Gavin confer near St. Vith on a cold winter's day in Belgium.

Right: Bastogne area. Weary infantrymen of the 110th Regiment, 28th U.S. Division, make their way through typical Ardennes country following the initial enemy breakthrough when their positions were overrun.

On 20 December Bastogne was completely surrounded. Although the "Screaming Eagles" had other units, including artillery, under command, McAuliffe did not have adequate supplies of ammunition, food and medical requirements to withstand a long siege. Moreover, an airborne division's scale of armaments, as the British 1st Airborne Division had found to its cost at Arnhem, was not sufficient to fight battles with Tiger tanks. At St. Vith, the 82nd began to give ground, with the 504th Parachute Infantry Regiment and the 325th Glider Infantry Regiment taking the brunt of the attacks. The 504th won its second Presidential Unit Citation at St. Vith, but it took heavy losses during the Ardennes offensive. The 82nd managed to hold the line and the 517th Regimental Combat Team with the 3rd Armored Division advanced through one night in freezing cold and deep snow drifts to capture Hotton.

When reports of the situation in the VIII Corps zone of operations began arriving at SHAEF, the Allied supremo ordered a major airlift of supplies by Douglas C-47s, which were hastily assembled by the U.S.A.A.F. IX Troop Carrier Command at airfields in England. Lieutenant General George S. Patton's U.S. 3rd Army, as well as British units, were ordered to the area — and "Old Blood and Guts" requested the 101st should be granted first priority on all air supply. On the night of the 17-18 December, this need had already been anticipated, but the severe flying conditions had prevented 23 Dakotas from taking-off from Greenham Common, Berkshire, with ammunition and medical supplies. The weather cleared the following day and the aircraft were airborne but after landing at an airfield in France, the mission was aborted when the pilots were unable to obtain any information on drop zones in the Ardennes.

At Bastogne, the Americans were taking a battering and by 22 December the supply situation was critical. Requisition of local stocks had replenished the food situation to some extent; but the shortage of artillery ammunition particularly was becoming very serious. A check-up revealed that except for one battalion that was using short-range 105mm ammunition and had several hundred rounds on hand, the batteries were down to less than ten rounds per gun. McAuliffe, a thick-set, diminutive, cigar-smoking general, after surveying the situation asked for 104 aircraft loads of ammunition and rations. The U.S.A.A.F. now began a frantic effort

to assemble the necessary supplies for long-term needs at airfields in England and in France.

Shortly after dawn on the morning of 23 December two C-47s dropped two pathfinder teams from the 101st Division into an open field north-west of Bastogne. They had jumped in the area of the 2nd Battalion,

Above: Grim-faced American paratroopers in Bastogne.

Below: Re-supply by C-47s and gliders was a major factor in the defense of Bastogne by the 101st Airborne Division. Here two "Screaming Eagles" drag in an airborne supply load.

327th Glider Infantry Regiment. Soon the navigation aids were working and the pilots had little difficulty recognizing their DZs. Shortly before noon, 21 Dakotas dropped their parachute containers and bundles to the 106th Infantry Division near St. Vith and within minutes the gray sky over Bastogne was filled with 239 Dakotas and 95 Republic P-47 fighter escorts. Altogether, 334 tons of supplies were dropped by parachute that day but eight transports were brought down by flak.

The day before, when the 101st's fortunes were at such a low ebb, Generalleutnant (Lieutenant General) Heinrich Graf von Lüttwitz, commanding XLVII Panzer Corps, had sent a captain, accompanied by two privates bearing white flags, through the American lines. The German general considered the "Screaming Eagles" position untenable and his junior officer bore the written threat that, unless the 101st surrendered, the Americans in Bastogne would be annihilated by his corps artillery fire. The ultimatum, which had been typed on a captured American typewriter, read as follows:

Below: A C-47 has crashed running supplies into Bastogne.

Inset: Troops of the 505th wrapped up against the severely cold Belgian winter. Note the snow chains fitted to the jeep in the foreground.

"To the U.S.A. Commander of the encircled town of Bastogne.

"The fortune of war is changing. This time the U.S.A. forces in and near Bastogne have been encircled by strong German armored units. More German armored units have crossed the river. ...

"There is only one possibility to save encircled U.S.A. troops from total annihilation. In order to think it over a term of two hours will be granted from the presentation of this note.

"If this proposal should be rejected, one German Artillery Corps and six heavy AA Battalions are ready to annihilate the U.S.A. troops in and near Bastogne. The order for firing will be given immediately after the two-hour term.

"All the serious civilian losses caused by this artillery fire would not correspond with the well-known American humanity.
The German Commander".

McAuliffe, who had been handed this note by one of his glider battalion commanders (the Germans had been placed under guard), briefly studied the note before reaching for a piece of paper and writing his reply. He folded his hand-written message and handed it to his colonel. When the German captain, who was authorized to negotiate further in the event of an American surrender, read it he was astonished, to say the least. The message read:
"To the German Commander
Nuts!
The American Commander"

"But this is war...," exclaimed the German, to which the American replied: "Good luck to you, Bud!"

The manna from heaven the following day put the Bastogne defenders in good spirit. The Americans now had plenty of 0.50 caliber machine-gun ammunition but there was still a shortage of 75mm and 76mm ammunition to fight the tanks. Also on 23 December, another body of troops was isolated in the town of Mercury and an attempt was made to drop 50 loads of supplies to them. Since the country around the town was thick with enemy troops, it was impractical to risk sending in a pathfinder team by parachute and when the pilots risked unloading their supplies by using map coordinates, the containers and bundles fell into German hands.

Meanwhile the 17th Airborne Division was being lifted from England by IX Troop Carrier Command into the U.S. airborne headquarter area in Reims. "Bud" Miley was the most senior in the way of service of all the American airborne generals, but somehow his turn to command a division in action had come late in the queue. The 17th "Golden Talon" Division consisted of the 507th and 513th Parachute Infantry and the 550th Glider Infantry Regiments. The 17th Airborne Division occupied positions on the west bank of the Meuse River and received its baptism of fire on 4 January when it went into action to seize key towns around Bastogne. In a few days, the "Golden Talons" had cleared the west side of Bastogne and attacked across the border into Luxembourg.

On the day before Christmas the weather improved for a short while and IX Troop Carrier Command made 160 sorties dropping 159 tons to the 101st Airborne Division. On Christmas Day, the weather turned so bad that the mission of 116 aircraft scheduled to carry supplies to Bastogne had to be canceled. The German corps bombardment promised by Lüttwitz did not materialize but the Panzers, supported by artillery fire, persisted in their attacks on Bastogne. The day after Christmas, SHAEF called for another air supply drop for the 101st. Flying weather over the U.K. was virtually impossible but over France it was better. The "Screaming Eagles" were desperate for ammunition for the artillery and gasoline for the jeeps, and these items could not be packed into parachute containers.

A staff officer of the 101st Airborne hit upon the idea of using gliders salvaged from Normandy and the Netherlands to carry the heavy supplies. On 26 December, ten gliders mainly loaded with ammunition and one carrying a surgical team and medical supplies floated into the Bastogne perimeter. A further 301 tug aircraft and gliders were standing by that day on runways in England covered in fog but they finally took off flying on instrument bearings and delivered 320 tons of supplies to the 101st Division. After completing the mission, a number of the C-47s had to land on airfields in France to wait for better weather before returning to their bases in England. The next day, 35 more gliders landed, but on the return journey 17 C-47s were shot down by flak. The heavy fog over the U.K. continued, but nevertheless 188 aircraft, scheduled to drop supplies by parachute, arrived safely over the target area.

During the first week of January, the U.S. 4th Armored Division relieved Bastogne and no further airlifts were necessary. During the

Left: Christmas Eve in Bastogne. Stunned paratroopers of the 101st face worse to come with an intense week-long battle in which the Germans spare nothing in their attempts to take Bastogne.

Below: Re-supply at Bastogne. This Waco appears to have landed intact with much-needed stores.

The German Ardennes Offensive by 2 January had failed and they were thrown back by the 19-day Allied counter-offensive that followed. The Germans were now on the defensive until the end of the war.

course of five days, IX Troop Carrier Command, assisted in the latter stages by Nos. 36 and 48 Groups R.A.F., had landed by glider 1,112 tons of supplies, of which 94 per cent went successfully into the division area. During the same period U.S.A.A.F. and R.A.F. crews had lifted 13,000 men of the 17th Airborne Division and dropped 1,800 tons of equipment. Some 96 per cent of ammunition and equipment were despatched accurately. Altogether the supplies landed by the two methods of delivery included 656 tons of ammunition, 98 tons of rations, 87 tons of mines and explosives, 26 tons of medical supplies, 19 tons of signal equipment, 319 mortars and howitzers, and 4,840 gallons of gasoline. Supplies arriving successfully by glider included 53 tons of artillery ammunition and 11,262 litres (2,975 U.S. gallons) of gasoline. The C-47 Dakotas – the work-horses of the Allied airborne forces – also provided the useful service of evacuating 4,264 casualties to the U.K.

McAuliffe's epic defense of Bastogne was just one aspect of one of the greatest pitched battles of World War II. In the period 16-19 December, in his last desperate bid to enjoy the glare of the limelight in the theater of Grand Guignol, Hitler had launched – on his own initiative – 24 divisions, ten of them armored, plus his 7th Army to cover the southern flank, against the American line thinly held by VIII Corps. Substantial reinforcements, American and British, were rushed to the Ardennes, and attacks and counter-attacks were carried out on a wide front. But the linchpin of the American line was centered on Bastogne where the efforts of 18,000 men resisted all attempts of the 5th Panzer Army to overrun the perimeter.

Although the 101st Airborne Division had on this occasion, moved overland to the combat zone, the fact that it was an airborne division contributed a great deal to its survival at Bastogne. To fight in a situation where it was surrounded by the enemy was normal to its role. It had had training and experience in working with the IX Troop Carrier Command on resupply by air. It had a rear organization outside the encircled area which could help coordinate the resupply missions. It had its own pathfinder teams, experienced in working with the division and the troop carriers, which were able to drop into the area of Bastogne and set up radar aids to ensure the arrival of the supply aircraft. Its staff and its soldiers were trained and experienced in recovering supplies dropped by parachute.

With the defeat of the great German Ardennes offensive, the forces of the Third Reich lost some 220,000 men (of which 110,000 were taken prisoner), as well as 1,400 tanks and assault guns destroyed or captured. But the Germans had one last defensive stratagem – the Rhine River – which, as the snow and ice melted with the warm expectancy of the spring, proved more difficult in the fighting along its approaches than in the crossing of it. Ridgway's XVIII Airborne Corps would be in the forefront of the assault into the heartland of Germany.

Far left: Two sharpshooters from the "Screaming Eagles" have spotted enemy troops on what looks like an ideal drop and landing zone for airborne supplies.

Across the Rhine

With Generalfeldmarschall (Field Marshal) Gerd von Rundstedt's decisive defeat in the Battle of the Ardennes, the Allies resumed their endeavors to break through the Siegfried Line and cross the Rhine River into Germany. Field Marshal Montgomery was now forced to abandon his plan to advance through the Netherlands and outflank the Siegfried Line in the area of the Reichswald. After an amphibious landing in October by Anglo-Canadian forces on South Beveland and Walcheren Islands to clear the estuary and open the port of Antwerp, the 21st Army Group (the British 2nd Army and the Canadian 1st Army) now faced east in the north-east corner of Belgium.

Extending southward, Lieutenant General Omar N. Bradley's U.S. 12th Army Group consisted of the newly-arrived 9th Army stationed in January 1945 on the Upper Roer on the Belgian border with Germany; the 1st Army advancing to a line extending from Köln to Koblenz; and the 3rd Army which was operating much farther south beyond the Saar River to Oppenheim. Further south still to the Swiss border Lieutenant General Jacob Dever's U.S. 6th Army Group comprised the U.S. 7th Army, which included the French 2nd Armored Division, and the French 1st Army operating just north of Strasbourg.

On 7 March, a two-battalion task force of the U.S. 9th Armored Division, probing east as part of the U.S. 1st Army's advance, unexpectedly found the Ludendorff railroad bridge over the Rhine at Remagen, which is situated between Bonn and Koblenz, still standing. Daringly seizing the bridge before

it could be blown up, these Americans changed the entire course of Eisenhower's planned campaign. By nightfall the 1st Army held a rapidly swelling bridgehead on the east bank. On 22 March, Patton threw the U.S. 5th Division across the Rhine, using bridging equipment, and in four days advanced 160km (100 miles) beyond the river. On 26 March the 6th Army Group also began to move across the Rhine. The 7th Army crossed in the Worms-Mannheim area. The French 1st Army soon followed at Gersheim (31 March).

The 21st Army Group's planned crossing was to be at the northern tip of the Allied line, striking from south of the Waal across the Rhine to capture Wesel. Two airborne divisions were to be used in the assault: the U.S. 17th Airborne Division (Major General William Miley) and the British 6th Airborne Division (Major General Eric Bols). The plan for Operation "Varsity," the code-name for the airborne operation, was based on a new concept for the employment of airborne troops. Lieutenant General Lewis Brereton's 1st Allied Airborne Army was to land not before but after land operations had begun. Lieutenant General Sir Miles Dempsey, whose idea this was, had two reasons: 1) to permit his lead ground assault units (the Commandos of the 2nd Army) to cross the river in landing craft in the pre-dawn darkness under cover of heavy preparatory fire on the Diersfordter Forest, which was the airborne objective on the highest terrain of the area; and 2) to allow the airborne troops to make their attacks in broad daylight from accurately located and compact DZ's and LZ's. Lieutenant General

Far left: The 17th Airborne Division (the "Talons"), newly arrived in France, make a practice jump in the Reims area. The aircraft is the Curtiss C-46 Commando, which was fitted with two doors for the simultaneous dispatch of paratroopers from both sides of the fuselage.

Above: The 17th Airborne arrive in trucks at their emplaning airfield in England in preparation for Operation "Varsity", the airborne drop across the Rhine. The "Talons" had already seen some action at the tail end of the Bastogne battle.

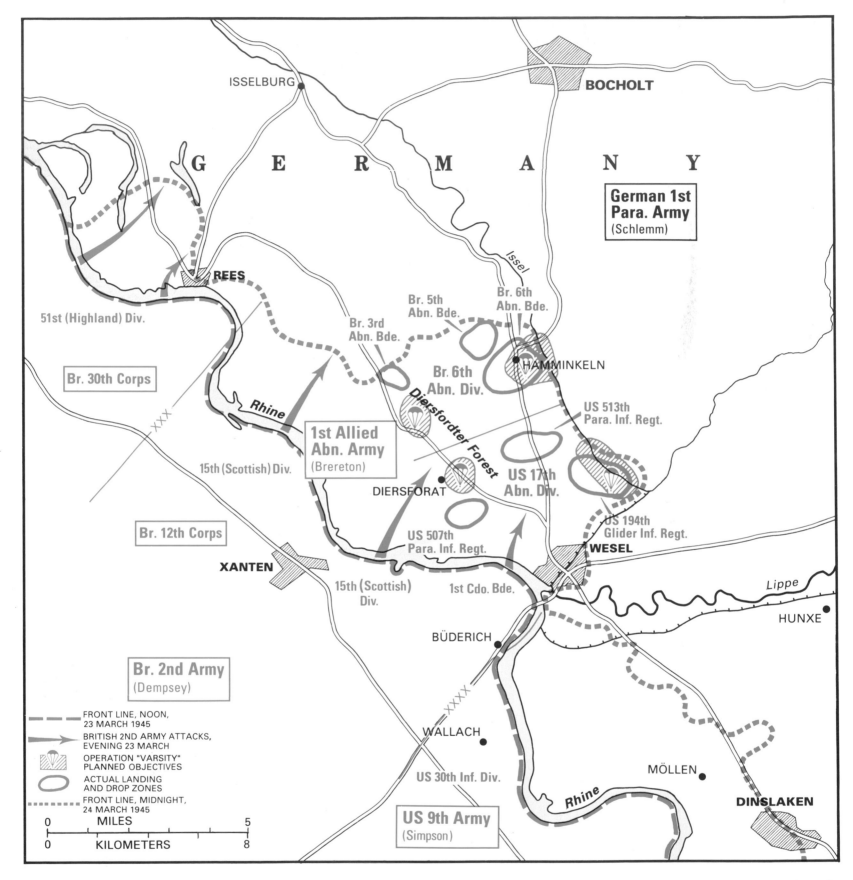

ISSELBURG

BOCHOLT

G E R M A N Y

**German 1st
Para. Army**
(Schlemm)

Issel

REES

Br. 6th
Abn. Bde.

Br. 5th
Abn. Bde.

51st (Highland) Div.

Br. 3rd
Abn. Bde.

HAMMINKELN

Br. 30th Corps

Br. 6th
Abn. Div.

Rhine

Diersfordter Forest

US 513th
Para. Inf. Regt.

**1st Allied
Abn. Army**
(Brereton)

15th (Scottish) Div.

DIERSFORAT

US 17th
Abn. Div.

Br. 12th Corps

US 194th
Glider Inf. Regt.

Lippe

WESEL

US 507th
Para. Inf. Regt.

XANTEN

HUNXE

15th (Scottish)
Div.

1st Cdo. Bde.

BÜDERICH

Br. 2nd Army
(Dempsey)

FRONT LINE, NOON,
23 MARCH 1945

BRITISH 2ND ARMY ATTACKS,
EVENING 23 MARCH

OPERATION "VARSITY"
PLANNED OBJECTIVES

ACTUAL LANDING
AND DROP ZONES

FRONT LINE, MIDNIGHT,
24 MARCH 1945

WALLACH

MÖLLEN

0   MILES   5

US 30th Inf. Div.

Rhine

DINSLAKEN

0   KILOMETERS   8

US 9th Army
(Simpson)

Matthew B. Ridgway was in overall command of the ground operations on the airborne sector with Major General Richard Gale, the former commander of the British 6th Airborne Division, as his deputy.

Dempsey's 2nd Army started crossing the Rhine between Xanten and Rees soon after nightfall on 23 March. It was a massive amphibious feat using all the latest landing craft, which the Germans attempted to attack

Left: The 17th paratroopers and glider men with troop transport, tug and glider pilots are briefed on 23 March for the Rhine crossing which will take place the following day. The plan is for the 17th and British 6th Airborne Divisions to land north of the German town of Wesel, in support of the British Second Army of Field Marshal Montgomery's 21st Army Group which will make the river assault by amphibious craft on the night of 23/24 March.

Below: A party of Glider infantrymen of the 17th Airborne wait to emplane in a glider for Germany on 24 March.

with frogmen. Shortly after daybreak on 24 March, 1,696 transport aircraft and 1,348 gliders brought 21,680 airborne troops to the battlefield in one single lift. The skytrain run by the U.S. IX Troop Carrier Command and Nos. 38 and 46 Groups, R.A.F., was escorted by nearly 1,000 fighters and twice that number supported ground operations. It was the largest single airborne landing of the war. The drop and landing zones were situated to the north, west and south of the Diersfordterwald, a forested area measuring roughly 41km² (16 sq miles). The largest settlement in the area was the small town of Hamminkeln, just 13km (8 miles) east of the Rhine. The 6th Airborne was assigned to the northern half and the 17th Airborne to the southern half of the sector.

The sky transport armada was made up of a huge assortment of aircraft: Douglas C-47 Dakotas, Curtiss C-46 Commandos and the R.A.F.'s converted Armstrong Whitworth Albemarles, Handley Page Halifaxes and

Short Stirlings. (The R.A.F. aircraft were also employed as tugs.) The glidermen were carried in the Waco CG-4As, Airspeed Horsas and General Aircraft Hamilcars. The Hamilcar had originally been built to lift the British Tetrarch, a light reconnaissance tank, but for the Rhine crossing these cargo gliders brought in a small number of American M22 Locust tanks. The C-46 Commando was the first transport aircraft to carry two sticks of paratroopers, jumping simultaneously from port and starboard doors. However, when hit the C-46 was liable to burst into flames and 22 of them were lost in this manner. (If a wing tank was punctured the fuel ran down the fuselage and an incendiary shell would set the whole aircraft aflame in a second.) Altogether 44 transport aircraft and 80 gliders

were destroyed by anti-aircraft fire.

The landings were made into brisk automatic rifle and machine-gun fire, and shrapnel from air bursts from enemy artillery showered down on the troops as they went into action. The anger of the 1st Canadian Parachute Battalion which formed part of the 6th Airborne was aroused when the men found their commanding officer, Lieutenant J.S. Nicklin, hanging dead from a tree. Nicklin had been shot by German marksmen while attempting to free himself from his parachute harness. The British and Canadians went quickly to work and had secured their objectives by late afternoon, by which time the 3rd Parachute Brigade had made contact with the advancing 2nd Army.

The U.S. 507th Parachute Infantry Regiment landed to similar opposition a short distance south of a road skirting the southern tip of the Diersfordterwald. The 513th Parachute Infantry Regiment was supposed to have dropped at the western tip of the forest, but the intense flak drove the pilots 1·6km (1 mile) or so to the north and the paratroopers were scattered in the British 6th Air Landing Brigade sector beyond a railway line on the outskirts of Hamminkeln. The 194th Glider Infantry Regiment was farther forward on the Issel 8km (5 miles) south of Hamminkeln. All the American objectives were taken by 2.00 p.m. of the first day of Operation "Varsity" and the 513th operating jointly with the glider men of the Oxford and Buckinghamshire Light Infantry captured Hamminkeln that afternoon.

Below: 17th paratroopers assembled on the morning of the drop at Wesel, 24 March. Curtiss C-46 Commandos are lined up in the background. The C-46 proved very vulnerable on operations, taking heavy losses when flak shells hit fuel tanks. This aircraft was used more successfully in the Pacific theater in the cargo supply role.

Insert left: Operation "Vanity." Interior of a Waco CG-4A in flight bound for Germany.

Operation "Varsity" was not entirely necessary. Late on 24 March, the 2nd Army was streaming unopposed across the Rhine. The Allied airborne troops had accomplished their tasks but their success did not justify the losses. The heavy toll of carrier aircraft, tugs and gliders has already been quoted. Forty-one aircrew were killed, 153 wounded and 163 posted as missing. The 6th Airborne Division lost 347 men killed and 522 wounded. The 17th Airborne Division's casualties, killed and wounded, were slightly less. About 1,000 British, Canadian and American troops were reported missing but many of them found their way back to their lines. General Ridgway was himself very nearly a casualty when a grenade exploded under his jeep and he tumbled out returning the fire of the attackers with a sub-machine gun.

Apart from a few small S.A.S. operations, there were no more airborne drops in the European theater. Spearheading the race of the 2nd Army to the Baltic, Ridgway's XVIII Airborne Corps crossed the Ems, Weser and Elbe; the Canadians of the 6th Airborne Division were the first on this sector to meet the Soviets on 1 May at the port of Wismar. The U.S. 7th Armored Division should have reached the Baltic coast first but as a gesture to Dempsey, Ridgway held open the Elbe bridges at Artlenburg and Lauenburg for tanks of the British 11th Armored Division. The "Red Devils" turned their berets inside out to make them look black like those of the tankers and climbing on top of the tanks rode triumphantly to meet the advancing Soviets.

Major General James Gavin's 82nd Airborne Division crossed the Rhine independently in amphibious craft in early April and captured Köln. The "All Americans" went on – now part of XVIII Corps again – to cross the Elbe at Bleckede using amtracs, which had first seen action in Europe on the Rhine crossing at Wesel. Gavin's division first met the Soviets in the small town of Grabow in Mecklenburg. Berlin fell on 5 May, but resistance was still expected in the so-called "National Redoubt" centered on Hitler's vacation retreat at Berchtesgaden in Bavaria. It was here that Major General Maxwell Taylor's 101st Airborne Division ended the war in Europe, arriving hot on the heels of the French 2nd Armored Division. With the Americans in the south advancing into Czechoslovakia and Austria, the Germans admitted defeat on 7 May and 8 May was declared Victory in Europe (VE) Day.

The 82nd and 17th moved back to the

"Champagne" country around Reims, where Gavin held a full-dress review of his division on 9 June. In July the "All Americans" were in Berlin to take up occupation duties in the American sector, the 508th Parachute Infantry being detached to fulfill the same duties in Frankfurt am Main. Two American units notified for reassignment to the Pacific were the 13th and 101st Airborne Divisions. Ridgway's XVIII Airborne Corps were also alerted for immediate redeployment but the dropping of the atomic bombs on Japan in August 1945 canceled all transfer orders for American units still in Europe. Later that month the 13th Airborne Division was shipped home and deactivated, and so also the following month was the 17th Airborne Division.

Taylor's "Screaming Eagles" were actively hunting down Nazi war criminals and unearthing stolen art treasures cached in secret hiding places. Taylor left the 101st Airborne Division to be Commandant of West Point, and his natural successor was Brigadier General Anthony McAuliffe who had commanded the division with such distinction at Bastogne. McAuliffe now received some exciting news which, in the event, turned a trifle sour on the "Screaming Eagles." The War Department had decided to disband the 82nd Airborne Division but maintain the 101st as an active division in the U.S. Army. The "Screaming Eagles" would be stationed at the airborne home at Fort Bragg.

McAuliffe was further informed that his division would receive a "ticker-tape" reception as it marched down Fifth Avenue, New York City. Each member of the division was issued with a silk parachute scarf to wear in the parade and a brand new pair of jump boots for the big day. But the "powers-that-be" thought again: the 82nd had longer service and more battle honors than the 101st, so the decision was reversed and the "All Americans" were retained as the only parachute division in the U.S. Army, and Gavin's men would make the big parade.

On 3 January 1946, the *Queen Mary* steamed past the Statue of Liberty to an outstanding welcome from the assembled ships and thousands of people who were gathered on a bitterly cold Manhattan morning to greet the returning heroes. It was a proud moment for "Jumping Jim" Gavin, still only 38 years of age, as he led the division down the gangplank of the great ocean liner, which was also seeing the conclusion of a brilliantly successful war service as a transatlantic troop transport. After practice drill and "spit and polish" at

Camp Shanks, the parade took place on 12 January. The temperature was well below freezing that day but there were warm hearts among the cheering onlookers all along Fifth Avenue; the entire division passed the reviewing stand presided over by the Governor of New York, Thomas Dewey, and the Mayor of New York, William O'Dwyer, in what came to be known as the New York City Victory Parade. The 101st was in fact disbanded but it was not to be long before it reappeared again in the order of battle of the U.S. Army.

Above: Glider troops of the 101st Airborne Division stand guard at the imposing entrance to Berchtesgaden, the scene of many historic meetings in the Fuhrer's days of power in the Third Reich.

Facing page, above: American glider infantry having landed near Wesel move off into action.

Facing page, below: Paratroopers of the 17th Airborne Division fight alongside British Coldstream Guardsmen on the road to Munster in early April.

The Pacific Theater, 1942-45

The Pacific land war was essentially a story of assault from the sea and the parachute arm was not as widely used as in Europe. General Douglas MacArthur's strategy, as commander of Allied forces in the Southwest Pacific, in 1942–43 developed into a major, two-pronged offensive aimed at the Philippine Islands. One line of advance lay from Guadalcanal up through the Solomons, while the other was from the Buna-Gona area westward along northern New Guinea's coastline. Much of this coastal littoral was useless, impenetrable jungle, and the Allies' most urgent need was for "staging posts" where airfields could be built to progressively extend the range of their bombers and fighters. MacArthur focused his eyes on the town of Salamaua, 320km (200 miles) to the west of Buna. Some 80km (50 miles) to the north of Salamaua was the town of Lae, the gateway to the Huon peninsula.

The Allied commander surmised that if he launched an amphibious assault on Salamaua first, the Japanese would send a heavy contingent of troops south from Lae to help in the former's defense. Once the Lae garrison was weakened, MacArthur planned to divert the Australian 9th Division, after the assault on Salamaua, to make an amphibious run up the coast and go ashore 32km (20 miles) east of Lae. While the Australians attacked the town, an American parachute regiment would drop the following day 35km (22 miles) west of Lae to seize an old abandoned airstrip near the town of Nadzab on the banks of the Markham River, and prepare for the air-landing of the Australian 7th Division.

The U.S. Army had only one parachute unit available to make the jump, the 503rd Parachute Infantry Regiment, which was commanded by Colonel Kenneth H. Kinsler. The 503rd had arrived in Australia from Fort Bragg in December 1942 and as an independent outfit was assigned to MacArthur's headquarters. The regiment included many of the first paratroopers to be trained in the United States. In June 1942, the 503rd's 2nd Battalion had been shipped out to England, destined to drop in North Africa the following November. When Kinsler and his two battalions sailed from California on 22 October, the ship sailed via Panama where the original 501st Parachute Infantry Battalion was embarked, bringing the 503rd Parachute Infantry Regiment up to full strength.

The regiment took off for the Nadzab drop on 5 September 1943 from its departure field near Port Moresby, New Guinea. Eighty-two Douglas C-47s were airborne before 9 a.m., and they were joined in flight by over 100 fighter escorts, as well as six squadrons of bombers specially rigged with eight .50 caliber machine-guns in their noses. High above the armada flew three heavily armed Boeing B-17 bombers, one with MacArthur on board to observe the drop. After climbing over the Owen Stanley Mountains, the skytrain on reaching the Markham River descended to 120m (400 ft). The paratroopers stood up and hooked up their static lines, each clutching his rifle at the port arms, standard jump procedure in the 503rd.

All three battalions were dropped with pin-

Far right: Noemfoor Island, west of Biak, New Guinea campaign, July 1944. The 503rd Parachute Infantry Regiment drops from C-47s onto the Kamiri airstrip, another potential base for General MacArthur's island-hopping campaign to the Philippines (July 1944). This photograph shows the first lift when the C-47s flew in two abreast. The DZ looks ideal but the sharp pointed, coral-covered surface of the airstrip caused the paratroopers splintered bones.

Also Kamiri airstrip was not quite wide enough to take two C-47s in line abreast. As a result of this miscalculation, many paratroopers had the misfortune to drift into the tall trees and others collided with trucks carelessly parked by American infantry already on the island on both edges of the airstrip.

point accuracy on the airfield, only four and half minutes elapsing before the entire regiment was on the ground. Unfortunately, the drop zone was covered in kunai grass, which was up to 3·7m (12 ft) high and had sharp, knife-like edges. Two men crashed to their death when their parachutes failed to open and a third was killed when, after landing in a tree, he released his harness and fell to the ground; 33 paratroopers sustained injuries caused by rough landings. The tall grass was an unexpected obstacle and the 503rd troopers had to hack paths to their assembly areas with machetes. By late morning, the temperature was nearly 38°C (100°F) and the going with heavy equipment was tough.

Three Dakotas shortly appeared overhead and dropped, from under their wings, two 25-pounder guns, which had been stripped down and packed in bundles, together with a 503rd artillery officer and a contingent of Australian jump volunteers parachuted in to man the guns. In the afternoon Australian engineers, who had trekked through the jungle from the south coast, linked with the paratroopers and set to work clearing the landing strip. The sappers worked all through the night and at first light, two Douglas C-47s landed at Nadzab with two bulldozers and 12 portable flamethrowers. At noon that day (6 September), Major General Vasey's Australian 7th Division air-landed at Nadzab and started its march down the Markham Valley toward Lae. The Australian 9th Division had landed successfully from the sea the previous day and Lae fell to the converging divisions on 16 September. American and Australian

casualties were slight, but over 3,000 Japanese died from wounds, illness and exhaustion.

The campaign in New Guinea was resumed in April 1944 when MacArthur's forces leap-frogged 640km (400 miles), landing simultaneously by sea at Aitape and Hollandia. In mid-May, American units landed on the offshore islands of Wakde and Biak, where the objectives were to seize airfields. The two regiments of the 41st Infantry Division landing on Biak Island on 27 May met fierce Japanese resistance, which after several days of fighting showed no signs of abating. Unknown to the Americans at first, the Japanese were ferrying in reinforcements and supplies by barge at night from Noemfoor Island, located 130km (80 miles) to the west of Biak. When MacArthur heard about this, he ordered the immediate seizure of Noemfoor.

Lieutenant General Krueger's U.S. 6th Army set sail for Noemfoor at sunset on 30 June

Above right: In the thick of the New Guinea jungle, 1943. An American team man a 37-mm infantry support gun. This weapon was adopted for use by airborne units and could easily be carried in a glider or dropped by parachute.

Right: "Diggers" of the Australian 7th Division, who were airlifted in C-47s into the Markham River Valley to reinforce 3,000 Americans and 31 Australians, who parachuted in to seize the Nadzab airstrip, eastern New Guinea, September 1943.

from the small New Guinea coastal town of Toem, aboard a fleet of landing craft and escorted by 21 American and Australian warships. Preceded by heavy air and sea bombardments, the LCMs the following morning churned through the surf to "Yellow Beach." Once ashore, Krueger learned indirectly from a Japanese prisoner that the island had been heavily reinforced to defend its three airfields. This unexpected piece of intelligence so alarmed the general that he ordered the 503rd to stand by for parachute operations; the 1st Battalion taking off at 6.30 a.m. on 4 July in 41 Douglas C-47s from Hollandia's Cyclops airfield. The DZ on Noemfoor was the Kamiri airfield, which was a cleared area 76 x 1,524m (250 x 5,000 ft), with a 30·5m (100 ft) wide runway extending the full length of the clearing.

The plan was for the Douglas C-47s to fly over the runway two abreast. The 503rd flew in just below 122m (400 ft) and at 10 a.m. 739 1st Battalion paratroopers began to land on Kamiri airfield. Seventy-two men were injured – half of them with severe bone fractures – when they landed on the coral runway, which was as hard as concrete, or collided with 6th Army bulldozers and other vehicles parked carelessly on the edges of the runway. The following morning, the 503rd's 3rd Battalion flew in in single file. This time the vehicles were pulled back into the jungle but, although most of the parachutists steered their way onto sandy areas alongside the airfield, some were not so lucky and 56 men splintered bones on the hard coral surface. In view of the DZ injuries the 2nd Battalion of the 503rd was re-routed to Noemfoor by sea.

The enemy on Noemfoor Island retired swiftly to the jungled interior and the 503rd Parachute Infantry was assigned to clearing the southern half of the island, which is covered in hills and where the jungle is thick. The paratroopers now became engaged in a six-week battle against small groups of a tenacious, elusive enemy, who made the Americans pay for every inch of ground. Time after time, the 503rd launched attacks on hill positions, only to find on reaching their crests that the Japanese had slipped away. The 6th Army headquarters officially declared Noemfoor Island secure on 31 August. During the nearly two months that the 503rd Parachute Infantry Regiment had fought on Noemfoor, the unit was credited with killing 1,000 enemy soldiers. Sixty paratroopers had been killed in action and another 303 wounded. The 503rd set up

Previous page, left: American paratroopers move off into action on Kamiri airstrip, Noemfoor Island, while others drift into the trees.

Previous page, above: Staff Sergeant Alton W. Davis of the 503rd Parachute Infantry Regiment finds himself lucky to be in one piece on the edge of Kamiri airstrip, Noemfoor Island.

Previous page, below: A medic tends a drop zone casualty on Noemfoor Island.

Below: American troops land on Leyte Island, October 1944.

camp at Kamiri airfield, with the 462nd Parachute Field Artillery Battalion; the new unit being named the 503rd Parachute Regimental Combat Team.

The 11th Airborne Division, which was last referred to in this book in training at Camp Mackall, North Carolina, in 1943, dropped anchor after the sea voyage across the Pacific from San Francisco at Milne Bay, New Guinea, in July 1944. Major General Joe Swing's division (the "Angels") consisted of the 511th Parachute Infantry Regiment and two glider infantry regiments, the 187th and 188th. During August and September, a glider school was opened at Nadzab airstrip and Swing's paratroopers were also trained in the glider role. Also during this period, the division was practiced in amphibious operations at Oro Bay. MacArthur's forces were now rapidly approaching the Philippine Islands and the "Angels" were assigned to Krueger's 6th Army

for the massive seaborne invasion of Leyte.

When the American threat loomed, General Tomoyuki Yamashita, the Japanese commander in the Philippines, decided to fight for Leyte and reinforcements were poured in from Luzon. The 6th Army's X and XXIV Corps began landing on Leyte, one of the large central islands in the eastern Philippines, during October. When on 18 November, the 11th Airborne Division landed from APAs (personnel transports), the bulk of their equipment stowed in AKAs (cargo ships), the fighting had progressed to the jungle, mountainous terrain that abounds on the island. On 22 November, Swing received this order: "The 11th Airborne Division will relieve the 7th Infantry Division along the line Burauen–La Paz-Bugho and destroy all Japs in that sector."

The 511th Parachute Infantry Regiment sent one battalion (the 1st) up into the

mountains where a base was set up on a small plateau called Manarawat. Colonel Orin D. Haughen, who commanded the 511th, made his HQ at Manarawat, while the 1st Battalion continued to advance through the mountains. Haughen, known as "Hardrock" or "Rock" to his men, decided to bring in some artillery support. A problem arose in that it would need 13 Douglas C-47s to drop one battery of 75mm "pack-hows," and only one Dakota could be found at the coastal airfield at San Pablo. The door was stripped off the solitary Dakota, the landing gear masked and pararacks fitted below the fuselage. By a simple calculation, the artillery commander, Colonel Stadtherr, reckoned that if five men and nine loads were lifted at a time, it would take 13 trips to put "A" Battery in position.

A drop zone was chosen in the west in the circle of mountains that made the Manarawat plateau resemble an island. Cliffs surrounded all four sides of the DZ, and tall mountains rose, to enclose it on three sides. Beautifully controlled flying by the pilot, who to reach the DZ had to follow a deep, moon-shaped canyon, as well as remarkably proficient jump-mastering by Stadtherr, who personally led each of the 13 flights, landed all the equipment and all the men in the center of the field. From that day "A" Battery of the 457th Parachute Field Artillery Battalion provided 360-degree support for all the infantry fighting in the mountains. The lack of Douglas C-47s forced the 11th Airborne to adopt a novel method of dropping troops in the Manarawat garrison. Cub spotter 'planes were used, and on one occasion, 11 Piper Cubs dropped one man each drawn from the 187th Glider Infantry Regiment. The Cubs were also used to parachute "scouts" onto muddy jungle trails.

The 511th's objective was to move west across the rugged moutains to descend on Ormoc Bay where the Japanese reinforcements were landed from Luzon. Apart from desperate "Banzai" charges by the Japanese, there were two major problems in crossing the mountains. One was the evacuation of the wounded by litter train, and the other the carriage of equipment. Surgical loads were man-handled over the treacherous, tortuous trail to Mahonag where a forward hospital was established. The only beast of burden was the carabao (a large animal of the ox family, the water buffalo), which could negotiate the trails if dry but not if covered with mud. Haughen's airborne troops continued their exhausting advance through the mountains before making contact with

the U.S. 32nd Infantry Division, which was also closing in on Ormoc.

The 511th Parachute Infantry Regiment was withdrawn after Christmas to a south coast base but the 188th Glider Infantry remained to fight a tough, two-day action to capture Purple Heart Hill. From this time on there was no organized resistance in the 11th Airborne Division's zone of responsibility on Leyte. The whole of the island was in American hands before the end of January 1945. Thus far, the American public had not heard of the "Angels" but this was rectified when General MacArthur sent the following communiqué to the press: "Operating in the central mountains region south-east of Ormoc, the 11th Airborne has been waging aggressive warfare along a wide sector...." The 11th Airborne's record looked good: 5,760 enemy counted dead during the campaign and 12 prisoners of war taken. Of the division, 128 men had been killed in action, a remarkably low casualty rate in the fiercely-contested battle in the torrid heat of the Leyte mountains of the Philippine Islands.

On 22 January 1945, General Joe Swing received orders to land the 11th Airborne Division in the thick of the fighting on Luzon. Swing's mission was to support a Subic Bay landing by the 6th Army's XI Corps by conducting a combined amphibious and parachute assault south of Manila, the Philippines' capital, to seize Tagaytay Ridge. The two glider infantry regiments – the 187th and 188th – were duly landed on 27 January at Nasugbo Bay, 80km (50 miles) south of

Below: The 11th Airborne Division drop on Tagaytay Ridge on Luzon Island in the Philippines on 3 February 1945. The ridge held a commanding view of Manila to the north.

Manila. The line of advance lay along Route 17 through mountainous terrain in which the dominant peaks were Mount Batulao and Mount Cariliao; deep, heavily wooded gorges marking the way from the port of Nasugbo to Tagaytay Ridge. The region was ideally suited to ambush operations and the Japanese were prepared to fight to the last drop of blood.

The 511th Regimental Combat Team, which had assembled on Mindoro Island, was ready for action. As the U.S.A.A.F. could spare only 48 Douglas C-47s for the lift, it was necessary to plan the drop in three echelons. At 8.15 am on 3 February, the first serial of the 511th began dropping on Tagaytay Ridge. The aircraft had come north from Mindoro over the scenic wonder of Lake Taal, formed in an extinct volcano. The drop zone was on the northern slope of the volcano, the terrain extending gently downward into Manila Bay. The most dangerous prospect for the paratroopers was the possibility of being blown off the ridge into the watery volcano. All the 511th paratroopers had landed on the DZ by noon and were joined by the 188th Glider Battalion, which had fought its way from Nasugbo, in a ridge-top sweep. The Japanese, who had hidden themselves in caves and tunnels, took some uprooting but on 5

Below: The 503rd Parachute Infantry Regiment land on Topside on Corregidor Island, 16 February 1945. The old U.S. Army barracks and headquarters can be seen on the left.

February, the 11th Airborne Division commenced its advance on Manila.

Japanese troops were still holding out against advancing Americans in downtown Manila when on 16 February Colonel George M. Jones's 503rd Regimental Combat Team executed the most unorthodox parachute assault attempted in World War II: a drop on tiny Corregidor Island. The recapture of the island, which for centuries has guarded the mouth of Manila Bay, was in 1945 of no strategic value in the re-conquest of the Philippine Islands. But there was a strong emotional reason for the recapture of "Fortress Corregidor," the last stronghold of American resistance in the Philippines in 1942. Shaped like a tadpole, with its bulbous head pointing toward the South China Sea, Corregidor's key terrain was high ground known to the U.S. Army as "Topside." Situated in the center of the tadpole's head, Topside's cliffs on two sides dropped precipitately to the sea. The small Japanese garrison had its headquarters on Topside and it was here on the old American parade ground and nearby golf course that Colonel Jones decided to drop with his paratroopers.

A strong wind was blowing when at 10 a.m. on 16 February the first stick to jump, acting as drifters to assess the wind direction, slammed into rocks and chunks of concrete scattered on the parade ground by the pre-drop air bombardment. Over the next 105 minutes, the 503rd continued to make bone-crushing landings amid Topside's rocks, broken concrete and shattered trees. The second echelon began jumping at 12.40 p.m. Though the drop this time in the area of the golf course was less painful, enemy ground fire was active. When the last man of the second echelon landed, Jones had 2,050 paratroopers on the ground. Fifty had been shot and killed while still suspended in mid-air. Eight others had died on the cliff-edges when their half-inflated 'chutes dragged them to their fate on the rocks below. Six more were killed on impact with partially destroyed concrete buildings and rocks. Another 210 troopers were put out of action by jump-related injuries and wounds. The Japanese HQ staff on Topside were quickly killed and the paratroopers were busy dealing with the suicide attacks from all directions. The Japanese resisted in isolated pockets on the island's low ground where American forces had landed from the bay.

On 2 March, General MacArthur returned to Corregidor, just nine days short of three years from his departure. As MacArthur faced

the 503rd RCT drawn up on the parade ground on Topside, Colonel Jones saluted and said: "Sir, I present you Fortress Corregidor." The general returned the salute, and congratulated the troops on the heroic achievement in reclaiming the island. His address completed, MacArthur glanced at the bent but unbroken flagpole behind him and said: "I see the old flagpole still stands. Have the troops hoist the colors to its peak and let no enemy ever haul them down." At that, a paratrooper flag detail rapidly hoisted "Old Glory" to the top of the pole. Six days after the flag-raising, Jones and all his paratroopers departed Corregidor aboard LCMs.

In the closing months of World War II, 11th Airborne Division was involved in the heavy fighting to clear northern Luzon. The "Angels" set up a base and jump training school at Lipa near Lake Thai. On 23 June 1945, "Gypsy Task Force" numbering 1,010 men was lifted in Douglas C-47s and Curtiss C-46s from Lipa airstrip to the Cagayen valley, in the northeastern tip of Luzon, to assist the 37th Infantry Division and Filipino guerrillas in a hard fight against fanatical "last-ditch" Japanese troops. For the first time in the Pacific theater, the skytrain included seven Dakotas with six WACO CG-4As and one CG-13 in tow. The landings on the Aparri drop zone by paratroopers and gliders were a success but casualties were caused by heavy ground winds, ruts and bomb holes on the DZ. The 11th Airborne Division's next posting was to Japan where the "Angels" served with the occupation forces until May 1949.

Above: Two 503rd troopers look out over Manila Bay from Topside on Corregidor Island.

The U.S. Airborne in the Korean War, 1950-53

Korea, annexed by Japan following the Russo-Japanese War of 1904-05, was promised its freedom by the Allies during World War II. When Japan surrendered in 1945, a hurried Allied agreement established the 38th degree of latitude as an arbitrary dividing line: north of this line the U.S.S.R. would accept surrender of Japanese forces in Korea, while those south of the line would surrender to U.S. troops. Following the surrender which took place with little friction, the U.S.S.R. held the 38th parallel to be a political boundary; along it the Iron Curtain dropped.

Two years of unsuccessful attempts to reach agreement were followed by U.S. referral of the problem to the United Nations, which undertook the establishment of an independent Korean government following free nationwide elections. The U.S.S.R. refused to cooperate. In the southern zone, the Republic of Korea was established on 15 August 1947 with Seoul as its capital. Declaring the action illegal, the U.S.S.R. set up a puppet state as the Democratic People's Republic of Korea with its capital at Pyongyang, and organized a North Korean Army (N.K.A.). Allegedly, Soviet troops evacuated the north in December 1948. U.S. troops completed their evacuation of the south in June 1949, although a small American military advisory group remained to organize a Republic of Korea (R.O.K.) Army.

On 25 June 1950, North Korean forces (seven infantry divisions, a brigade of Soviet T-34 tanks, and supporting troops, under Marshal Choe Yong Gun) drove rapidly south and captured Seoul. The U.N. reacted by ordering General Douglas MacArthur, commanding U.S. forces in the Far East, to cover R.O.K. defense with air and sea forces. MacArthur effected naval blockade of the North Korean coast and furnished the South Koreans with air support. Reconnoitering the front in person on 28 June as Seoul fell, he reported that the R.O.K. Army would be incapable of stopping the invasion even with American air support. President Harry S. Truman accordingly authorized use of American troops on 30 June.

Aside from the U.S. 7th Fleet and the Far East Air Force (eight complete combat groups) the forces at MacArthur's disposal consisted on the ground of two skeleton army corps stationed in Japan. When reinforced these became known as the U.S. 8th Army. The R.O.K. Army was little more than a national police force, and consisted of about 100,000 men in eight divisions with little supporting artillery. It lacked medium and heavy artillery, tanks, combat aircraft and reserves. Naval strength on both sides of the opposing Korean forces was negligible.

From the beginning of August to mid-September, Lieutenant General Walton H. Walker's 8th Army held a line extending along the Naktong River some 145km (90 miles) north of Tsushima Strait, thence east for 95km (60 miles) to the Sea of Japan. The perimeter embraced the south-east edge of the Korean peninsula, including Pusan, the one available harbor. The Korean conflict was developing in the same pattern as World War II with two notable exceptions: carrier-

Above: 82nd Airborne Division artillery men are emplaned for a jump at Fort Bragg, 1951. The aircraft used at times for paratrooping were Fairchild Packet C-119s known as the "Flying Boxcar."

Far left: 1st Airborne Rangers emplaning for a practice jump at Yojo, Korea, April 1951.

A mass jump from C-119s takes place at Pope Air Force Base, Operation "Flashburn," 1954.

Below: The 11th Airborne Division on occupation duty in Japan after World War II make a practice jump from a Curtiss C-46 Commando over a DZ at Camp Crawford, Hokkaido Island.

based aircraft no longer controlled the outcome of naval battles and the 7th Fleet (now augmented by an Australian squadron) launched its aircraft in the wide-ranging ground attack role. Jet aircraft now also took part in the air war.

Between 15 and 25 September the 8th Army broke out, the 1st Cavalry Division leading, from the "Pusan Perimeter." At the same time (15 September) the U.S. IX Corps under Major General Edward M. Almond made a major amphibious landing over the difficult and treacherous beaches at Inchon on the west coast more than 240km (150 miles) north of Pusan, and some 32km (20 miles) to the south-west of Seoul. The Inchon landing was one of the great strategic strokes of history in conception, execution and results. The U.S. 1st Cavalry and 7th Infantry Divisions met as Seoul was liberated. More than 125,000 prisoners were taken and the N.K.A. scattered into the roadless, rugged countryside. Less

than 80km (50 miles) to the north of Seoul lies the 38th parallel, and the 8th Army and R.O.K. forces were now poised to take the war into North Korea.

At the onset of the Korean War, the parachute element was not considered an all-important element of tactical maneuver. As the heterogeneous forces of the U.N. assembled under MacArthur's command, with the exception of the U.S.A. no nation supplied parachute troops. It was natural that for airborne support MacArthur should look to the 11th Airborne Division, which had served him so well in New Guinea, the Philippines and during the occupation of Japan. The 187th Airborne Regimental Combat Team, commanded by Colonel Frank J. Bowen, Jr., was accordingly compounded from three infantry and one field artillery battalions with "engineers." When Pyongyang, 95km (60 miles) north of the border, fell on 18 October, the 187th Regimental Combat Team formed part of the strategic reserve at Kimpo airfield near Seoul, where they were supported by the new Fairchild C-119 Flying Boxcars of the 314th Troop Carrier Group and the Douglas C-47s of the 21st Troop Carrier Squadron, which was based in Japan.

After the fall of Pyongyang, the U.N. Forces formed a giant pincers movement heading for the Yalu River, beyond which lies Manchuria. The 8th Army (less X Corps) thrust rapidly toward Chusan in the west, while X Corps, which had taken part in the landing at Inchon, was diverted to make another amphibious landing at Wonsan on the east coast. Once ashore at Wonsan, which had already been captured by the R.O.K. I Corps, the U.N. objectives embraced the Chosin Reservoir area, Hyesanjin virtually on the Yalu, and a point farther east, south of the river and 80km (50 miles) from the Sea of Japan. On 16 October, MacArthur issued orders for an airborne operation north of Pyongyang.

The 187th Regimental Combat Team's tasks were to harass the communist withdrawal and secure allied prisoners who were being sent to remote areas of North Korea. Two drop zones were chosen: one near Sukchon and the other close to Sunchon. The two towns lay 11km (7 miles) apart, lying on the arms of the V forming the road and rail routes converging on Pyongyang, 43km (27 miles) to the south. The U.S. Combat Cargo Command canceled all supply commitments of the 314th Troop Carrier Group and 21st Troop Carrier Squadron to ensure that enough aircraft were fully ready for the operation.

The two drops were scheduled for 20 October, and 116 aircraft were assembled at Kimpo airfield for the purpose.

On the morning of 20 October, equipment and supplies were loaded and the paratroopers emplaned in 76 C-119s and 40 C-47s. The aircraft were crowded. The C-119 was, however, a large enough plane, the first designed both as a military cargo and a troop carrier. The Flying Boxcar had a greatly increased payload as compared with its similar predecessor the Fairchild C-82 Packet, which was not used in the paratroop assault role. The C-119's loaded weight was 34,675kg (76,455 lb), its maximum speed 306km (190 mph) and its range 3,925km (2,440 miles). It could carry up to 67 troops, but a typical load was two sticks of 23 paratroopers, jumping simultaneously from port and starboard doors placed toward the end of the fuselage. (One advantage of jumping from a C-119 was that the doors were placed diagonally in the tapering central nacelle, and the jumper could make his exit virtually straight into the prop wash rather than abruptly sideways into it, the principle effect of which was fewer twists in the rigging lines than when leaping through the door of a C-47.) In addition to dispatching the 46 paratroopers, the C-119 could handle 15 monorail bundles and four door bundles. As a paratroop support aircraft it could dispatch field guns mounted on platforms through the nacelle's cargo door. The Flying Boxcar also saw action in the French Indochina War of 1946–54 and it was also used by British paratroopers for training exercises in Europe during the same period.

After take-off from Kimpo on 20 October, the skytrain assembled in a group over the Han River estuary then turned north along the west coast, escorted by aircraft of the 5th U.S. Air Force. U.S.A.F. General Tunner acted as airborne commander for the lead aircraft before the drops, 75 North American F-51s, 62 Lockheed F-80s and five Douglas B-26s bombed and strafed the DZ areas, the pilots claiming the destruction of 57 vehicles (including four tanks), five fuel and ammunition dumps, 23 oxcarts and a field artillery gun. The drop at Sukchon started at 1.00 p.m. and the second drop at Sunchon at 2.20 p.m. Altogether the aircraft had delivered 2,860 paratroopers and 301·2 tons of cargo to the DZs by 3.00 p.m. The airborne deliveries included 12 105mm (4·13 in) howitzers, 39 jeeps, 38 1/4-ton trailers, four 90mm (3·54 in) anti-aircraft guns and four 3/4-ton trucks, as well as ammunition, gasoline, water, rations and other supplies.

Above: Operation "Flashburn," Pope A.F.B., 1954. A party of paratroopers are about to emplane in a C-119. The boom of the "Flying Boxcar" could be opened up to take a jeep or a medium caliber field gun for dropping on platforms by parachute.

At Sukchon, the regimental combat team's 1st Battalion, followed by the 3rd Battalion, captured the town and took control of the area, including Hill 92, which occupied a commanding position overlooking Sukchon. The N.K.A. opposition came mainly from snipers. The 2nd Battalion, jumping over Sunchon, met with no opposition and quickly set up road blocks to trap the escaping N.K.A. troops. As a result of the regimental combat team's block on the gap between the 1st Cavalry and 1st R.O.K. Divisions advancing from Pyongyang, 30,000 communists were caught in the triangle – as it happened, only a small proportion of the North Koreans who fell back to the Yalu River. The airborne operation developed into the Yongu battle, which lasted two days (21–22 October). With the help of the 27th Commonwealth Brigade, the regimental combat team was credited with destroying the 239th N.K.A. Regiment: the paratroopers took 3,818 prisoners, but did not encounter any Allied prisoners of war being conveyed north.

MacArthur, who had witnessed the 187th's drop, declared in Tokyo a few days later that "The war is very definitely coming to an end shortly," but his optimism was short-lived. On the night of 25–26 November, the communists launched a counter-offensive in the west from the Yalu River against the U.N. Forces' right flank. Some 180,000 Chinese troops, in 18 divisions, shattered and ripped through the R.O.K. II Corps, hit the U.S. 2nd Division on the right flank of IX Corps, and threatened envelopment of the entire 8th Army. Walker threw in his reserves, the U.S. 1st Cavalry Division and the Turkish and 27th Commonwealth Brigades, who between them staved off the envelopment, the Turks in particular taking heavy casualties. The 8th Army now withdrew in good order to the general line of the 38th parallel, slightly north of Seoul, a loss of ground since 24 November of 210km (130 miles).

Between 5 and 15 December, X Corps, which had been attacked by 120,000 Chinese in the east, was evacuated from Wonsan by sea. In the fighting which had preceded the withdrawal, the 1st Marine Division had made an epic stand in isolation at the Chosin Reservoir set among mountains before breaking out in the severe winter conditions for the embarkation at Wonsan. In all 105,000 R.O.K. and U.S. troops were lifted by the U.S. Navy with 98,000 civilian refugees. About 350,000 tons of cargo and 17,500 vehicles were also carried by sea. The Far East Air Force also evacuated 3,000 troops, 200 vehicles and 1,300 tons of cargo. On arrival at Pusan, X Corps came under 8th Army control again as part of the strategic reserve. Toward the end of December 1950 Walker was killed in an automobile accident, and was succeeded in command of the 8th Army by Lieutenant General Matthew B. Ridgway, a familiar name in our story of the United States airborne forces.

During the first two weeks of January 1951, the Chinese launched their next massive offensive. Some 400,000 Chinese, with an additional 100,000 of the reconstituted N.K.A. pushed the 200,000-man 8th Army back toward Seoul, which was evacuated on 4 January, the third time the South Korean capital had changed hands. Stubborn resistance of ground troops, plus the Far East Air Force's close support and interdiction of the now-exposed communist lines of communication, slowly checked the

momentum of the drive. By mid-January the U.N. positions had stabilized 80km (50 miles) south of the 38th parallel, from Pyongtaek on the west coast to Samchok on the east. All Allied efforts were directed toward the relief of Seoul.

Operation "Ripper" (7–31 March) was designed to recapture the capital, inflict as many casualties on the enemy as possible, and to eliminate a large communist supply base which had sprung up at Chunchon. By 10 March, the enemy resistance on the Han River had collapsed, and the communists began retreating out of Seoul two days later. Seoul was taken again by the Allies on 14 March. On the next day the U.N. ground troops seized the communications center at Hongchon. As the communists broke cover, the Far East Air Forces launched more than a 1,000 sorties to destroy them. The advancing allied forces captured Chunchon on 21 March.

In the hope of exploiting the communists' retreat, the 187th Regimental Combat Team was alerted on 21 March to attack their line of retreat from Seoul. At noon on that day Brigadier John P. Henebry, commanding the U.S. 315th Air Division, received planning information that the 187th would be air-dropped at Munsan, north-west of Seoul, on the morning of 23 March. Henebry and his two wing commanders, accompanied by now Brigadier General Frank S. Bowen, Jr., the 187th's commander, made a late afternoon aerial reconnaissance of the objective area, and at 5.30 p.m. they met with Generals Partridge and Ridgway to confirm D-day as 23 March and set H-hour for the drop at 9.00 a.m. About this time about 12,000 N.K.A. troops were believed to be in the vicinity of the Munsan area.

In anticipation of a drop on Chunchon, which was canceled, the U.S. Air Force had assembled at "K-2" (Taegu airfield) 80 C-119s of the U.S. 314th Troop Carrier Wing and 55 Curtiss C-46s of the U.S. 437th Troop Carrier Wing, which grouped together formed the U.S. 315th Air Division. The 187th was already based at Taegu. The date was 21 March. Weather on the morning of D-day was perfect for the operation, and for 30 minutes before the drop the 5th Air Force used 56 B-26s of its 3rd and 452nd Bombardment Wings to soften up the objective area with 227kg (500 lb) air-burst bombs. At Taegu Airfield dust made transport take-offs hazardous, but pilots maintained ten-second intervals and no one got into trouble. These transports were escorted by 16 F-51 Mustangs. Promptly as scheduled,

Right: General Matthew B. Ridgway, who succeeded General Douglas MacArthur as C.-in-C. United Nations Command, is seen here visiting the 2nd U.S. Infantry Division in Korea, May 1951.

at 9.00 a.m. the first serial of C-119s began dropping paratroopers in the north drop zone, and five other serials launched paratroopers and dropped equipment during the day.

Only one error marred the drop. When a lift of C-46s was about to take off, the lead aircraft carrying the command section of the 1st Battalion lost one of its engines. The Commando was temporarily airborne before making a successful emergency landing at Tongmyong airstrip (K-37). The deputy commander took over but, losing the formation, headed independently for the south drop zone. As a result of an error in low-level navigation, however, the aeroplane missed the assigned DZ and dropped its men on the north DZ. Meanwhile, the regular battalion commander at K-37 had found a spare C-46 and took off with his staff, dropping on the south zone, only to find they were like castaways on a desert island. They were the only troops on the DZ at the time, so the 30 men were "rescued" by a company sent over from the north DZ to retrieve them.

Except for this incident, the Munsan airborne operation went satisfactorily but without achieving significant results. Seventy-two C-119s dropped 2,011 paratroopers and 204 tons of supplies and equipment, while 48 C-46s unloaded 1,436 paratroopers and 13.5 tons of ammunition, food and signal equipment. During the operation five C-119s incurred minor damage from enemy small-arms fire, and one C-119, evidently struck by enemy fire, burst into flames and crashed enroute for home, killing the pilot and co-pilot. In order to support the 187th Regimental Combat Team and U.N. ground forces driving north from Seoul, the 5th Air Force during the daylight hours of 23 March flew 168 sorties involving F-51, F-80, F-84 and 56 B-26 attack aircraft and bombers. Several airborne relay aircraft (C-47s) provided tactical co-ordination and reconnaissance over the drop zones. In direct support of the parachutists, the relay aircraft directed 31 flights of fighter aircraft. Ridgway, who landed from a small liaison plane in the 187th operational zone, commented that the fighter support was the best he had seen in any airborne operation.

Although the deployment of the 187th Regimental Combat Team at Munsan enabled the U.S. I Corps to close up to the Imjin River, the paratroopers did not account for many of the enemy: 200 were killed and 84 captured; although precise casualty figures are not available, the Americans lost considerably less men. Aerial resupply of ground troops by the U.S.A.F. was becoming increasingly efficient in the Korean War and, as an example, in the airborne element of Operation "Ripper" on 24 March 36 C-119s dropped 40 men and 187.7 tons of supplies. Four C-46s dropped 10 tons of supplies on 26 March, and on the next day 12 C-119s dropped an additional 65.8 tons of supplies.

Early in April, the U.N.'s co-ordinated air ground actions had driven the communist forces back to the 38th parallel and, to pre-empt another communist offensive MacArthur and Ridgway decided on farther advance toward the "Iron Triangle" – Chorwan – Kumhwa – Pyongyang, the major assembly and supply area, as well as the communications center for the Chinese. At this juncture MacArthur, who had been pressing for support for an all-out offensive into China and the use of nuclear weapons, was summarily ousted by President Truman from his dual command of U.N. forces in Korea and of U.S. forces in the Far East. Ridgway was appointed in his place and Lieutenant General James A. Van Fleet was hurried out from the United States to command the 8th Army.

There were no more airborne operations in the Korean War. The U.N. advance to the "Iron Triangle" continued until 21 April when on the following day the Chinese and N.K.A. launched the first phase of their spring offensive, 1951. This was followed by the second phase on 14 May, but although Allied pressure on the "Iron Triangle" was blunted, threats of Soviet intervention now caused the U.N. to do nothing to risk World War III and in June a cease-fire proposal was made in the U.N. Assembly by Soviet Ambassador Malik. In November, peace negotiations started at Panmunjon and dragged on interminably throughout 1952 and for the first half of 1953. During that long time, the "stalemate" Korean War was largely a matter of attacking and defending hill-top outposts, each representing little tactical importance but bitterly contested nonetheless. On 27 July 1953 the armistice was signed. The *de facto* boundary was the existing battle front and the line of demarcation with its "Iron Curtain" exists to this day. Exchange of prisoners who desired repatriation followed the cease-fire; 77,000 communists against 12,700 U.N. men – of whom 3,597 were American and 945 Britons.

The U.S.A.'s overt involvement in Vietnam dates back to 1961 when President John F. Kennedy sent his military advisor, General Maxwell D. Taylor, to South-East Asia to report on the growing communist military threat to the people of South Vietnam, and to suggest the ways and means of supporting President Ngo Dinh Diem's government forces in their mounting struggle to suppress the Viet Cong guerrillas. After the defeat of the French and the end of colonial rule in 1954, the country had been divided by treaty on the 17th parallel between two nations: the communist People's Republic of North Vietnam, with its capital at Hanoi; and the Republic of South Vietnam, a capitalist democracy with its capital at Saigon. The Viet Cong operated from jungle lairs making opportunist attacks on units of the Army of the Republic of Vietnam (A.R.V.N.) as well as government police and para-military forces before, in the classic guerrilla role, swiftly disappearing into the tropical undergrowth from which they had emerged. Converting the southerners, more especially in the rural areas, to the communist creed – by fair means or foul – was also a prime objective of the Viet Cong, an ever-increasing threat to the stability of the Diem regime.

The geography of Vietnam and climatic conditions were an all-powerful influence on Taylor's survey. Vietnam appears on a map of Asia as an elongated figure of eight along the eastern edge of the Indochinese peninsula. It is made up of two river basins – those of the Red and the Mekong Rivers – separated by a narrow chain of mountains backing on even narrower coastal plains. The Red River delta is separated from the coastal lowlands to the south by low-lying hills that also served as the boundary between the old provinces of Tonkin and Annam. Elsewhere the delta is surrounded by rugged mountains that jut abruptly out of the alluvial plain to form the frontier shared with China and Laos.

South Vietnam, formerly Cochinchina, has 6,400km (3,975 miles) of navigable waterways. The Mekong, which is one of the world's longest rivers, rises in South Tsinghai Province in China and flows for 4,185km (2,600 miles) through South-East Asia into the South China Sea. The Mekong delta extends from Saigon south and west to the Gulf of Thailand and the border with Cambodia. The delta, its geography and climate are worth looking at in some detail since the maze of waterways was the scene of major conflict between the U.S. and the South Vietnamese navies against the Viet Cong.

With an area of about 40,000km^2 (24,860 sq miles) and an estimated 8,000,000 inhabitants, the Mekong delta constituted about one-fourth of the total land area of South Vietnam, and the flat alluvial plain created by the Mekong River and its tributaries contained about one-half of the country's population. Much of the land surface is covered by rice paddies, making the area one of the world's most productive in rice growing. It was by far the most important economic region in Vietnam.

The delta had poor overland communications, the low, badly drained surface being subjected to extensive and

Above: Communist troops are seen in the Haiphong area of North Vietnam.

Far left: Vietnam. Troops of the 1st Air Cavalry Division (Airmobile) load onto a C-123 Provider aircraft at the An Khe airbase for a flight to Bong Son at the start of Operation "Masher," 25 January 1966.

prolonged inundation. There was only one major hard surface road, Route 4 (which extended from Saigon south to Ca Mau) traversing the delta and linking many of the larger towns; the secondary roads were poorly surfaced and in the mid-1960's had deteriorated through lack of maintenance. In short, the road network was of little use for military action. Any movement by road was best during the dry season (November to March) when paddies were dry and could support light tracked vehicles and artillery pieces; it was poorest during the wet season (May to October) when paddies were flooded. It was restricted all year round by the network of rivers, canals, streams and ditches. Swamps, marshes and forests bordered the sea coast. One especially swampy area, which concealed a main Viet Cong base, was the Rung Sat Special Zone, in the Vietnam War the only territorial command of the South Vietnamese navy.

In sharp contrast to its limited land transportation, the delta had a highly developed inland waterway system. There is evidence that the inhabitants of the region discovered the means of improving natural drainage as long ago as A.D. 800 and succeeding generations have continued the work. As a result, in the mid-1960's the 2,400km (1,490 miles) of natural, navigable waterways were supplemented by almost as many miles again of landcut canals in varying depth and width, and in condition between good and poor. From mid-May through to early October, the south-east monsoon drenches the lowlands with rain accumulated from its passage over thousands of miles of ocean. Unleashing a torrent of savage thunderstorms in May, the weather then lapses into a monotonous pattern of afternoon showers. The rainfall and the cloudiness reaches a peak in July and August, when heavy downpours often wash out the horizon and reduce the visibilty to zero. The fall transition period lasts barely a month before the north-east monsoon season, which brings cool, dry weather from early November until March. The wet season permits the deliberate flooding of the rice paddies, but also brings unavoidable flooding as rivers overflow their banks, further restricting the cross-country traffic of military ordnance and equipment.

One-third of the delta is marsh, forest or swamp forest. In the north lies a flat grassy basin, the Plain of Reeds. During the wet season it is inundated to a depth of 2–3m (7–9 ft). During the dry season much of the plain dries out to the extent that large grass fires are frequent.

As a result of his visit to South Vietnam, Taylor reported that lack of adequate roadnets, lines of communication, and means of mobility contributed heavily to the problems of the Diem government. As a result of Taylor's recommendations, President Kennedy approved an active support program to South Vietnam to assist in the fight against the Viet Cong. Generally, the support included the establishment of a joint headquarters for directing the program; increasing the number of U.S. advisors for the South Vietnamese armed forces (a few such instructors were already "in country"), and additional support through U.S. Army aviation, communication units and U.S. Navy and U.S. Air Force units. Thus began a chain of events culminating in the arrival of U.S. helicopter units in Vietnam and the new era of airmobility.

On 11 December 1961, the aircraft carrier U.S.N.S. *Card* docked in downtown Saigon with 32 Piasecki H-21 "Flying Banana" helicopters and 400 men. The 57th Transpor-

Below: A student patrol from the 101st Airborne Division "Screaming Eagle" Replacement School starts down the road in patrol formation.

tation Company (Light Helicopter) from Fort Lewis, Washington, and the 8th Transportation Company (Light Helicopter) from Fort Bragg, North Carolina, had arrived in South-East Asia. Just 12 days later those helicopters were committed to the first airmobile combat action in Vietnam, Operation "Chopper." Approximately 1,000 Vietnamese paratroopers were airlifted into a suspected Viet Cong headquarters complex about 16km (10 miles) west of the Vietnamese capital. The paratroopers captured an elusive underground radio transmitter after meeting only slight resistance from a surprised enemy. Major George D. Hardesty, Jr. of the 8th and Major Robert J. Dillard of the 57th could report that their units had performed outstandingly under the first baptism of fire.

The arrival of the "Flying Bananas" in Saigon was the culmination of a decade of debate in the U.S.A. on the possible use of the helicopter in the counter-guerrilla role. American observers had watched with interest how the French had adapted the rotorcraft as a gunship in Algeria, and also the helicopter's suitability as a reconnaissance platform in the hands of British pilots during the Malayan Emergency. In Korea, the U.S. Army had learned that the difficult terrain in that land mass and the numerical superiority of the enemy combined to provide the communists with an advantage that was not easy to match. Many helicopters – turned ambulance – flitted up and down the steep

hills with effortless agility. It was not hard to envisage the possibilities inherent in hundreds of larger machines carrying combat troops up and over the deadly slopes. The U.S. Marines had already demonstrated the possibility of a small unit being carried into combat, and the helicopter itself was beginning to mature with more power and more dependability.

After Korea many senior commanders restudied the lessons of the war and compared actual campaigns with hypothetical airmobile operations under the same conditions. Major General James M. Gavin's article in *Harpers* magazine (April 1954) entitled "Cavalry and I Don't Mean Horses" suggested that "Jumping Jim" thought the future role of the paratrooper was limited and that there was a new scenario for the U.S. Cavalry in assault from the sky. About this time a small group of pioneers at Fort Rucker, Alabama, was making its first crude experiments with armed helicopters. Colonel Jay D. Vanderpool formed a "Sky-Cav" platoon which became notorious for its hair-raising demonstrations of aerial firepower. By 1957 this provisional unit, redesignated the Aerial Combat Reconnaissance Platoon, had somehow acquired two H-21s, one Piasecki H-25 and one Sikorsky H-19, all bristling with a variety of unlikely weapons.

In late September, Secretary of Defense Robert S. McNamara began urging the step-up of the U.S. Army's aviation plans, and

Left: Men of the 17th Cavalry, 82nd Airborne Division, unload from H-34A Choctaw cargo helicopters.

Above: A jeep is driven off a Sikorsky H-37 Mohave helicopter of the U.S. Air Force. The piston-powered Mohave, which saw service in the early days of the Vietnam War, was the precursor of the Boeing-Vertol Chinook as a heavy weapons and equipment carrier.

Above right: A Bell H-13 Sioux helicopter is being used for a mock casualty evacuation by the U.S. 82nd Airborne Division in the Fort Bragg area in 1958. The Sioux, which could carry two casualties in externally strapped litters, was used successfully in the Korean War to move casualties from the battlefields to the Mobile Army Surgical Hospitals (MASH).

Facing page, top: The twin engined DHC-4 Caribou of the U.S. Army was designed and manufactured by de Havilland of Canada. This transport aircraft saw much service in Vietnam where it was used for air-landing troops and parachuting. In this role the Caribou could carry 32 troops or 26 parachutists.

Facing page, below: UH-1D Iroquois helicopters of the 1st Air Cavalry Division land and pick up troops during a search-and-destroy mission 5 kilometers south-west of Landing Zone Uplift in October 1967.

in April of the following year General Hamilton H. Howze, Commanding General of the Strategic Air Corps and of the XVIII Airborne Corps at Fort Bragg, was appointed to form a board for framing the establishment of an air cavalry division. The final report of the Howze Board was submitted on 20 August 1962. An air assault division consisting of 15,787 officers and men, 434 aircraft and 1,600 air-portable vehicles was to be formed without delay. The establishment of the division was to be along the usual infantry pattern but with much reduced firepower from support weapons and vehicle allocation. Artillery consisted of only 105mm (4·13 in) howitzers and Little John rockets. The troop transport first allocated to the division was the Bell UH-1B Iroquois (better known as the "Huey") and the prime mover of artillery and other heavy equipment was the Boeing Vertol CH-47 Chinook.

The "test" division was activated at Fort Benning, Georgia, on 11 February 1963 and was named the 11th Air Assault Division, to revive the colors of the 11th Airborne Division. Brigadier General Harry W.O. Kinnard was selected to lead the 11th Air Assault Division, and he handpicked his key officers and gave them the widest possible latitude in accomplishing their particular roles in the mission. Lieutenant John B. Stockton's 227th Assault Helicopter Battalion – the first in the U.S. Army – spent much of its time experimenting with flying the Hueys over long distances through low cloud and maintaining tight formation flying at night. Meanwhile the Chinook battalion under Lieutenant Colonel Benjamin S. Silver Jr.

devised new methods of moving the artillery and key supplies.

The newly formed 10th Air Transport Brigade, under Colonel Delbert L. Bristol with a combination of fixed-wing de Havilland Canada C-7 Caribous (a STOL transport aeroplane type) and Chinooks, devised the first workable air line of communications. Throughout the early formation and training period of the air assault test units, there was a continuous cross-feed of people, information, equipment and ideas between what was going on in Vietnam and what was happening at Fort Benning. In addition, the division formed a total of six airmobile companies that were sent to Vietnam during the testing period. It must be remembered at this time that the U.S.A. was not committed to combat action in Vietnam, but that there was much to learn from the U.S. advisors already "in country" and from the Vietnamese paratroopers already airmobile in American helicopters.

The Howze Board emphasized the quantitative and qualitive improvements that would be necessary for U.S. Army aviation personnel programs. Its proposal would require 8,900 aviators in 1963, growing to 20,600 in 1968. The board foresaw an increased need for warrant officer pilots and recommended an officer to warrant officer ratio of one to one by the end of five years. It also recommended major changes in the officer career program to enhance their training, administration and utilization. When recruit pilots started to arrive at Fort Benning, they were told there was no truth in the rumors that they were going to Vietnam.

Like most Americans at the time, the trainee pilots knew little or nothing about the political situation in Vietnam, but they were eager to fly. During their nine-month period of flight training discipline was harsh and the fall-out rate high, but those with the right aptitudes relished the new and thrilling experience of flying helicopters.

Training started at the U.S. Army Primary Helicopter School at Fort Wolters, Texas, where the pilot candidates underwent one month of pre-flight training and four months of primary flight training. This preliminary course was designed to reject the pupils who did not have the aptitude and could not take the discipline. The candidates listened attentively to the instructors explaining aerodynamics, helicopter control and maneuvers. They learned that the names of the controls in a helicopter refer to their effect on the rotating wings and tail rotor. The disk formed by the rotor blades is what makes the helicopter bird fly. The collective control stick is located on the left side of the pilot's seat. Pulling it up increases the pitch angle of all main rotor blades, at the same time, collectively, causing the disk and the helicopter to rise. Lowering the collective reduces the pitch and the disk descends. The cyclic control stick rises vertically from the cockpit floor between the pilot's legs. Moving the cyclic stick in any horizontal direction causes the rotating wings to increase their pitch and move higher by one half of their cycle while feathering the other half. This cyclic change of pitch causes the disk formed by the blades to move in the same direction as the cyclic stick is pushed.

Having grasped the theory and practise of raising a helicopter from the ground, flying in a particular direction and landing, the pilot candidates logged 85 hours of flight time over four months in Hiller H-23 Raven trainers. The time had now come to fly 88 hours over the same four-month period from Fort Rucker in the H-19, more correctly designated the UH-19D Chickasaw, whose mission included transportation of cargo or up to ten passengers, together with rescue and observation operations (cargo was carried externally). During the last month at Rucker, each pilot would log 27 hours in the ship all were lusting to fly – the UH-1B – which in its wide-ranging roles was to be the universally recognized silhouette in the Vietnam skies. The pilots found that with its gas-turbine engine the Huey was light and easy to fly. Its streamlined design allowed for a maximum cruise speed of 204km/h (127 mph), about

56km/h (34.5 mph) faster than the H-19.

When the UH-1B was first introduced in Vietnam, it usually carried ten (or at times 11) combat-equipped Vietnamese soldiers. An investigation determined that the average helicopter was grossly overloaded with this many soldiers. A combat-equipped Vietnamese soldier averaged 76kg (167 lb). When the personnel were loaded into the Huey with a full load, a U.S. Army crew of four, armor plate, a tool box, a container of water, a case of emergency rations, weapons and armored vests for the crew, the Huey grossed 3,946kg (8,700 lb), or 953kg (2,100 lb) over normal gross weight. Not only that, the center of gravity had shifted beyond safe limits. As a consequence, the standard procedure was to limit the UH-1B to eight combat troops except in grave emergencies.

The "early years" in Vietnam (1961–65) when the A.R.V.N. became airmobile can be divided into two phases. The first was the period when U.S. Officers taught the South Vietnam commanders how to effectively employ helicopter tactics, while at the same time the American pilots were learning by experience, trial and error; the second phase was characterized by battalion-size air assaults of selected Vietnamese units including paratroopers, Rangers, and the regular infantry. It was the success of the second phase that forced the North Vietnamese government to step up the flow of supplies, which now poured along the Ho Chi Minh Trail complex and across from the Cambodian border. It was during this phase that the Huey came into its own. The turbine-engine helicopter with its great power, its reliability and its slight requirement for maintenance, was the technological turning point so far as air-mobility is concerned. Actually, the key improvement of technology was the trio of the Huey as a troop-lift bird, the Huey again as a fledgling attack helicopter, and the Chinook with its larger capacity for re-supply. These three together allowed the U.S. Army to take a giant step forward at this time.

In those early days there was still a school of thought in the air-conditioned halls of the Pentagon that the helicopter was too vulnerable for military operations and indeed could be shot down by any damned Tom Sawyer with a catapult. However a North Vietnamese instruction pamphlet captured on 16 November 1962 included the following appreciation of the new American airborne techniques employing helicopters.

1. Careful planning and preparations are possible together with complete mobility in an attack, support and relieving role.

2. Secrecy can be preserved and surprise strikes can be accomplished.

3. Landings can be effected deep into our rear areas with the capability to attack and withdraw rapidly.

4. An appropriate means of destroying our forces while they are still weak.

The following strike operation involving the 57th Transportation Company may be described as typical of its kind, and took place in the early weeks of 1962.

As was their custom every day, the pilots assembled before dawn in the ready room of their Saigon base. They were dressed in gray-blue nylon coveralls and busily strapped on pistol belts, checked sector maps and read notices on the operations board. The pilots were mostly warrant officers and lieutenants, with a few captains. The pilots were issued with navigation maps with plastic overlays and allocated frequencies for radio communications. When they were ready to go they pulled on heavy flak vests with bullet-resistant fiber-glass plates. After exchanging jokes in their own jargon about the prospects of the day, they made their way along the muddy paths to the flight line, still clothed in the darkness of night.

Inside the banana-shaped H-21 Shawnees, dull blue cabin lights glowed. The two pilots climbed up into the plexiglass-covered cockpits and slipped on heavy white flight helmets. Switches were flicked and red instrument lights gleamed from the dashboards. At each helicopter, the gunners waited for the signal from the pilot and co-pilot to climb aboard. The forward man took his position at the open door on the left side near the tail where the combat troops made their entry into the helicopter. The Vietnamese soldiers were small of stature and with heavy packs, so the rear gunner had a tough job pulling them aboard. There were no seats for the troops, so they sat or squatted on the aluminum floor. (In the Vietnam War, the "grunts" often sat on their helmets, believing that their rear quarters were more in need of protection than heads in the prevailing circumstances!)

Idling motors speeded up, transmission shafts along the ceiling of each craft began to whine, and the twin rotors began to turn. Red signals beacons on each helicopter were now blinking along the flight line. The helicopters rolled forward, out on to the runway, one behind the other. Pilots revved up their engines and lifted their collectives to see if there was enough power to lift the machines. The signal came and the helicopters roared down the runway: a loaded H-21 took off forward like any other aeroplane. The target this morning was a group of several hundred Viet Cong based in a village in the Mekong delta. The heavily-laden helicopters ascended to 915m (3,000 ft), soon leaving the pre-dawn lights of Saigon behind.

The sunrise began to flood the cabins with light. The watery green patchwork of rice fields, rivers, streams, canals and palm trees slid below. Farmers' dwelling places with their surrounding fruit trees were dotted about everywhere and made a pleasant break from the featureless rice paddies. Ten minutes to go and the helicopters descended swiftly into an open rice field, causing herds of water buffalo to stampede in every direction. The sudden change of air pressure was hard on the ears but the 12 troopers in each helicopter wasted no time in leaping out of the rear doors to a hail of fire from a tree line that separated the landing zone from the Viet Cong positions. With rotors flapping wildly, the helicopters rose from their watery berth. The ground operation would last several days but they would be back to pick up the survivors. Meanwhile, Saigon and cool drinks for the crew were only half an hour away.

In March 1965, when President Lyndon B. Johnson had already committed combat troops to the Vietnam War, a tentative decision was made to convert the 11th Air Assault Division (Test) to a fully-fledged fighting division, and it was decided it would carry the colors of the 1st Cavalry Division, which was then deployed in Korea. On 28 July, the men of the division knew for certain that they were on their way to Vietnam. On that day President Johnson announced on television: "We will stand in Vietnam" and "I have today ordered to Vietnam the Air Mobile Division." The games were over, and life was about to get serious for the "Air Cav." The division staged out of Mobile, Alabama and Jacksonville, Florida on the U.S.S. *Boxer*, three military sea transportation ships, six troop carriers and seven cargo ships. Approximately 80,000 man hours were required to process the cargoes of Hueys, Chinooks, and the fixed-wing Caribous and Grumman OV-1 Mohawks crammed aboard the four aircraft carriers for protection against sea conditions. The U.S.S. *Boxer* proceeded via the Suez Canal while the other vessels crossed the Pacific.

An advance party of 1,000 men was airlifted and landed in the Republic of Vietnam on 25 August. They moved immediately to An Khe, which was situated about halfway between the coastal towns of Qui Nhon and Pleiku on the 160km (100 mile) east-west stretch of road called Route 19, and which was to be the highlands base for the "Air Cav" in the heart of Viet Cong territory. An Khe itself was a tiny village 3·2km (2 miles) off the main highway, and here the advance party commenced work clearing the surrounding countryside for what was to be the world's largest helipad. The ships dropped anchor in Lang Vei Bay, south of Qui Nhon, during the second week of September after about a month at sea. The vinyl coating applied to those lashed to the flight-decks was peeled off and thrown overboard, and boxes of rotor blades were brought up to the decks to be sorted out and attached to their mountings. More helicopters were stored in the hangars, and these also needed assembling before the flight to An Khe. The U.S. Cavalry was about to add a new chapter to its proud history.

Below: Men of the 173rd Airborne Brigade (the "Sky Soldiers") make a practice landing from a Bell UH-1 Iroquois helicopter, Vietnam. The "Sky Soldiers" were the first combat men to fly into Vietnam, landing at Bien Hoa airbase near Saigon on 5 May 1965.

The Early Helicopter Operations

The first major unit of the U.S. Army to be deployed to Vietnam was the 173rd Airborne Brigade, comprising two battalions of infantry and one of artillery. The 173rd, which was to earn the sobriquet "Sky Soldiers" from the Viet Cong, had been stationed on Okinawa for rapid deployment in the event of an emergency in South-East Asia. Arriving on 5 May 1965, Brigadier General Ellis W. Williamson immediately put the men of his brigade into training in jungle conditions. Emphasis was given to grasping the technique of counter-ambush but the men, who were all paratroopers and up-to-date on jump practice, had also to learn how to ride in helicopters. Getting in and out of the helicopters quickly was essential, and the first procedure once on the landing zone was to move as rapidly as possible in the right direction into the woodlines. There was no time to take cover on the way, but the paratroopers were assured that most of the metal flying around would be expended cartridges or belt links falling from their own helicopter gunships. The brigade's first assignment was to guard the major air base at Bien Hoa and the airfield at Vung Tau. During June the 173rd was joined by the 1st Battalion of the Royal Australian Regiment. The Australians would be working directly with the brigade for some months, and would also be joined by a field artillery battery from New Zealand.

On 28 June the 173rd Airborne Brigade participated in the largest troop-lift operation conducted in South Vietnam up to that time. Over 144 U.S. Army aircraft, including 77 troop transport helicopters (called "slicks" by the soldiers), lifted two battalions of the Vietnamese 2nd Airborne Brigade and the 1st and 2nd Battalions of the 503rd Infantry deep into War Zone D north-east of Saigon. In all, nine battalions were involved: five infantry battalions, one artillery battalion, one support battalion, one composite battalion of cavalry, armor and engineers, and the Australian battalion. This was the first time any large force of friendly troops had operated in this area for more than a year. Many caches of weapons and rice were destroyed, and casualties inflicted on the Viet Cong were 25 killed and 50 more wounded. After a two-day fire-fight the forces were extracted. On 6 July, the 173rd returned to War Zone D and in conjunction with the Australians and South Vietnamese infantry made multiple air assaults just north of the Song Dong Nai River. Some 1,494 helicopter sorties were flown in support of the operation. Fifty-six Viet Cong were found dead on a body count. Twenty-eight prisoners of war were taken and 100 tons of rice plus literally tons of documents were captured. Reviewing these early operations, Williamson said he was frankly surprised to find as many enemy as they did in the target areas. The vulnerability of transport helicopters in the assault phase to ground fire was inevitable, but was more than balanced by the fire-power of the gunships and fixed-wing attack aircraft. But it was not only vital for the disembarked troops to move off "on the double," it was equally necessary for the men to be evacuated swiftly from surrounding jungle areas after

Above: Elements of the 173rd Airborne Brigade participate in a joint sweep with South Vietnamese forces just north of Saigon near the town of Ben Cat in the Binh Duon Province. Here the paratroopers are moving through dense jungle growth in a previously unexplored area under Viet Cong control, September 1965.

Far left: Soldiers of the 25th Infantry Division move toward the woodline after being airlifted to a landing zone in the Xa Ba Phuoc Province during Operation Wahiawa in May 1966.

Main picture: The "Sky Soldiers" prepare to board Bell UH-1 helicopters shortly after their arrival in Vietnam.

Inset below: Members of Company "B," 2nd Battalion, 173rd Airborne Brigade, apply blacking to their faces prior to moving out from Bien Hoa in a search-and-destroy mission in the infamous Zone D 19km (12 miles) to the south-east, June 1968. The 173rd pioneered the tactics for airmobile attacks in Vietnam.

Inset right: The "Sky Soldiers" operating with the ARVN conduct a two-day sweep in the Bien Hoa area. Two captured suspected Viet Cong are loaded aboard a jeep, 1965.

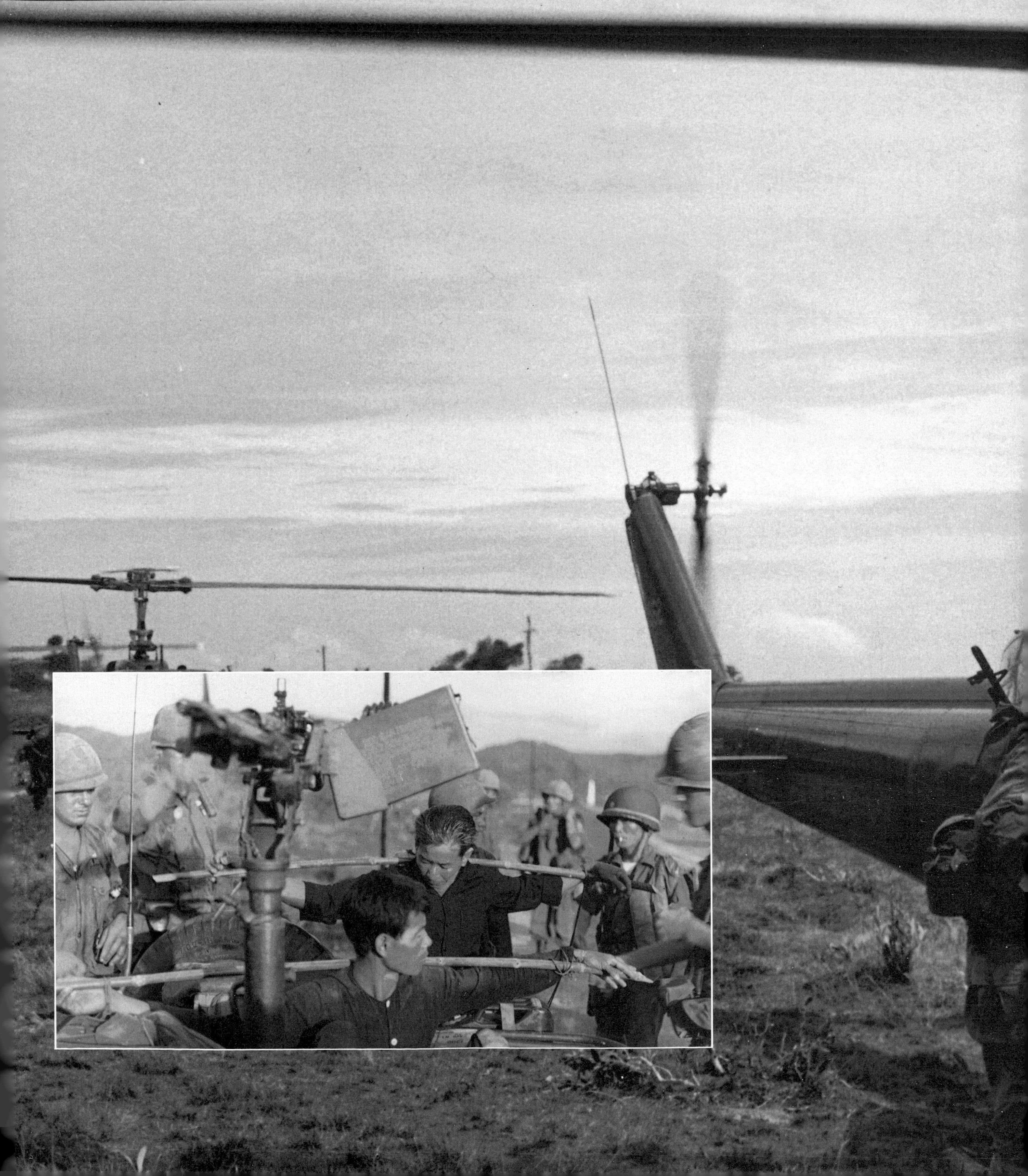

Above: Members of the 1st Brigade, 101st Airborne Division, jump from a U.S. Army Caribou aircraft during ceremonies held upon the arrival of the 1st Brigade at Cam Ranh Bay, Vietnam, July 1965. The "Screaming Eagles," now an airmobile division, were not destined to make an operational jump in the Vietnam War.

the engagement was over. On the Song Dong Nai River operation, some 3,000 troops had been pulled out of the jungle and emplaned in three hours and ten minutes, a not unsatisfactory achievement. The gunships had described an ever-decreasing circle of fire around the retreating troops and the 173rd's own 105mm (4·13 in) artillery sited on the LZs had put up an effective protective barrage of fire during the withdrawal. In the words of Lieutenant Colonel Lee E. Surut, commanding officer of the 3rd Battalion, 319th Artillery: "Once again the artillery lent dignity to what otherwise would have been a vulgar brawl."

On 29 July, the 1st Brigade of the 101st Airborne Division arrived in South Vietnam from Fort Campbell, Kentucky, manned a defensive perimeter in the Cam Ranh Bay area, and began to establish a base camp. The 1st Brigade was quickly employed securing the An Khe base area for the 1st Cavalry Division. During Operation "Highland" (22 August to 2 October), one battalion conducted an airmobile assault in conjunction with a battalion-size ground attack to open the An Khe Pass and to clear and secure Route 19 from Qui Nhon to An Khe. The "Air Cav" was fully in position at An Khe by 2 October and was assigned a roving commission over an area 240 x 240km (150 x 150 miles). The 1st Brigade was to operate in the highland province of Pleiku, which included the Chu Pong Mountains; the 2nd Brigade was given Kontum Province; and the 3rd Brigade was allocated the populous coastal province of Binh Dinh. The Cavalry Squadron was charged with a wide-sweeping reconnaissance mission throughout the entire area, but most particularly around the Special

Forces camps at Pleime, Duc Co, Plei Djereng, Plei Murong and Dak To that dotted the western highlands. After some experimentation, it was decided to deploy the UH-1B helicopters in what from the ground looked like rough "V" formations. The choppers would fly in the stepped "V" configuration, taking care and keeping distance to avoid turbulence from each other's large rotors. Escorts would fly slightly ahead of, to the side, and to the rear of the "slicks," and would arrive over the target area a few minutes before the troop carriers, open fire to soften up the area, and attack clearly identified targets. Keeping the landing zone protected was of prime importance, and if the LZ was on firm ground and lacking obstacles the Americans felt that a 12-Huey "slick" formation could unload its troops and be back in the air within two minutes, minimizing the helicopters' exposure to enemy fire.

Like most other theories in the Vietnam War, the two-minute interval proved to be wildly optimistic and was possibly only feasible in the most ideal of conditions; the amount and accuracy of enemy fire obviously also posed a threat to the two-minute notion. Other factors also had to be considered, the most important being the surface of the LZ. If it happened to be a rice paddy or an area with an unstable ground mass, the helicopters would go into a hover as low as possible from the ground while the troops made the best of jumping overboard. The hovering not only increased the time of operation but the additional height also made the "slicks" easier targets, although the fixed-wing element assisted greatly in providing safety on the landing zone.

Above: Elements of the 25th Infantry Division take off in Huey helicopters to participate in Operation "Fort Smith" in the Ap An Bien Province near their base camp at Gu Chi.

This division was famous for providing the "tunnel rats," the men who crawled down the shafts of the underground tunnels connecting the subterranean base areas built by the Viet Cong, 1966.

Left: A Bell UH-1D Iroquois lands in thick growth near the Demilitarized Zone to offload troopers of the 101st Airborne Division for a jungle sweep, 1969.

Above: A UH-1D Medevac ("Dust-Off") helicopter takes off to pick up an injured member of the 101st Airborne Division near the Demilitarized Zone, 1969.

The ideal battlefield situation was to have all the "slicks" land and take-off together. The mass envelopment of the helicopters distracted the enemy fire from concentrating on one particular machine and also permitted the landing of a massed body of airborne soldiers who would soon be firing into the enemy positions. However, the landing phase was not easy to accomplish for several reasons. The noise from a combined number of "slicks" was extremely loud and the landing "V" patterns could be disrupted if Viet Cong fire was accurate. Landing simultaneously was made more difficult because of the stepped altitude of the formation, the rotor wash encountered during the descent, and the uncertainty of finding a suitable touchdown spot for each of the ships. In practice, no terrain in areas of combat provided absolutely

ideal conditions for landing. In the Mekong delta, water was sometimes chest deep and rather than maintaining a low hover and risk drowning the troops, the ship was held with its skids just under the water level. In jungle areas, grass 3-3·6m (10-12 ft) high was also encountered. The two-minute landing intervals, even assuming they were achieved, nevertheless seemed like an eternity to the crews.

Developed from the UH-1A, the UH-1B helicopter initially had a 716kW (960 shp) Lycoming T53-L-5 turboshaft, replaced in later machines by the 820kW (1,100 shp) T53-L-11. The UH-1B, with its more powerful lightweight engine, had some power to spare as compared with the UH-1A. It could hover and take off with ten passengers and a crew of two, and it was also quieter, started more

Above: UH-1s in action in Vietnam in September 1967.

easily, and was simpler to maintain. A U.S. Army training film shown to pilot candidates flying UH-1Bs at Fort Rucker boasted that the T53-L-11 engine developed 820kW (1,100 shp) yet weighed only 227kg (500 lb). The film went on to explain that a turbine is basically a jet engine with a fan placed in the exhaust. An animation showed an engine cutaway illustrating the 30·5 cm (12 in) diameter turbine fan spinning in the gas behind the jet engine. The single turbine fan was connected by a shaft running back through the engine to the transmission. The pressure of the gas pushing through this fan generated sufficient force to turn the single 13·41m (44 ft 0 in) diameter main and 2·4m (8 ft 0 in) diameter tail rotors, and thus lift the 2,041kg (4,500 lb) machine together with a load of 3,039kg (6,700 lb) into the air. The animation

then dissolved to a Huey banking away to swoop down on the jungle, followed by a view of the helicopter sitting in a clearing before rising vertically. The announcer said at this point: "Though not recommended, the Huey is capable of hovering vertically up to an altitude of 10,000 feet on a standard day." The film then went on to show how the UH-1B was variously configured as an air ambulance (nicknamed "Medevac" or "Dust-Off") carrying a pilot, co-pilot, crew chief, medical orderly and three stretchers, as a gunship ("Guns") lifting pilot, co-pilot and two gunners, one of whom was the crew chief, operating machine-guns, rockets, or grenade launchers, and as a troop carrier ("Slick") with space for eight soldiers and two crew-operated door guns.

Along with the "slicks," the armed UH-1B

Above: A U.S. Navy Huey of the Helicopter Attack (Light) Squadron (HAL 3) based at Vung Tau fires a rocket at a Viet Cong manned vessel in the Mekong Delta. The "Seawolves" operated in support of the riverine craft of the Brownwater Navy.

Above right: A UH-1B Huey pilot looks over his MXL machine-guns externally mounted on his helicopter. The guns were operated by remote control by the co-pilot.

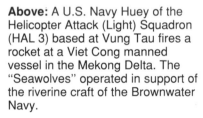

Far right: A Boeing-Vertol CH-47 Chinook helicopter brings in a load of artillery shells to a landing zone northwest of Tuy Hoa during Operation "Bolling," a search-and-destroy mission in Phu Yen Province, 1967.

Huey gunships saw much action in the service of the "Air Cav." During 1966, the U.S. Army developed a gunship helicopter program which saw a platoon of gunships (eight UH-1Bs) assigned as an element of each helicopter assault company. This plan gave the company instant protection which could be relied upon to protect troop helicopters during landing and take-off from a landing zone. Of the eight ships in each platoon, five were kept at operational readiness while the remaining three were undergoing maintenance or being held in reserve. When sent into action, the Hueys would fly in two pairs called light fire teams while the fifth helicopter could join one of the teams when needed.

The gunships were called upon to do hazardous work, and the Huey's relatively low speed and less than snappy maneuverability made it a good target for the enemy. However, it could sting back hard and often. Various armament systems could be installed in and on the helicopter. The UH-1B was armed with four 7·62mm M60 machine-guns, a 40mm grenade launcher, 48 70mm (2·75 in) rockets and an M22 guided missile. The XM3 armament system boasted two rocket pods (one on each side of the Huey), each of which could hold 24 70mm (2·75 in) unguided folding-fin rockets, while the XM16 armament included two rocket pods, also located one on each side of the Huey and each holding seven 70mm (2·75

in) unguided folding fin rockets. Two M60 machine-guns were provided for the door gunners, and there were also two flexiguns, externally mounted M60CA1 7·62mm machine-guns. The standard M60 rate of fire (2,400 rounds per minute) had been uprated in the M60CA1 to 4,000 rpm, but they were restricted to a three-second maximum firing time with a momentary automatic stop between firings. To feed the weapons, 12 feeder ammunition boxes were located in the cargo compartment, as used by the troop transport. The rockets could be fired in a combination of ways: singly, in pairs, or in massive salvos from the pods.

A few UH-1Bs were fitted with the French SS.11 missile system. This system, which employed a wire-guided armor-piercing missile, had been used in Vietnam since the arrival of the 1st Cavalry Division, but the lack of suitable targets had reduced its usefulness. The system had been standardized in the U.S. Army since 1960, when it replaced the lighter French SS.10 missile, and since then hundreds of gunners had been trained at Fort Rucker in the use of the SS.11. Hueys mounting the SS.11 were alerted in April 1968 when North Vietnamese PT-76 tanks were sighted in the Lang Vei area during an attack on the Special Forces camp, but no missiles were used on that occasion.

During the Vietnam War three versions of the CH-47 Chinook were in service. The

Right: A CH-47 lands in a clearing. Four CH-47s were converted to ACH-47A, "Go-Go Birds" and served as gunships during the Vietnam war.

CH-47A was the initial production model, and was consigned with its Huey escorts to serve the 1st Cavalry in Vietnam in 1965. Twin-engined with two sets of rotors (one above the cockpit and one at the rear), the CH-47A was fitted with two Lycoming turboshafts, either 1,640kW (2,200 shp) T55-L-5 or 1,976kW (2,650 shp) T55-L-7 units. The CH-47B, which first came off the assembly line on 10 May 1967, had uprated 2,125kW (2,850 shp) T55-L-7C engines, redesigned rotor blades with a cambered leading edge, and other minor modifications to improve flying qualities. The CH-47C, with its 2,796kW (3,750 shp) T55-L-11 engines and increased integral fuel capacity, was by far the most powerful of the early Chinooks. The first flight of a CH-47C was made on 14 October 1967, and deliveries of the production aircraft began in the spring of 1968; they were first deployed to Vietnam in September of that year. By the beginning of 1969, some 270 CH-47Cs were in action there, and had logged more than 300,000 hours of combat flight. On one occasion no fewer than 147 refugees and their possessions were evacuated by a single such helicopter, and by that time Chinooks had picked up 5,700 disabled aircraft and flown them to repair bases.

If the Huey was the cavalry horse and endowed with the tradition of the U.S. Cavalry of "Old Army" years, the Chinook was more akin to Hannibal's elephants. One battalion of Chinooks was assigned to the 1st Cavalry Division. The most spectacular mission in Vietnam for the Chinook was the placing of artillery batteries in mountain positions inaccessible by any other means, and then keeping them supplied with large quantities of ammunition.

For centuries the infantryman has depended on artillery for support whether on the offensive or in retreat. The artilleryman in turn has depended on the infantry to secure his positions and keep his supply routes open. In Vietnam, no simple solutions were available to continue this long-established team work. It was not until World War II that field guns, originally hauled by teams of horses achieved mobility with the use of wheeled and tracked vehicles powered by the internal combustion engine. Tank-like self-propelled guns, which are an item of artillery, can move more or less at will, but much sweat is still needed, especially in muddy conditions, to manhandle guns into and out of their firing lines. The nature of the guerrilla war in Vietnam with its jungled highlands, lowlands and labyrinthine delta waterways meant that there was no front line which the allies – or the enemy – could advance from or fall back to. As for the infantry, the helicopter provided the means of mounting short-term "search and destroy missions" with adequate fire support. The early designers of the airmobile division had recognized that they would have to sacrifice the heavy 155mm howitzer and be content with moving the 105mm howitzer with the Chinook helicopter.

The 1st Cavalry Division found that its Chinooks were limited to a 3,175kg (7,000 lb) payload when operating in the mountains, but could carry an additional 454kg (1,000 lb) when operating near the coast. The early Chinook design was limited by its rotor system, which did not permit full use of the installed power, and the users were anxious for an improved version which would upgrade the system. As it turned out, a 155mm howitzer battalion was continuously attached to the 1st Cavalry Division. It was teamed with the Sikorsky CH-54 Tarhe "sky crane" to become an integrated part of the Air Cavalry's fire support. The Little John rocket had been included in the original line-up, but when the 1st Cavalry Division deployed to Vietnam, the Little John was left out as a result of tactical and manpower considerations.

The Bell AH-1 HueyCobra came into being as a result of an urgent program initiated by the U.S. Army when the Vietnam War revealed the need for a fast, well-armed helicopter to provide escort and fire support for the UH-1 Huey and CH-47 Chinook. Relatively small, the HueyCobra had a low silhouette and narrow profile with a fuselage width of only 91cm (3 ft). Although the noise of their rotors betrayed approaching AH-1 helicopters, these features helped to conceal the "Snakes" (to use the HucyCobra's Vietnam nickname) when approaching a landing zone and on the ground where they could be hastily covered by the camouflage nets or moved into the cover of trees. The greater agility of the AH-1G armed helicopter as compared with fixed-wing aircraft, and its performance in speed and maneuverability in particular were outstanding. Tandem seating for the crew of two provided a maximum all-round field of view for the pilot and co-pilot/forward gunner, another advantage that helicopters had over the fixed-wing attack aircraft and gunships when supporting troops on the ground. If the Viet Cong opened fire from their jungle lairs, they were apt to lose the advantage of cover and concealment, and a corollary of this advantage of spotting and firing on the enemy was the ability to spot "own troops" and to place supporting bursts of machine-gun fire just a few yards ahead of them. In normal operation the co-pilot/gunner controlled and fired the turret armament, using a hand-operated pantograph-mounted sight to which the turret was slaved.

The gunner's field of fire was 230 degrees, 115 degrees right and left of the centerline, and the turreted weapons could be depressed 50 degrees and elevated 25 degrees. In addition, the gunner had the capability of

Below: The first Bell AH-1 HueyCobra flew on 7 September 1965. The version seen here is the AH-1S.

Above: A close-up of one of a Cobra's externally mounted wing stores – a rocket gun pod, which was fired by the co-pilot/gunner by pressing a button in the cockpit cabin.

firing the wing stores. The pilot could only fire the turreted weapons when in the stowed position (the TAT-102A or XM28 turret returned to the stowed position automatically when the gunner released his grip on the slewing switch) but he usually fired the wing stores, utilizing the XM73 adjustable rocket sight. Rockets were fired in pairs, one rocket from each opposing wing station; any desired number of pairs from one to 19 pre-selected on the cockpit-mounted intervalometer. The inboard wing stores were equipped to fire either the XM18 or XM18C1 Minigun pod, and all wing stores were totally jettisonable. Two rates of fire were provided for the 7·62mm six-barrel Minigun in the TAT-102A and XM28 installations, namely 1,600 and 4,000 rounds per minute. The lower rate was for searching or registry fire, while the higher rate was used for attack. Rate of fire was controlled by the gunner's trigger. A 40mm grenade launcher was paired with the Minigun in the XM28 turret, and this XM129 fired at a single rate of 400 rounds per minute. In 1969, an XM35 20mm cannon kit was added to the weapons available for the AH-1G. Designed jointly by Bell and General Electric, the XM35 subsystem consisted of an XM195 six-barrel 20mm automatic

cannon, two ammunition boxes and certain structural and electrical modifications. Mounted on the inboard stores attachment of the port stub-wing, the XM35 had a firing rate of 750 rounds per minute, and the two ammunition boxes, fared flush to the fuselage below the stub wings, held 1,000 rounds. The total installed weight of the system was 532kg (1,172 lb). The crew were protected by seat and side panels made of armor manufactured by the Norton Company, and similar panels protected vital areas of the aircraft.

As an example of the firepower available in 1971, in addition to its turret armament the AH-1G could carry the 70mm (2·75 in) rocket with a 7·7kg (17 lb) warhead the very effective flechette rocket of the same caliber, and the XM35 20mm cannon pod. The firepower of the 1st Cavalry Division was also enhanced by the intelligence-gathering capability of seismic intrusion devices, which were dropped by UH-1H helicopters along known infiltration routes. Once enemy movement had been detected, a small unit was lifted into the area ahead of the enemy's determined course of movement and established an effective ambush with artillery and gunships standing by.

With the success of the Chinook as a prime

artillery mover and heavy cargo carrier, its intended role as a medium assault helicopter was quietly forgotten. However, an armed version of the CH-47, unique to the 1st Cavalry Division, was the "Go-Go Bird," so named by the infantry. This was a heavily armed Chinook which the 1st Cavalry was asked to test in combat. Three test models were armed with twin 20mm Gatling guns, 40mm grenade launchers and .50 caliber machineguns, along with assorted ordnance. Though anything but graceful, the type had a tremendous morale effect on the friendly troops who constantly asked for its support. From the G.I.'s viewpoint, when the "Go-Go Bird" came the enemy disappeared, and the pilots who flew these test machines performed some incredibly heroic deeds to prove the type's worth. However, the armed Chinook required an inordinate amount of maintenance support and the 1st Cavalry found that it could keep three Chinook lift ships in the air for the price of one "Go-Go Bird." When two of the armed Chinooks became unairworthy through attrition, the final "Go-Go Bird" was transferred to the 1st Aviation Brigade. Although judged a mistake, the troopers who had enjoyed its support never forgot it.

The CH-47 was also deployed as a "bomber" over South Vietnam. The Viet Cong developed an ingenious and wide-ranging underground fortification and tunnel system throughout Binh Dinh Province. Many of these fortifications could withstand almost any explosion, so tear gas was introduced to drive the enemy into the open. During Operation "Pershing" in 1967, the 1st Cavalry Division dropped a total of 12,247kg (27,000 lb) of tear gas from CH-47 helicopters using a simple, locally fabricated fuzing system on a standard drum. Initially the drums were merely rolled out of the back of the open door and the fuzing system was armed by a static line after it was free of the helicopter. Using this method, a large concentration of tear gas could be spread over a suspected area with accuracy. Napalm was rigged and dropped in a similar manner during the same period: a single CH-47 could drop 2 1/2 tons of napalm on an enemy installation. Naturally, this was only used on specific targets where tactical air support could not be effectively used.

Above: A Bell AH-1J SeaCobra follows a river line over the Vietnam jungle. This helicopter is the Marine Corps version of the Army's HueyCobra, which came into being to provide escort and fire support for the CH-47A Chinook, first arriving in Vietnam in September 1967.

The Jungle Birds in Action

By mid-October 1965, the North Vietnamese Army had begun its major operation in the Central Highlands. There is every reason to believe that the N.V.A. planned to cut South Vietnam in two, for three N.V.A. regiments had assembled in western Pleiku Province and adjacent Cambodia. On 19 October, the enemy opened the campaign with an attack on the Pleime Special Forces Camp 40km (25 miles) south-west of Pleiku. On 27 October, General William C. Westmoreland, the overall U.S. military commander in Vietnam, directed Brigadier General Harry W.O. Kinnard to move his 1st Cavalry Division to seek out and destroy this enemy force consisting of the 32nd, 33rd and 66th N.V.A. Regiments. This became the month-long campaign known as "The Battle of the Ia Drang Valley."

Initially, the 1st Cavalry Division reinforced the South Vietnamese army in relieving the Pleime Camp, and the N.V.A. regiments broke contact and disappeared into the jungle. Little was known about the enemy's direction of movement except to speculate that the departing units had gone west towards the Cambodian border. The 1st Brigade of the 1st Cavalry was given the mission of organizing a systematic search for the elusive enemy. It was apparent that the Pleime Camp had been hit – and hit hard – by the enemy and it seemed inconceivable to the Air Cavalry Squadron that thousands of Viet Cong and North Vietnamese soldiers could completely disappear. On 1 November, Captain William P. Gillette, the Air Cavalry Squadron intelligence officer, spotted some unusual

activity just 8km (5 miles) west of the Pleime Camp, and the squadron was quick to capitalize on this information. Before the day was over, the Cavalry Squadron had committed most of its rifle and gunship platoons into the skirmish that developed. They killed 78 of the enemy and captured 57 prisoners. It was obvious that the "Air Cav" had uncovered a major base area which included a well-equipped hospital.

In this first skirmish of the Ia Drang Valley campaign the cavalry troopers were initially taken back at the almost suicidal short ranges at which they came to grips with the enemy. The bulk of the enemy attack force was within 18m (60 ft) of their perimeter before it was discovered, and the enemy's "bear hug" tactics made supporting fire extremely difficult to place safely. Emergency medical evacuation landing zones had to be literally hacked out of the jungle with hand axes. Infantry reinforcements arrived at the site too late to take full advantage of this enemy contact. The best estimate was that the major enemy force had moved along the Ia Drang Valley close to the base of the Chu Pong Mountains and the 1st Squadron, 9th Cavalry, was given the mission of establishing an ambush in the area. A site was chosen and named Landing Zone "Mary." Here the troopers of this swashbuckling outfit, to be known more familiarly as the "Cav of the Cav," fought their first major battle.

LZ "Mary" was unique in that it was the first time that the 1st Cavalry Division had mounted a successful night ambush and reinforced their attack with a night lift of an

Above: The 4th Battalion, 503rd Parachute Infantry Regiment, of the 173rd Airborne Brigade is heli-lifted by UH-1D Hueys to the brigade operational base camp at Xuan Loc Province after successfully completing a search and destroy mission.

Far left: Troopers of Company "A," 1st Cavalry Division (Airmobile), check out a hut during "Irving," the second phase of Operation "Thayer," 1966. The "Air Cav" was given the mission of clearing a mountain range where an estimated two battalions of North Vietnamese regulars (N.V.A.) were thought to be massing for attack on Hammond airstrip, 1966.

infantry company. Also they had developed their fire procedures to the point that armed helicopters were able to fire within 50m (165 ft) of the friendly troops during night operations. By 4 November, the Cavalry Squadron had developed the battle to a point where it could be turned over to the infantry battalions. Over 150 enemy casualties had been accounted for, and so far only nine American soldiers had been killed. The Ia Drang battle was now fully under way. On 9 November, the 1st Brigade was relieved by the 3rd and the latter's commander, Colonel Thomas W. Brown, decided to make the initial assault with the 1st Battalion, 7th Cavalry, commanded by Lieutenant Colonel Harold G. Moore.

Moore's battalion began the pivotal operation on 14 November. LZ "X-Ray" was chosen, and a reconnaissance revealed that the landing zone could take eight to ten UH-1Ds at one time. Two artillery batteries were in position to support the landing. Preparatory fire began at 10.17 a.m. and was timed with the lead elements of the assault company. The aerial artillery came on the heels of the tube artillery fire and worked over the area for 30 seconds, expending half the load of the helicopters, which then went into orbit nearby to be on call. The lift battalion gunships, immediately ahead of the troop-transport Hueys, took up the fire. The terrain was flat with scrub trees up to 30m (100 ft) high, thick elephant grass varying in height up to 1·5m (5 ft), and ant hills up to 2·4m (8 ft) high. Along the western edge of the LZ the trees and grass were especially thick and extended through the jungle to the foothills of the Chu Pong Mountains. Company "B" made the initial assault.

Once four companies were on the ground, enemy 60mm and 81mm mortar fire began falling on the LZ and several helicopters were hit. In spite of this, the Huey pilots and crews ran the gauntlet of enemy fire to take off the wounded. Fierce fighting continued during the day but the 1st Battalion, 7th Cavalry, was able to hold its own against heavy odds. In the early morning hours savage close-range fighting went on throughout the battalion perimeter. There was considerable hand-to-hand fighting. For example, the 1st Platoon leader of Company "C" was found killed with five dead enemy in or near his command post fox hole. Nearby one "Air Cav" trooper was found killed in action with his hands on the throat of a dead Vietnamese soldier. Brown radioed Kinnard for another battalion, and was informed that the 1st

Battalion, 5th Cavalry, would begin arriving at brigade headquarters the following morning. Late on 14 November, the brigade commander had moved the 2nd Battalion, 5th Cavalry, into LZ "Victor" but the enemy continued to attack strongly.

By 26 November, the 1st Cavalry Division had completed its mission of pursuit and destruction. Altogether the "Air Cav" and A.R.V.N. troops killed an estimated 1,800 North Vietnamese troops. The 1st Battalion, 7th Cavalry, lost 79 troopers dead and 121

wounded. During the 35 days of the campaign, the aircraft delivered 5,048 tons of cargo from the C4 supply terminals to the troops in the field. In addition they transported 8,216 tons into Pleiku from various depots (primarily Qui Nhon and Nha Trang). Whole infantry battalions and artillery batteries were moved by air, and approximately 2,700 refugees were rescued from the Ia Drang valley. In all this flying, 59 aircraft were hit by enemy fire – three while on the ground – but only four were shot down. Of these four, three were recovered by "sky crane" helicopters. Westmoreland stated: "The ability of the Americans to meet and defeat the best troops the enemy could put on the field of battle was once more demonstrated beyond any possible doubt as was the validity of the Army's airmobile concept."

The earlier helicopter units developed a task force called an "Eagle Flight." An "Eagle Flight" was defined by Headquarters U.S. Military Assistance Command, Vietnam, as "a tactical concept involving the employment

Below: "The Cav of the Cav." Elements of the Blue (Rifle) Platoon, "B" Troop, 1st Squadron, 9th Cavalry, 1st Cavalry Division, are seen in action in the An Lao Valley, Operation "Pershing," 1967. The 1st Squadron, 9th Cavalry, was the "eyes and ears" of the division.

Right: A squad of Company "B," 503rd Infantry Regiment, of the 173rd Airborne Brigade jump out from an M-113 armored personnel carrier during a training exercise near Bien Hoa. The M-113 PC could be lifted by a CH-47 Chinook slung by ropes attached to the belly of the fuselage and was used on search and destroy missions.

of a small self-contained, highly-trained heliborne force." A typical "Eagle Flight" would consist of the following: one armed Huey serving as the command and control ship, and having on board the U.S. Army aviation commander; seven unarmed Hueys gave the fire support and escort to the troop carrying helicopters; and one Huey usually designated as a medical evacuation ship. The "Eagle Flights" were usually on a standby basis or sometimes even airborne searching for their own targets. Not only were the "Eagle Flights" immediately available for those missions which required a minimum of planning, but they also provided the basis for larger operations. Several "Eagle Flights" were used against targets that when developed proved to be too large for a single unit.

On 1 January 1966, the 173rd Airborne Brigade moved to the Mekong delta to operate in the notorious Plain of Reeds. The brigade had moved from Hau Nghai Province into the delta by land and air. The air elements came into Bao Trai airstrip and comprised the 1st Battalion (Airborne), 503rd Infantry; the 2nd Battalion (Airborne), 503rd Infantry; the 1st Battalion, Royal Australian Regiment; and Battery "C", 3rd Battalion, 319th Artillery. Air assaults were immediately made on the east side of the Oriental River. The 173rd Brigade was soon involved in some heavy fighting in the rice paddies. Effective use was made of artillery fire to pound the Viet Cong but the armored personnel carriers had difficulty in moving over the marshy terrain. On D+5 of Operation "Marauder," the 173rd demonstrated its growing skills in airmobile techniques. Three "Eagle Flights," one consisting of 144 men and the others of 72 each, orbited their targets just beyond visual range. Each flight made brilliantly co-ordinated landings under covering fire. Three companies were quickly at work searching for Viet Cong, and accomplished their tasks in much less time than a much larger force would have taken. Operation "Marauder" ended on 8 January after the decimation of the Viet Cong 267th Battalion and part of the 506th Battalion.

During the first half of January 1966 the 1st Brigade of the 1st Cavalry Division conducted Operation "Matador" to find and destroy the enemy in Pleiku and Kontum Provinces. During this operation, the 1st Cavalry saw the enemy flee across the border into Cambodia, confirming that the enemy had well developed sanctuaries and base camps inside that country. After Operation

"Matador," the 1st Cavalry Division shifted its weight toward Binh Dinh Province. Some of its forces had been committed into the area soon after its arrival in Vietnam in the summer of 1965, but the major effort in the Ia Drang valley occupied most of the 1st Cavalry's attention throughout 1965. The heavily populated rice plains in the Binh Dinh area had a population of nearly half a million people, of whom at least 200,000 or more were firmly under the control of the guerrillas. These latter were supported by the 3rd N.V.A. Division.

The 1st Cavalry's first major operation in this area was called "Masher" in the first phase, and "White Wing" in its second, third and fourth phases that ended on 17 February. The fighting covered a full circle around Bong Son. The 1st Cavalry Division, in close co-ordination with the 22nd A.R.V.N. Division, began with air assaults into the Cay Giep Mountains then moved to the Bong Son

Left: Troops and equipment of the 1st Air Cavalry Division are about to be loaded at a main Vietnam airbase at the commencement of Operation "Masher-White Wing," 1966. The DHC-4 Caribou of Canadian design was used by the U.S. Army in Vietnam as a troop and load lifter, parachute and ambulance aircraft.

Right: Operation "Crazy Horse,"
northeast of An Khe, 1966. "O"
Battery, 2nd Battalion, 19th Artillery,
1st Cavalry Division, site their
105mm howitzer guns for a fire
mission in support of the 1st
Battalion, 5th Cavalry Regiment, on
a mountain-top position.

The Vietnam War saw the
replacement of the mule for carrying
loads up steep mountain tracks by
the helicopter. The prime mover of
artillery and ammunition pallets was
the CH-47 Chinook but the Sikorsky
CH-54 Tarhe "Sky Crane" could be
used for the purpose as well.

Mountain tops were ideal sites for
fire support positions dominating
the valleys with, on a good day,
clear visions of the target areas.
Army 0-1 Bird Dogs helped spot
enemy movements and
concentrations. In the absence of
an enemy air force over the South
Vietnam skies, these artillery
batteries were unassailable and
could be easily re-supplied with
ammunition by helicopter.

Plains, the An Lao valley, the Kim Son valley,
and finally back to the Cay Giep Mountains.
As a result of the "Masher-White Wing"
operations, the airmobile division and the
A.R.V.N. infantry forced the N.V.A. regulars
out of the area and temporarily broke their
hold on the population. As it turned out, the
1st Cavalry would find itself preoccupied in
Binh Dinh Province for a long time to come.
In the after-action report of the 3rd Brigade,
it was reported that 893 enemy had been
killed, and that a large quantity of equipment
and small arms had been captured along with
24,000 rounds of ammunition. The U.S. and
A.R.V.N. losses were 82 killed in action and
318 wounded.

The origins of many of the major operations
in Vietnam can be traced to some minor
contact which was quickly exploited by
airmobile forces. Often this was the only way
the elusive enemy could be forced to fight.
Operation "Crazy Horse" was a good example
of the determination of the "Air Cav" to seek
out and destroy the enemy. The 1st Cavalry
was finishing Operation "Davy Crockett" on
15 May when a Civilian Irregular Defense
Group (see chapter 20) patrol from a nearby
C.I.D.G. camp working in the mountain valley
immediately to the east discovered evidence
that a mortar post was in the process of
preparation to bombard the camp. One
company of the 1st Cavalry Division air
assaulted into the hills east of the C.I.D.G.
camp at 10.00 a.m. on 16 May to search out
the area. Company "B," 2nd Battalion
(Airborne), 8th Cavalry, landed on a small
patch of elephant grass about halfway up the
side of the largest mountain east of the
C.I.D.G. camp. After a hard climb to the
ridgeline of the mountain, marked only by
one punji stake, the company began moving
eastward along the razorback.

Hitting a Viet Cong ambush, the company
split by platoon to counter-attack the Viet
Cong. It was early afternoon and the
temperature scorching, but the fire-fight took
place in semi-darkness; the 60m (200 ft) high
jungle canopy of the trees admitted little
sunlight, made worse by a torrential downpour
which drenched the battlefield. The heavy
rains continued unabated into the evening
when a company of the 12th Cavalry
(Company "B," 1st Battalion) fought together
side-by-side for nearly two hours. Enemy
riflemen came within a few feet of the foxhole
positions before being killed, but the
ammunition still available to the Americans
was running dangerously low. Another relief
company (Company "C," 1st Battalion, 12th

Cavalry) moved up from LZ "Hereford," and
this forced the enemy to break contact. As
the Viet Cong riflemen melted away into the
jungle, the Americans had fixed bayonets and
had loaded their last magazines into their
rifles. For Company "B" the remainder of
17 May was spent evacuating dead and
wounded. For the 1st Cavalry Division,
Operation "Crazy Horse" had really begun.

The rest of the action took place in the most
mountainous and heavily forested area in the
province, far from the lowlands. Because of
the extraordinarily difficult terrain, helicopter
commanders found themselves carrying a
maximum load of only two or three soldiers
as they went into "elevator shaft" single-
helicopter LZs in the triple canopy hilltops,
where the aircraft would barely fit in a circle
of giant tree trunks. Chinooks hovered over
the jungle so that the men could climb down
swaying "trooper ladders" through the triple
canopy. Nevertheless, in the three weeks of
"Crazy Horse," over 30,000 troops moved
by helicopter – an excellent example of the
tactical value of airmobility in mountain
operations. The battleground was a complex
morass, 915m (3,000 ft) from bottom to top
and 20km (12·5 miles) square. In the fighting
it soon became clear that the 2nd Viet Cong

Regiment was bottled up in these rugged hills, but the 1st Air Cavalry Division's individual companies were having trouble in finding and attacking the elusive enemy.

A new plan was devised to move the companies into pie-shaped sectors in which the outer edges would be held on all sides and a double row of ambushes set up. The artillery then as a daily routine fired 12,000 to 13,000 rounds into the enemy concentrations. The U.S. Air Force assisted with tactical attacks and also hit the enemy with Boeing B-52 bomber raids. When North Vietnamese regulars came under attack they attempted to escape out of the area, and ambushes were hastily set up to hinder their flight. During the final phase of Operation "Crazy Horse" Republic of Korea forces maintained contact with an enemy battalion for four days, inflicting heavy casualties. In this operation, the 1st Cavalry Division evacuated or destroyed 45 tons of rice, 10 tons of salt, a weapons repair shop, and several large caches of ammunition and medical supplies. Captured documents revealed the extent of the Viet Cong guerrillas in north-east Binh Dinh. It was this intelligence that provided targets for ensuing operations. After "Crazy Horse" there was a pause in

the Battle of Binh Dinh that lasted until early September, while the 1st Air Cavalry Division concentrated on the battlefields to the west and south. With overlapping Operations "Paul Revere" (Pleiku Province), "Hawthorne" (Kontum Province) and "Nathan Hale" (Phu Yen Province) taking place many miles apart, the 1st Cavalry Division's logistic planning was put to a severe test.

Meanwhile the 1st Brigade, 101st Airborne Division – no longer a parachute formation – was learning helicopter rappeling techniques for descending into dense jungle terrain which did not have accessible landing zones. The training was particularly concentrated in the reconnaissance elements and the engineer LZ clearing teams. The engineer teams roped often into an unknown area, their equipment being air-dropped or delivered by sling with the object of felling enough trees to permit several helicopters to land simultaneously. Vietnam abounds with many large hardwood forests which are extremely difficult to cut, even with the best heavy equipment. To add to the frustration of clearing operations, the engineer teams found the chain saws were of little value in bamboo forests. Vines became easily entangled with the saws and the bamboo splinters caused many lacerations.

Above: Strategic Air Command's B-52 intercontinental bombers release their 750-pound bombs over a suspected Viet Cong stronghold in 1965.

In the 101st Airborne's operations in the highlands during this period, an airmobile company was placed in direct support of each infantry battalion and the same company usually supported the same battalion. The brigade found this scheme worked well. By now the use of a command and control helicopter had become routine for each infantry battalion commander and he used this helicopter for liaison, communications relay with subordinate units, assisting units to pinpoint their locations, guiding units to terrain objectives, and locating potential landing zones.

Another problem in the dense jungle was the evacuation of the wounded. The Huey flying ambulance in 1966 had no hoist suitable for the task of lifting a stretcher to a hovering helicopter. The hoist of the Chinook was adequate, but too slow for personnel evacuation. Brigadier General Willard Pearson, commanding general of the 101st Division's 1st Brigade, was responsible for the introduction of the improved winch systems for both the Huey and the Chinook.

During the fall of 1966, the 1st Cavalry Division also launched Operation "Thayer" on 15 September. The "Air Cav" jumped off in the attack with the simultaneous air assault of two brigades. Three battalions were lifted from An Khe and two from Hammond into the mountains of the Kim Son valley. The five assaulting battalions secured the high ground all the way round the claw-shaped

valley and then fought their way down to the valley floor against elements of the 18th N.V.A. Regiment. In the action that followed the 3rd Brigade was committed, putting a full airmobile division into combat on a single tactical operation for the first time. Later in the fight, the cavalrymen were reinforced by the 3rd Brigade of the 25th Division, which increased to 11 the number of battalions controlled by the 1st Cavalry Division, operating with nine battalions of the 22nd A.R.V.N. Division and two to three of South Vietnamese marines and airborne troops.

On 20 September, the battle area shifted to 506 Valley as the 18th N.V.A. Regiment attempted to move to the east and break contact. Three cavalry battalions made air assaults to the east to follow their trail. The brigade fire base at Hammond was attacked on the night of 23 September, in what was apparently a move to take the pressure off the enemy in the Kim Son and 506 Valleys as they moved eastward. Also on 23 September, the Capitol ROK Infantry Division moved into the Phu Cat Mountains in force, opening up a new phase of the Allied effort in Binh Dinh Province. With the 18th Regiment now withdrawing to the coast, "Thayer" came to a close at the end of September with over 200 enemy killed and 100 tons of rice captured.

After the 196th Light Infantry Brigade ran into a major enemy force south of Sui Da but failed to prevent the destruction of the

U.S. Special Forces C.I.D.G. camp in the area, General Westmoreland responded to the enemy's success by sending in the 1st Infantry Division, contingents of the 4th and 5th Infantry Divisions and the 173rd Airborne Brigade. Some 22,000 U.S. and Allied troops were committed to the battle which became known as Operation "Attleboro." The battle raged from 19 October until 24 November, during which over 1,000 enemy were killed and large quantities of weapons, ammunition and supplies were captured. The 9th Viet Cong Division would not be seen again until the following year. The 1st Cavalry Division concluded 1966 with Operations "Thayer 21/2" and "Irving." Operation "Paul Revere IV" was also in progress on the Cambodian border. By the end of 1966, the United States would have 385,000 military personnel in South Vietnam and would be in a position for the first time to go over to the offensive on a broad and sustained basis. Westmoreland remarked: "During 1966, airmobile operations came of age. All maneuver battalions became skilled in the use of the helicopter for tactical transportation to achieve surprise and out-maneuver the enemy."

Far left: A UH-1B Huey releases two Navy Sea-Air-Land commandos (SEALS) into a Viet Cong-held jungle zone in the Mekong Delta. The SEALS were usually inserted by air by the abseiling method, sliding down ropes into the jungle, and evacuated from river banks by fast patrol boats (PBRs). A SEAL operation involving at most about four men inflicted significant casualties on the Viet Cong in raids lasting up to 48 hours.

Left: A soldier of the 101st Airborne Brigade setting alight a Viet Cong hut during Operation Van Buren, January 1966.

Left: A trooper of the 1st Brigade, 101st Airborne Division, leads a night ambush patrol with his scout dog in the Vietnamese Highlands, 1966.

At 9.00 a.m. on 22 February 1967, Brigadier General John R. Deane, Jr. stood in the door of a Lockheed C-130 aircraft. When the green light flashed, Deane jumped as leader of the first U.S. parachute assault in Vietnam, and the first such since the Korean conflict 15 years earlier. This drop by the 2nd Battalion, 503rd Infantry, signaled the beginning of "Junction City Alternate" as an operation involving the 1st and 5th Infantry Divisions, the 11th Armored Cavalry Regiment, the 196th Light Infantry Brigade, elements of the 4th and 9th Infantry Divisions and A.R.V.N. units, as well as the 173rd Airborne Brigade. Their targets were enemy bases north of Tay Ninh City. The decision to make a parachute assault was based on the urgency to place a large force on the ground as quickly as possible and still have enough helicopter assets to make a sizable heliborne assault as an immediate follow-up.

The requirement for a helicopter lift on D-day was substantial. The 1st Infantry Division had five infantry battalions to put in by air assault and the 173rd had three infantry battalions. In addition to the requirement for the Bell UH-1 Huey "slicks" there was a vital need for a Boeing Vertol CH-47 Chinook lift to position artillery and stocks of ammunition. The 173rd had calculated that it would free 60 Hueys and six Chinooks for support of other forces by using the parachute assault technique. The paratroopers were assigned DZs farthest to the north, areas that would have cost many extra minutes of flying time for lift helicopters. The 173rd was placed under the operational control of the 1st Infantry Division for the operation and developed an

elaborate deception plan to avoid possible compromise of the drop zone.

The cover plan designated a larger alternate drop zone outside the planned area of operation. This permitted all the necessary staging preparations which must precede an air drop and all necessary coordination with the U.S. Air Force. The actual drop plan was not distributed to the units until 5.00 p.m. on 21 February, the evening before D-day. After Lieutenant Colonel Robert H. Sigholz, the Airborne Task Force commander, had briefed his troops for the operation, he sealed off his battalion area as a security measure. Thirteen C-130s were used for the personnel drop and eight C-130s for the heavy drop of equipment. Jump altitude was 305m (1,000 ft). The 173rd was a proud brigade: the "Sky Soldiers" had been flown from Okinawa into Vietnam immediately upon President Johnson's decision to send combat troops, and the brigade had already seen some tough fighting, but now at last they had a chance to prove the worth of their parachute brevets and moreover justify their jump pay.

The battalion dropped on schedule and by 9.30 a.m. on D-day all companies were in their location around the DZ. Out of 780 combat troops who made the assault only 11 sustained minor injuries. The heavy equipment drop commenced at 9.25 a.m. and continued throughout the day. The 1st Battalion, 503rd Infantry, conducted a heliborne assault into two other close LZs at 2.40 p.m. and phase one of "Junction City Alternate" was over. During this operation the 173rd Brigade was supported by the 11th, 145th and 1st Aviation

Above: Staff Sergeant Clarence D. Neitzel, Company "D," 2nd Battalion, 503rd Regiment, 173rd Airborne Brigade mans an M-60 machine-gun post in preparation for the final assault on Hill 875 near Dak To (1967). Hill 875 was the "Sky Soldiers'" toughest battle in Vietnam.

Far left: "Sky Soldiers" of the 173rd Airborne Brigade move through Than Dien Forest on patrol in the southern section of the "Iron Triangle" during Operation "Cedar Falls," 1967.

Battalions. Over 9,700 sorties were flown in support of the operation and U.S. Army aviation lifted 9,518 troops and a daily average of 50 tons of cargo. While the parachute assault received most of the publicity, the subsequent moves were made by helicopter and the momentum of the operation depended on this support.

The combined operation, begun so dramatically by the 173rd Brigade, continued until mid-May. The enemy lost over 2,700 dead along with substantial amounts of ammunition and medical supplies, and more than 800 tons of rice. The area north of Tay Ninh City, which had been an exclusive stronghold for many years, was now vulnerable to the allied forces at any time of their choosing. In retrospect, there is no question that the parachute assault which began "Junction City Alternate" was not effective. As it happened, this was the first and last parachute assault of any scale in the Vietnam War. Every man with jump wings was eager to prove his mettle. However, parachute drops were not always suited to the terrain and for fighting the Viet Cong. Nevertheless, it was firmly believed by

the U.S. Army that there would be a continuing requirement for parachute units for many years to come.

The year 1967 saw the peak of the airmobile operations in Vietnam. In March, the 2nd Battalion, 5th Cavalry, was landed at short notice to relieve the U.S. Marines, who had been conducting "search and clear" missions in the area since the beginning of the year. It was immediately obvious that if more reinforcements were to be called in, the first requirement would be the building of a heavy duty airstrip for support by U.S. Air Force aircraft. The decision was made to build a de Havilland Canada C-7A Caribou strip at LZ "Montezuma," which could be expanded to accommodate Fairchild C-123 Provider aircraft. At "Montezuma" there would also be space enough to build a parallel Caribou strip while the first airstrip was improved and surfaced to handle the larger and heavier C-130 aircraft. On 7 March a company of U.S. engineers arrived at "Montezuma" and immediately began a thorough reconnaissance of the airfield site.

During the next two days 31 pieces of heavy

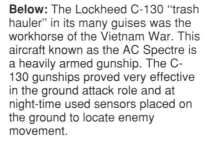

Below: The Lockheed C-130 "trash hauler" in its many guises was the workhorse of the Vietnam War. This aircraft known as the AC Spectre is a heavily armed gunship. The C-130 gunships proved very effective in the ground attack role and at night-time used sensors placed on the ground to locate enemy movement.

engineer equipment weighing over 200 tons were airlifted into Duc Pho. This move required 29 Sikorsky CH-54 and 15 Chinook sorties. Much of the equipment (including bulldozers and road graders) had to be partially disassembled to reduce the weight to a transportable helicopter load. By midnight, six hours after construction began, 25 per cent of the Caribou strip was completed. LZ "Montezuma" was composed of light sandy soil, and the heavy rotary-wing traffic soon generated monumental, semi-permanent dust clouds. By 4.30 p.m. on 8 April, the 457m (1,500 ft) Caribou strip had been completed. Work continued on the strip to expand it to 700m (2,300 ft) for C-123 use. On 13 April, the engineers began the construction of the second Caribou airstrip parallel and west of the completed C-123 strip. The second strip (for the C-130s) was finished 25 hours after

3,173m³ (4,150 cu yards) of earth had been moved.

LZ "Montezuma" was the scene for the launching of Operation "Lejeune," which combined the efforts of the U.S. Army, the U.S. Marine Corps, the U.S. Air Force and the U.S. Navy. The U.S. Air Force Caribou pilots were slightly wary of accepting the hastily constructed airstrip but they made 159 sorties into "Montezuma" carrying 1,081 passengers and 229 tons of cargo. During the first eight days of operations, tactical air power dropped 115 tons of bombs and 70 tons of napalm. The U.S. Navy provided gun support with a total of 2,348 rounds from its two ships offshore. Operation "Lejeune" was terminated at noon on 22 April. Although contacts were light throughout the operation, 176 of the enemy were killed and 127 captured by the 2nd Brigade, 1st Cavalry.

Above: A Sikorsky CH-54 Tarhe helicopter is seen without its detachable pod at the 1st Cavalry Division's base at An Khe. The mission of the "Sky Crane" was to lift heavy outsized loads, recover downed aircraft, and, by use of its pod, to transport personnel, vehicles and equipment.

Right: Paratroopers of the 173rd Airborne Brigade move into the attack on Hill 875. The hill position was strongly fortified and held by North Vietnamese regulars. The hillsides were thick with vegetation, mixed bamboo, scrub brush, and tall trees.

Right: Hill 875. The first attack by the 2/503rd resulted in the battalion being cut off at the top of the hill, the N.V.A. surrounding the paratroopers on the thickly wooded slopes. The 4th Battalion was sent to the rescue and the hill was cleared of enemy after four days of heavy fighting (November 1967). These are members of the 4th Battalion.

In June 1967 the "Air Cav" was in the thick of the fighting in the Kontum-Dak To area of the Central Highlands. On 23 June the 2nd Battalion, 12th Cavalry (with an artillery battery) flew into Dak To using 24 C-130 aircraft and two C-123s. They were almost immediately thrown into combat. The next day two more battalions followed, and the third day the remainder of the direct support artillery. The remainder of the 1st Cavalry Division at the time occupied locations north and south of the Bong Son River. Throughout the Battle of Binh Dinh, one airmobile battalion task force was detached from divisional control to operate in support of pacification activities around the city of Phan Thiet. The task force was created and moved at 24-hour notice. Although scheduled for an operation lasting 60 days, it remained on duty for 17 months. The task force contained a very significant part of the division's assets. In addition to the 2nd Battalion, 7th Cavalry, it included a scout section from the Air Cavalry Squadron, a platoon of engineers, a battery of 105mm howitzers, a platoon of aerial rocket artillery, lift helicopters, a signals team, and intelligence and civil affairs personnel, plus a forward support element for logistics.

Binh Thuan is situated about 160km (100 miles) north-east of Saigon in an area 320km (200 miles) south of Binh Dinh and bordering on the South China Sea. The principal port city, Phan Thiet, was surrounded by a heavily populated rice-growing area. Forty per cent of the province consisted of forested mountains, which supplied some of the best timber in Vietnam. These woodlands also provided clandestine bases and rest areas for the Viet Cong. The "Air Cav" in Operation "Byrd" was given the task of protecting the vital port of Phan Diet and, in close conjunction with South Vietnamese forces, of defeating the enemy forces in the area. Initially the task force established a fire base and a command post on the Phan Thiet airfield, from which infantry rifle companies were airlifted into LZs within the range of the direct support of the artillery battery. The first operations relieved pressure on Phan Thiet and the nearby district capitals. The task force then began combined operations with the South Vietnamese, taking advantage of U.S. Navy ships for fire support. The area of influence of the task force was broadened by the establishment of fire bases at steadily increasing distances from Phan Thiet.

As it continued, the operation isolated the enemy in the heavily forested areas, away from the populated zones. In the close-in areas, the task force concentrated on the Viet Cong network and on measures to build confidence in the population and the friendly armed forces. The task force ended up with an amazing record. During the 17 months of Operation "Byrd," the 2nd Battalion, 7th Cavalry had 34 troopers killed, while 849 enemy were killed and 109 captured.

The small but vitally important air assaults

Below: These "Sky Soldiers" have discovered a Viet Cong tunnel complex in the Thanh Dien Forest of the "Iron Triangle." Four V.C. prisoners are to be seen squatting in the foreground.

of "Byrd" emphasized the advantage of vertical envelopment as opposed to penetration as a tactic. The air assault concept permits a cheaper, faster and more decisive vertical envelopment approach, which makes the conventional battlefield more fluid than ever. The great variety of air assault concepts fall under two main headings – surprise and security. The air assault must rely on speed, scheme of maneuver, locally available fire power (aerial rocket artillery), and command and control from an aerial platform. Additionally a reinforcing capability to exploit success or to assault the enemy from another direction must be immediately available to the commander.

In August 1967, the 1st Cavalry Division, which operated mainly in the Vietnam War in the II Corps Tactical Zone, moved with three battalions (under the 3rd Brigade) north to assist the U.S. Marines in I Corps Zone. (I Corps, or "eye" corps, or Marineland as the U.S. Marines called it, with their base at Chu Lai, had been a Marine responsibility since they had first waded ashore at Da Nang

in April 1965.) The "Air Cav" at once launched a major reconnaissance in force into the Song Re valley in Quang Ngai Province. The picturesque terrain consisted of numerous hillocks in the valley floor, fertile fields of rice, and well-fed livestock. Previous aerial reconnaissance had drawn heavy anti-aircraft fire. Although the valley appeared prosperous only a few inhabitants had been actually observed. On 9 August 1967, the 2nd Battalion, 8th Cavalry, commenced a battalion air assault in the valley 51km (32 miles) south-west of Quang Ngai City. The selected zone, named LZ "Pat," was situated on a ridgeline 1,303m (1,425 yards) south-west of an abandoned airstrip at Ta Ma.

This landing zone was chosen because it was the only high ground large enough and clear enough of obstructions to allow six lift ships to land, and because it was in an area which would give an assaulting company the advantage of reconnoitering from high ground down to the valley floor. The assault started at 9.36 a.m. after a short artillery preparation. After the 1st Platoon had landed, intense anti-

aircraft fire came from the surrounding hills. Two Hueys were shot down almost immediately. Company "A" of the 2nd Battalion was faced with a pitched battle for the next four hours. The enemy situation, reconstructed later from information gained from prisoners-of-war, captured documents and a survey of the battle area, disclosed that the LZ was right in the midst of well-prepared enemy positions. Looking down on the LZ were at least 80 North Vietnamese with three 12·7mm anti-aircraft weapons, 82mm mortars and 57mm recoilless rifles. A Viet Cong rifle company, recruited from the Montagnards (the nomadic mountain tribes) was on the same hill mass. The ridgeline was rimmed with fox-holes and well-concealed bunkers almost flush with the ground. Company "A" had landed in a snake pit.

The "Air Cav" had learned by now how to react to a hot situation with terrific fire power and by extracting their men from almost untenable positions when necessary. The aerial artillery fired 576 rockets in support of the reconnaissance and two armed Chinook helicopters delivered eight tons of ordnance on possible escape routes. Tactical air power did a magnificent job of supporting the ground forces with a total of 42 sorties. What could have been a disaster turned out to be an effective assault, killing 73 of the enemy while losing only 11 men. Two enemy units were flushed out of hidden positions and a major anti-aircraft site was destroyed. The skirmish at LZ "Pat" was the principal encounter with the Viet Cong during the reconnaissance in force of the Song Re valley. This reconnaissance was a preview in miniature of major operations of the 1st Cavalry for the remainder of the American involvement in the Vietnam War.

The "Air Cav" was in constant action until the end of the year. The year 1967 had proved many important facets of the airmobile concept. Perhaps the most important facet that had been demonstrated was the value of the Air Cavalry Squadron. This unit, especially in its operations in the I Corps Tactical Zone, had demonstrated its unique capability of uncovering the elusive Viet Cong. Practically every major engagement was started with a contact by the 1st Squadron, 9th Cavalry, and the enemy was very slow in discovering means of coping with this reconnaissance in force. The Air Cavalry Squadron's success in the airmobile division convinced high authority that more air cavalry squadrons should be assigned to Vietnam to operate with non-airmobile infantry divisions.

Right: The Bell AH-1B HueyCobra Lycoming helicopter was born as a result of the need in the Vietnam War for a fast gunship to support the CH-47A Chinook cargo carrier. Known as the "snake" to the troops in Vietnam, the HueyCobra was driven by a shaft turbine engine which gave it a speed of 219 mph (352 km/h) and a range of 387 miles (622 km). There was a crew of two (pilot and co-pilot/gunner), no passengers.

Armament was provided by the GAU 2B/A minigun six barrel 7.62mm machine-gun with 8,000 rounds; the XM-28 subsystem mounting either two miniguns with 4,000 rounds each, two XM-129 40mm grenade launchers with 300 rounds each, or one minigun and one XM-129; four external stores attachments fitted beneath the stub-wings, which accommodated various loads including a total of 76 2.75in rockets in four XM-159 packs, 28 similar rockets in four XM-157 packs, two XM-18E1 minigun pods, one XM-35 20mm gun kit, or two pods each containing four ToW wire-guided missiles.

The Tet Offensive

Since the U.S. Marines first landed at Da Nang the South Vietnamese armed forces, the Americans, and other fighting units from the free world, had engaged for two and a half years in a daily battle to support the Republic of South Vietnam against the communist guerrillas operating in that country. All that time, the North Vietnamese Army seemed reluctant to join in the fight. So far the firefights had ranged through the jungled highlands, lowlands and the watery maze of the Mekong delta. The Viet Cong had launched short, sharp attacks on the U.S. military installations at coastal centers but the war had not touched the large cities and towns of South Vietnam.

As 1968 dawned the Vietnamese people, both north and south of the Demilitarized Zone (D.M.Z.), were looking forward to their New Year celebrations. Tet, the Chinese lunar year, is celebrated by the Chinese, Vietnamese and other communities of Chinese origin and association on its eve, 29 January. In the preceding years of the Vietnam conflict, a truce for the holidays had been arranged. The night before Tet is spent in much the same way as an American family enjoying a birthday, the Fourth of July and Thanksgiving all rolled into one. Special dishes are prepared, presents exchanged, and fire-crackers fill the air.

A half hour into the New Year, Tuesday 30 January, a South Vietnamese corporal guarding the government radio station at Nha Trang, a city of 129,000 inhabitants situated half-way up the coast of South Vietnam, noticed two small cars pull up to a nearby pagoda and discharge passengers. The travelers appeared to be wearing Army of the Republic of Vietnam (A.R.V.N.) uniforms, but there was something suspicious in their hurried manner. Suspicion that the men might be communists proved correct two hours later when some 800 regulars of the 18-B N.V.A. Regiment moved into action at Nha Trang. When early on Tuesday morning reports of fighting in both I and II Corps Zones began pouring into General Westmoreland's command center at Tan Son Nhut Air Base, Saigon, it was immediately obvious to Westmoreland and his staff that the communists had broken the truce and launched an all-out offensive. The carefully coordinated series of communist attacks commencing that morning was in fact aimed at over 100 towns and cities in South Vietnam. An estimated 70,000 N.V.A. and Viet Cong effectives were thrown into the offensive. "Tet" was to be the turning point of the Vietnam War.

Within three minutes after the alert at Tan Son Nhut, two "Razorback" fire teams, consisting of four armed helicopters from the 120th Assault Helicopter Company, were airborne and in action against Viet Cong guerrillas attacking the air base. Another area of heavy activity in Saigon was at the U.S. Embassy. Chief Warrant Officer Richard Inskeep of the 191st Assault Helicopter Company was the first to land a chopper on the embassy, which was under siege by Viet Cong who had infiltrated the city disguised as civilians. Shortly after troopers of the 101st Airborne Division landed on the embassy's

Above: The U.S. Ambassador Ellsworth Bunker views damage within the embassy grounds in Saigon after it had been attacked by Viet Cong at the commencement of the Tet Offensive. This photograph was taken on 31 January 1968.

Far left: After the failure of the Tet Offensive, which was launched on 30 January 1968, the N.V.A. and Viet Cong continued to mount attacks on urban populations in South Vietnam for another six months.

This photograph shows an area off Plantation Road adjacent to Tan Son Nhut airbase, on the outskirts of Saigon, which has been devastated by infiltrating enemy forces (May 1968).

The airfield at Tan Son Nhut, which was built by the French, also housed the headquarters of Military Assistance Command Vietnam (M.A.C.V.).

Right: Troopers of the 101st Airborne Division conduct a house-to-house search for Viet Cong in Bien Hoa during the Tet Offensive (February 1968). The tank is an M-48 Patton of the 11th Armored Cavalry Regiment.

Above: Members of the 30th Ranger Battalion search for Viet Cong in a village near Saigon during the Tet attacks.

helipad to form a stronghold. When reports of the beginning of the offensive reached the headquarters of the 1st Cavalry Division, it was decided to concentrate the whole of the "Air Cav" in the I Corps area. They were joined in the north by the 2nd Brigade of the 101st Airborne Division, newly arrived in Vietnam. The heavy concentration of U.S. and South Vietnamese forces in the north was aimed at blocking the passage of N.V.A. reinforcements over the parallel.

Company "B" of the 1st Battalion, 12th Cavalry, immediately assaulted into an LZ east of Quang Tri city and a few minutes later were followed by Company "C". Even while landing, the "Air Cav" came under heavy fire and it was at once obvious that they had landed in the middle of the enemy positions in the area. The 1st Battalion, 5th Cavalry, now assaulted east of Quang Tri with two companies. They also had landed directly on enemy positions. The N.V.A. troops were quickly demoralized by the air assaults, gunships and aerial rocket artillery of the 1st Cavalry Division. Although well equipped, the N.V.A. regulars were inexperienced in battle and completely foxed by airmobile tactics. By noon on 1 February, Quang Tri and its environs had been cleared of the enemy and the 1st Battalion, 502nd Airborne, initiated pursuit.

Far to the north of southern Vietnam lies the ancient city of Hué. At one time the capital of Vietnam and now its third largest city, Hué had so far escaped the ravages of war, and its ornate, historic buildings remained intact. Hué is actually two cities. The interior city called the Citadel, is a walled fortress patterned after the Imperial Palace of Peking. A rough square of about 3·2km (2 miles) on each side, built on the banks of the Perfume River, the Citadel once served as the residence for Annamese emperors. The wonderful palaces and temples of Hué were reconstructed by the Emperor Gia Long in the 19th century to replicate the seat of the Chinese emperor (Vietnam's patron) in Peking. The kingly residences included the imposing Palace of Peace. The Citadel is protected by an outer wall 4·9m (16 ft) high and varying in thickness from 18 to 61m (60 to 200 ft). The Citadel actually stands on the north bank of the Huong Giang (the River of Perfumes), which flows out into the ocean. On the southern bank of the river lies the South Side, a new residential district.

Like Saigon, Hué had been infiltrated over a week or more by Viet Cong in various disguises. The 1st Squadron, 9th Cavalry, was actively engaged on reconnaissance after the commencement of the Tet offensive on the outskirts of Hué, and the 1st Cavalry Division was given the mission to interdict and destroy enemy units moving along all routes to the city from the west. The 2nd Battalion, 12th Cavalry, began to seal off the city from the west and the north with its right flank on the Perfume River on 2 February. (By this time the city interior was completely in the hands of the enemy and the communist flag flew over the Citadel.) Weather conditions were poor with ceilings of at most 46 to 61m (150 to 200 ft). Nevertheless, helicopters kept flying and placed the troops close to the assault positions even if they could not make actual air assaults. The helicopter base at Camp Evans and its supply route had to be secured. The 1st Cavalry Division was spread particularly thin at this time, the 1st Brigade with four battalions being completely occupied at Quang Tri.

The job of recapturing Hué was naturally assigned to the U.S. Marine Corps in whose demesne the city stood. The battle for Hué quickly developed into some of the most furious combat that had taken place in Vietnam since the beginning of the war. The two cavalry battalions initially committed to the battle were reinforced by two more battalions. The main road from Da Nang had been cut but more circuitous supply routes were kept open by the helicopter gunships. The U.S. Air Force did a tremendous job

Right: The port facility at Da Nang in Tua Tien province of South Vietnam. In the background can be seen the Annamite mountains. Da Nang was the headquarters of the United States Marine Corps forces that manned the 10,000 square miles of I Corps territory located immediately to the south of the Demilitarized Zone (DMZ).

It was on the beaches of Da Nang that the first Marine combat troops to land in South Vietnam on 8 March 1965 were garlanded with flowers. The scene was never again so peaceful. Da Nang was the center of one of the major battles of Tet '68 when Ho Chi Minh's regulars and the Viet Cong took the war to the cities and towns of South Vietnam for the first time.

in flying parachute supply missions to Camp Evans. At times they were dropping supplies with ceilings at around 91m (300 ft) using Air Cavalry pathfinders and ground approach control radar. It was eerie to see the parachutes come floating in out of the clouds minutes after the C-130s had passed. Sikorsky CH-54s and Boeing Vertol CH-47s first flew out to sea to pick up supplies from naval vessels lying off the Da Nang shore before flying them back to Camp Evans.

Air strikes were very difficult to call in because of the bad weather and low ceilings. Most helicopter operations were flown at "nap-of-the-earth" altitude of about 7·6m (25 ft). The Air Cavalry succeeded in cutting off one of the enemy's main supply lines and captured the heavily fortified tactical headquarters at La Chu on Hué city's outskirts. While the U.S. Marines fought street by street and house by house in Hué, the Air Cavalry did an excellent job of preventing enemy reinforcements reaching the city. At least three N.V.A. regiments moving from around Khe Sanh between 11 and 20 February were stopped in their tracks. The final note of the Tet offensive in Hué was struck on 20 February when the elite Black Panther Company seized the flag tower at the south wall of the Citadel and ripped down the National Liberation Front flag, which had flown there since 31 January. In its place the soldiers raised the yellow and red banner of the Republic of Vietnam, and moved into the inner courtyard of the Nguyen Palace. The communists had vanished. In what the "Air Cav" called Operation "Jeb Stuart," the 1st Cavalry had acquitted itself well.

The Tet offensive resulted in a major communist defeat. The N.V.A. and the Viet Cong lost 32,000 killed in action, 5,800 were captured, and 7,000 individual weapons and almost 1,300 crew-served weapons were seized. By choosing Tet for their attack, they had alienated a major portion of the people of South Vietnam, who considered the birth of the New Year as sacred. The communists had brought the battle into the very midst of the most heavily populated areas, causing many casualties to civilians who were caught in the crossfire.

The government of South Vietnam did not collapse under the Tet offensive. On the contrary, it rallied in the face of the threat with unity and greater purpose than that which had ever been displayed up to that time. From the American point of view, however, Tet was the beginning of the end. President Johnson concluded that whereas the N.V.A. could be beaten in a set battle, the Viet Cong guerrillas could never be uprooted from their jungle lairs. Johnson, consequently, did not seek re-election and in November 1968 Richard Nixon was elected to succeed him. Pursuing the "Vietnamization" policy begun by the Johnson administration, Nixon gradually reduced U.S. combat strengths in Vietnam, but five more years were to elapse before the Americans departed the battlefield for good.

Below: An OH-13 Sioux reconnaissance helicopter prepares to land at an Air Cavalry LZ in the National Forest Reserve near Quang Tri during Operation Jeb Stuart III, Vietnam, 1968.

Weeks before the Tet offensive, the eyes of the world had been focused on Khe Sanh as all the signs pointed to a major enemy attack on this U.S. Marine outpost. Located some 24km (15 miles) south of the Demilitarized Zone and barely 11km (7 miles) from the eastern frontier of Laos, the Khe Sanh base functioned primarily as a support facility for surveillance units watching the Demilitarized Zone and probing the outer reaches of the Ho Chi Minh Trail in nearby Laos. Khe Sanh was almost completely surrounded by towering ridges and stood in the center of four valley corridors leading through the mountains to the north and north-west of the base. To the south, Khe Sanh overlooked Highway 9, the only east-west road in the northern province to join Laos and the coastal regions. The base itself was laid out on a flat laterite plateau. It was shaped somewhat like an irregular rectangle and covered an area approximately 1·6km (1 mile) long by 805m (2,540 ft) wide. A key feature of the base was a 914m (3,000 ft) aluminum mat runway, which during favorable weather conditions could accommodate fixed-wing aircraft up to the size of Lockheed C-130 transports.

When the North Vietnamese Army struck on 21 January, the Khe Sanh garrison consisted of about 6,000 U.S. Marines and South Vietnamese Rangers. At that time the 1st Cavalry Division and two brigades of the 101st Airborne Division (located in the northern provinces) were alerted to support in the defense of Khe Sanh. As the siege of Khe Sanh progressed, air-delivered fire support reached unprecedented levels. A daily average of 45 Boeing B-52 sorties and 300 tactical air attacks, by U.S. Air Force and U.S. Marine aircraft were flown against targets in the vicinity of the base. The U.S. Navy provided additional aircraft sorties from carriers. Some 1,800 tons of ordnance were dumped in the area, laying waste to huge swathes of jungle terrain. In 70 days of air operations, 96,000 tons of bombs were dropped, nearly twice as much as was delivered by the U.S. Army Air Forces in the Pacific during 1942 and 1943. B-52 "Arc Light" attacks were particularly effective against the enemy and had a great psychological impact on their troops.

The C-130s were the Khe Sanh garrison's main means of supply, but the "Herk" pilots quickly discovered that apart from the obvious dangers of landing on the runway and presenting sitting targets to the N.V.A. automatic fire, mortars and artillery, the air strip was not really long enough to land on and take-off from with ease, which could scarcely be achieved anyway under the constant pressure of attack. In the early days of the Khe Sanh siege, the C-130s, after touching down on the runway, managed somehow to disgorge their loads while taxiing, before turning round and hurtling forward to take-off without pausing to rest on the ground. Although some success was obtained with these frenetic efforts to resupply Khe Sanh, the daily runs into the firebase by the C-130s were perfected when low-altitude parachute extraction and free-fall methods were used to drop supply pallets, heavy

Above: A patrol of the 82nd crosses a field on a search-and-destroy mission shortly after the 3rd Brigade arrived in Vietnam (1968).

Far left: Company "O," 508th Infantry, 3rd Brigade, 82nd Airborne Division, step out from a C-141 Starlifter upon their arrival at Chu Lai airbase, February 1968. The "All Americans" found themselves in the thick of the fighting in the Tet Offensive.

Top left: A Boeing-Vertol CH-46A Sea Knight offloads wounded Leathernecks aboard U.S.S. *Tripoli*, Vietnam waters, 1967.

Top center: UH-1 helicopters operating from U.S.S. *Harnett County*, one of the afloat bases or mother ships which served the coastal and riverine fleets. This ship was a converted World War II tank landing ship (*LST-821*).

Top right: A Boeing-Vertol CH-46 U.S. Navy Sea Knight based on the amphibious assault ship U.S.S. *Okinawa*, is about to lift a netload of supplies from the store ship U.S.S. *Vega*, off the coast of Vietnam.

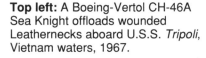

Far right: Seabees of the U.S.S. Naval Mobile Construction Battalion 133 (MCB-133) have just completed the resurfacing of the runway at Phu Bai. A C-130 Hercules can be seen taking off from the improved airstrip, 1968.

equipment and bundles from the open cargo doors as the aircraft flew over the runway. Many heroic and skillful landings were made, however, to evacuate the wounded. In these circumstances the U.S. Marine medics had to act swiftly to load the casualties onto the aircraft, so that the pilots could make a quick get-away. The other fixed-wing aircraft that made an important contribution to the Khe Sanh supply was the Fairchild C-123, but the plucky Provider did not have anything like the load capacity of the C-130 Hercules.

Although the full range of the 1st Cavalry Division's helicopters was deployed for the relief of Khe Sanh, Operation "Pegasus" that was launched on 1 April 1968, it was the Boeing Vertol CH-46 Sea Knight, in variants designated CH-46A and CH-46D by the U.S. Marines and UH-56A and UH-46D by the U.S. Navy, that played such a large part in the Khe Sanh campaign. The U.S. Army had considered the CH-46 (designed as a medium transport and assault helicopter) too heavy for the assault role and too light for the transport role, and it was this decision which led the U.S. Army to upgrade the more maneuverable Bell UH-1 as a tactical troop transport, and to acquire a heavy troop transport in the form of the CH-47 Chinook from the same Boeing Vertol stable. Both the U.S. Marines and the U.S. Navy wanted the Model 107 as the Sea Knight, and other versions of the Model 107 were also supplied for military purposes to other countries.

Used for routine supply work, cargoes of up to 4,524kg (9,973 lb) could be loaded by

one man in the CH/UH-46D, which superseded the CH/UH-46A in 1966. To simplify stowage on the decks of aircraft-carriers, a powered blade-folding system enabled the rotor blades to be folded quickly by a pilot-operated control. The CH/UH-46Ds with three crew accommodated 24 fully armed troops or, in the rescue role, 20 men, or 15 stretcher cases with two medical orderlies. The D model was generally similar to the A variant apart from its two uprated General Electric turboshaft engines to permit the carriage of a heavier payload. The U.S. Navy's Sea Knight was ordered for deployment from combat supply ships; they were utilized to transfer supplies, ammunition, missiles and aviation spares from these ships to combatant vessels under way at sea. Secondary tasks included transfer of personnel, and search and rescue. The UH-46As had been deployed with the U.S. 7th Fleet in the South China Sea from mid-1965, but the Vietnam War, as it developed, led to innovations in ship resupply, including bad-weather vertical replenishment by day and night with the aid of small signal lights.

The Sea Knight, probably because of its more mundane duties, did not share in the limelight enjoyed by its larger brother, the U.S. Army's CH-47 Chinook. U.S. Marine Sea Knights were nevertheless greatly praised for running in supplies in the monsoon rains to the U.S. Marines and A.R.V.N. manning the hilltop outposts outside the Khe Sanh perimeter from mid-January to late April 1968. Like the U.S. Marine Sikorsky H-34

helicopters also employed on the Khe Sanh sorties, the Sea Knights were unarmed and had to rely on the HueyCobra escorts to protect them. The UH-34D Seahorse could carry 16-18 troops, or eight litters, or supplies weighing 2,313kg (5,100 lb), but gained prominence in Vietnam as a search and rescue helicopter. On 6-7 March, however, the type went to the aid of the Green Berets besieged at Nam Dong, and between 20 January and 1 April was deployed at Khe Sanh, playing a gallant role in the transport of supplies into the garrison area and the evacuation of casualties. During the siege the U.S. Marines' UH-34s and CH-46s (as well as the U.S. Army's UH-1E Hueys) were continually subjected to a murderous barrage from N.V.A. heavy automatic weapons emplaced on the top of the outlying hills.

On 2 March the Air Cavalry presented their plan to the U.S. Marine headquarters at Da Nang for the relief of Khe Sanh. By this time, observers in Vietnam envisaged a disaster-at-arms on the level of the defeat of the French at Dien Bien Phu in 1954, which marked the end of French rule in Indochina. In Operation "Pegasus" the 1st Cavalry Division would be augmented by the 1st Marine Regiment, 3rd A.R.V.N. Task Force, and the 37th A.R.V.N. Ranger Battalion. In all, the relief force numbered 30,000 troops. It was decided that the construction of an airfield in the vicinity of Ca Lu would be a key factor in mounting the operation. This airstrip, which came to be known as Landing Zone "Stud," had to be ready well before

D-day on 1 April 1968. The airstrip was built on schedule by 1st Cavalry Division engineers, U.S. Marine Corps engineers and a U.S. Navy Mobile Construction Battalion. On completion LZ "Stud" consisted of a runway 457m (1,500 ft) long by 183m (600 ft) wide, ammunition storage areas and vehicle refueling facilities; extensive road nets were also built into the vicinity of "Stud."

The bad weather on D-day was to haunt the 1st Cavalry throughout "Pegasus." Seldom were airmobile moves feasible before the early afternoon. "Good weather" was considered to be any condition where the ceiling was above 152m (500 ft) and range visibility was more than an hour and a half. The bad weather, however, proved the soundness of establishing LZ "Stud" as the springboard for the assaults. Troops, ammunition and supplies could be assembled there ready to go whenever the weather to the west opened up. Marshaling areas farther away would have dramatically deteriorated response time. By D+1 on 2 April, the 1st Marine Regiment was pushing along the axis of Highway 9. Two U.S. Marine companies made limited air assaults to support the 1st Marine's momentum. The 3rd Cavalry Brigade was also in action with the 2nd Battalion, 7th Cavalry. Meanwhile the 2nd Cavalry Brigade had moved into LZ "Stud."

The initial thrusts had met with less enemy resistance than had been expected, so in order to push home the advantage, the U.S. commander, Brigadier General John J. Tolson, on D+3 ordered a battalion-size attack south of Khe Sanh to seize Hill 471, a strategic piece of terrain affording a commanding view of the base. Following a heavy artillery bombardment, the U.S. Marines successfully took the hill, killing 30 of the enemy. On the same day, the 2nd Brigade of the 1st Cavalry Division launched one battalion into an old French fort south of Khe Sanh: initial contact resulted in four enemy killed. On D+4 the 2nd Brigade continued its attack, meeting heavy enemy resistance. Enemy troops attacked the U.S. Marines on Hill 471 but were repulsed with 122 enemy left dead on the battlefield. The tempo of this battle was one of the heaviest during the operation. The 3rd A.R.V.N. Airborne Task Force was alerted to prepare to airlift one rifle company from Quang Tri to effect link-up with the 37th A.R.V.N. Ranger Battalion located at Khe Sanh.

On D+5 the 1st Marine Regiment continued its operations on the high ground north and east of Route 9, moving to the west toward Khe Sanh. On the same day, troops of the 1st Cavalry Division were airlifted to Hill 471, relieving the U.S. Marines at this position. In the afternoon, the "Air Cav" landing on LZ "Snapper" were attacked by an enemy force using mortars, hand grenades and rocket launchers. Shortly afterward, the 84th Company of the Vietnamese 8th Airborne Battalion was airlifted into the Khe Sanh perimeter and linked up with elements of the 37th Ranger Battalion. On 7 April the Vietnamese 3rd Airborne Task Force air-launched three battalions into positions north of the road and east of Khe Sanh to block escape routes toward the Laotian border. Fighting throughout the area was sporadic as the enemy attempted to withdraw. American and South Vietnamese units now began picking up significant quantities of abandoned weapons and equipment. Soon all the enemy strongpoints around Khe Sanh had been completely secured.

At 8.00 am on 8 April, Khe Sanh had been relieved. This was accomplished after the 2nd Battalion, 7th Cavalry, successfully cleared Highway 9 as far as the base and linked up with the 26th Marine Regiment. On the following day the 1st Battalion, 12th Cavalry, seized the old Lang Vei Special Forces Camp 6.4km (4 miles) west of Khe Sanh against light enemy resistance: Lang Vei was the site of an enemy attack in mid-February when N.V.A. troops, supported by armor, overran the camp. Early on 10 April a helicopter from "A" Troop, 1st Squadron, 9th Cavalry, had located a PT-76 tank and called in a tactical air attack on the vehicle. The tank was destroyed along with 15 enemy troops. The excitement that prevailed when the 1st Cavalry Division with attached airborne units finally reached the Khe Sanh compound, relieving the hard-pressed and battle-weary defenders, can be compared with a night at the movies with the cavalry galloping to the rescue of a fort in the Wild West besieged by Red Indians. The mode of travel was now different but the spirit of the U.S. Cavalry remained the same!

In the same period as the battle for Khe Sanh, the U.S. 9th Infantry Division was conducting airmobile operations in the IV Corps' Mekong delta zone. Conditions in the Mekong delta for the airborne infantry were rather different to other parts of the country. The entire area is subject to frequent flooding. Extensive embankments had been built over the centuries to channel water into the fertile rice-producing fields. Mud flats and mangrove swamps encircled the delta regions along the

rugged coastline. Road networks were limited but hard-surfaced major roads did exist. Most of the canals carried a heavy burden of traffic throughout the area. The helicopter pilots consequently found suitable landing zones in the watery terrain. Also the Viet Cong proved even more elusive than they were in the jungles of the Central Highlands and the lowland plain. The 9th Division, which was assigned in part to the "Brown Water Navy"

Above: South Vietnamese marines are embarked aboard U.S. Navy inshore patrol craft (PCFs) during a patrol on a river in the Ca Mau peninsula, 1969.

(the riverine assault flotillas) nevertheless acquitted itself well in heliborne operations in the Mekong delta.

After the completion of Operation "Pegasus," the 1st Cavalry Division was moved into the A Shau valley, which lies between two mountain ranges on the western edge of the Republic of Vietnam. On both sides of the valley the mountains climb sharply with the angle of slope varying from 20 to 45 degrees. The Laotian border lies less than 10km (6 miles) away. Three abandoned airfields were spread along the valley floor which runs north-west to south-east. The North Vietnamese forces had been in control of the valley since March 1966, when they overran the Special Forces camp in the southern end.

Since that time the North Vietnamese had built a major base for the infiltration of personnel and supplies from North Vietnam through Laos along Route 547 into Thua Thien Province and the northern I Corps Tactical Zone. Final preparations for Operation "Delaware-Lam Son 216" were conducted during the last days of Operation "Pegasus."

The 1st Squadron, 9th Cavalry, began an extensive aerial reconnnaissance of the A Shau valley to select flight routes, locate anti-aircraft and artillery weapons, and to develop targets for tactical air and B-52 strikes. During the period 14-19 April, over 100 B-52 sorties, 200 U.S. Air Force and U.S. Marine fighter sorties, and numerous aerial rocket artillery missions were flown against targets in the valley. The 1st Brigade of the 101st Airborne Division and the A.R.V.N. Airborne Task Force were moved to pre-assault positions ready to make a separate attack on D-day east of the A Shau valley. "Delaware" was to be a coordinated airmobile and ground attack on two axes using elements of three divisions – the 1st Cavalry, the 101st Airborne and the 1st A.R.V.N. Division. One prong was to attack along and astride Routes 547 and 547A, while the main attack was the assault on A Luoi and Ta Bat on the valley floor.

The 3rd Brigade of the 1st Cavalry Division made the initial assault into the A Shau valley on the morning of 19 April. Before the assault six B-52 attacks had been delivered in the northern part of the valley and two attacks had been made on the roads to the east. Tactical aircraft and artillery hit numerous targets just before the helicopters set down. Despite the large amounts of preparatory fire, enemy anti-aircraft fire was intense. The

5th Battalion, 7th Cavalry, air assaulted into LZ "Tiger" near the winding road into Laos, and was soon followed by its support artillery battery. The 1st Battalion, 7th Cavalry, went into LZ "Vicki" on the slope north-east of "Tiger." Among the initial assaults those of the 1st and 5th Battalions, 7th Cavalry, were virtually unopposed by ground action, but subsequent assault lifts received heavy anti-aircraft fire. In these later assaults, 23 helicopters were hit by ground-to-air fire and ten aircraft were destroyed. Because of the intense anti-aircraft fire, deteriorating weather conditions, and the extensive engineering effort required to prepare artillery positions at LZ "Vicki," insertion of the direct support artillery battery into that landing zone was aborted for that day.

To the east, the 1st Brigade of the 101st Airborne Division started operations out of Fire Support Base "Bastogne" with one battalion attacking to the south-west. Later in the morning of 19 April another battalion air assaulted into the landing zone near the junction of Routes 547 and 547A. These battalions made only slight contact with the enemy during that day. The weather during "Delaware" was atrocious. Heavy clouds, fog, thunder storms and low ceilings made bravery and daring on the part of the pilots commonplace. The pilots of the supply and strike aircraft more often than not had to take pot luck diving through the low clouds and heavy mists to reach their landing grounds or hit their targets. Not only were conditions bad in the A Shau valley, but even the weather conditions at the departure area at Camp Evans were so poor that the helicopter pilots had to climb up through an overcast on instruments, assemble in formation on top of the clouds, fly to the target area, and then – if they were lucky – find a hole in the clouds before making their descent. What should have been a simple 20-minute flight was usually 80 minutes of stark horror. The Hueys, Chinooks and Tarhes were flown to the limit of their capabilities.

With a slight improvement in the weather conditions on 22 April, the 3rd Brigade, 1st Cavalry, continued to improve its bases in the northern part of the A Shau valley and to bring in needed supplies and equipment. The 1st Battalion, 7th Cavalry, had completed an overland attack and secured an LZ farther south. The battalion was now in position to support the coming assault on the A Luoi airfield and the central area of the A Shau valley. On 24 April, the 2nd Battalion, 8th Cavalry, led the assault of the 1st Cavalry

Left: Fairchild C-123 Providers find a gap in the heavy cloud cover over the A Shau Valley in South Vietnam (May 1967). Atrocious weather conditions during the battle made re-supply missions both difficult and dangerous to perform.

Left: Air Cavalrymen unload supplies and equipment from a CH-47 Chinook helicopter during Operation "Delaware" in the A Shau Valley in 1968.

Above: South Vietnamese troops sit aboard a C-130 prior to being airlifted on an operational mission, 1968.

Main picture: An AC-130 Hercules, which was the "Spectre" gunship used in Vietnam. This one, at Tha-Trang Air Base in October 1967, carried four 7·62mm Miniguns and four M-61 Vulcans. AC-130 Hercules aircraft were converted from C-130 transports.

Right: A C-130 delivers supplies strapped to a pallet by the low-altitude parachute extraction system (LAPES). This involved flying in at a very low level when the palletized supplies or guns or vehicles were extracted through the boom of the "Herk" by cargo parachutes. This re-supply method was used successfully by the C-130 pilots during the siege of Khe Sanh in Vietnam in 1968. The Marine Corps runway on the firebase was too short for the Hercules to land or take off from without turning around at the end of the strip. This made the aircraft very vulnerable to mortar and machine-gun fire from the N.V.A. manning posts in the surrounding hills. Thus LAPES more than halved the time a C-130 needed to be over the Khe Sanh perimeter.

Brigade into an LZ a short distance from the A Luoi airfield. The 1st Battalion, 12th Cavalry, and the 1st Battalion, 8th Cavalry, completed the brigade movement the following day when they air assaulted the airfield itself. The 1st Brigade then began reconnaissance in force operations moving to the south and west, uncovering numerous caches of enemy communications equipment, vehicles and weapons. The cavalry troopers were also finding on the ground the heavy anti-aircraft weapons that had hit them so hard during the air assaults. They also found caches of 23mm and 37mm ammunition.

The 1st Cavalry Division continued to consolidate in the valley while supplies poured into the landing and drop zones. As an example of the dedication of the pilots, on 26 April a C-130 ran into enemy anti-aircraft fire after breaking out of an overcast too far south of its parachute drop zone. Attempting to land at a helicopter LZ and losing altitude rapidly, the C-130 came under small arms fire as it tried to turn and crashed, exploding into flames. Unlike the helicopter, the C-130s could not pick holes in the clouds for their descent. They were vectored to the A Shau valley by the intersection of the beams of two radio stations on the east coast. From there they began an instrument approach into the valley using their own on-board radar to avoid the mountains. No matter how reliable the gauges, it took a lot of guts to nose your way down through the clouds that might be full of solid rock! The pilots and crews, including the quartermaster despatchers of

the C-130s, did a tremendous job under extreme pressure.

By 1 May 3rd A.R.V.N. Regiment was on the ground landing at LZ "Lucy." The 8th Engineer Battalion of the 1st Cavalry Division had been working on the airstrip at A Luoi since 29 April with the heavy equipment that had been brought in by the CH-54s. The field was ready to accept fixed-wing Caribou aircraft by noon on 1 May, but it was not until the following day that the first cargo aircraft, a C-7A Caribou, landed at LZ "Stallion" in the late morning. The engineers continued their work on this airstrip so that it could handle C-123 Providers and C-130 Hercules. The 89th Engineers completed the upgrading of the A Luoi airfield to take the C-130s on 3 May.

While the 1st Cavalry Division was operating in the A Shau valley, the 101st Airborne Division had been conducting major operations to the east. Together with the 3rd A.R.V.N. Airborne Task Force, it had concentrated on blocking possible enemy escape routes from the A Shau Valley. Frequent contact with the enemy had uncovered major supply caches. The 101st had built up two large fire support bases, "Veghel" and "Bastogne," which played an important role throughout "Delaware." After dark on 3 May an A.R.V.N. battalion interrupted a ten-vehicle convoy heading past their location, destroying two of the trucks with artillery fire.

The Allied mission in the A Shau valley was successfully completed, and on 17 May

"Delaware-Lam Son 216" was officially terminated. A large amount of weapons, equipment and supplies had been captured, including 90,000 pages of documents. In what was described later as "one of the most audacious, skillfully executed and successful combat undertakings of the Vietnam War," the 1st Cavalry Division had gone into the A Shau valley in the face of the heaviest enemy air defense ever encountered in airmobile operations up to that date. The enemy had planned and interlocked their fire zones over a period of some years. While the "Air Cav" lost 21 helicopters on these operations, the fact that it was able to go into the A Shau valley at all against these defenses and in such weather conditions was a fitting tribute to the airborne concept.

On 28 June 1968 the 101st Airborne Division was redesignated the 101st Air Cavalry Division. During the period 10-20 September, the "Screaming Eagles" participated with the A.R.V.N. forces and the U.S. and South Vietnamese navies in a combined operation on Vinh Loc island, situated 24km (15 miles) east of Hué. The island is sub-tropical with sandy beaches, palm trees and rice paddies. It is almost completely flat with the exception of two small hills on the south-eastern end. The Tet offensive had left a power vacuum on the island since most of the island's South Vietnamese Regional and Popular Force units (the "Rough Puffs," as the Americans called these militiamen) had been pressed into service. Viet Cong forces promptly moved into this vacuum and established a sanctuary, prepared defense positions and established caches. As a symbol of their authority, they had staged the execution of a village elder and a 13-year-old girl to demonstrate the consequences which the villagers could expect if they failed to support the Viet Cong.

During the night of 10-11 September, the U.S. and South Vietnamese navies converged around the island and at first light on 11 September the encirclement of the island was complete. At roughly 7.30 a.m. three companies of the 1st Battalion, 501st Infantry, conducted air assaults into three landing zones on the seaward side of the island and started reconnaissance in force to the south; the three companies included National Police Field Forces men. The 1st Battalion, 54th A.R.V.N. Regiment, conducted an air assault into three landing zones at the same time to the north-west of the American battalion. Numerous "Eagle Flights" were used to conduct ambushes and to rapidly exploit intelligence as it developed. In the round-up of the Viet Cong, 154 were killed and 56 rallied to the government cause. Of the friendly forces two were killed and nine wounded.

Left: Popular Forces troops, a militia force, act as Viet Cong making a simulated attack on a village at the Long Hai training center, 1970.

Cambodia, Laos and the Flight from Saigon

During the period 1969-1973, the Americans gradually wound down their forces but the elements that remained were primarily concerned with assisting the South Vietnamese in their continuing war against the Viet Cong. In 1969-1970, the 1st Cavalry Division was actively engaged in mounting airmobile operations with Army of the Republic of Vietnam (A.R.V.N.) troops in the Mekong delta. But the "Air Cav" was also involved in operations across the South Vietnam border in Cambodia. Beginning in the fall of 1968, the 1st Cavalry Division had straddled the enemy trails leading southward from the Cambodian border to Saigon. The Viet Cong and North Vietnamese Army (N.V.A.) made desperate attempts to keep their supply routes open, with an obvious aim of repeating the attacks of the Tet offensive of 1968. Beginning early in 1969 the 1st Cavalry Division fought a series of heavy skirmishes along these trails as three separate N.V.A. divisions attempted to gain positions closer to the capital. The enemy effort was not successful. The Air Cavalry, whose operational zone covered 14,000km² (5,400 sq miles) blocked all the trail systems leading to Saigon.

The area of Cambodia that borders III Corps Tactical Zone of the Republic of Vietnam had been used extensively by the Viet Cong and N.V.A. since 1961. Although allied forces had approached the border in large operations such as "Junction City" and "Attlebord," and more recently with the operations of the 1st Cavalry Division, the enemy had always had the advantage of being able to withdraw to the safety of Cambodian sanctuaries. The Air Cavalry was alerted to mount co-ordinated attacks on these sanctuaries.

The operational zone was to be the "Fishhook" of Cambodia, which extended from generally flat plains adjacent to Mimot north-east to the dissected hills and low mountains near O'rang. Multi-canopied, dense undergrowth forest was the dominant natural vegetation throughout the area. Rubber plantations were found primarily in the western section. Open areas with dry crops, upland rice or marshes were scattered throughout. Because of its inaccessibility and dense vegetation cover, this area was extremely favorable to guerrilla warfare and restricted heliborne and mechanized operations. Generally, concealment from both aerial and ground observations was excellent.

D-day was 1 May 1970 when the air assaults were preceded by six serials of B-25s dropping their bombs on hard targets within the primary objective area. The ever-faithful and long serving 1st Squadron, 9th Cavalry, began an aerial reconnaissance tour early on D-day. After locating a suitable landing zone code-named "East," the A.R.V.N. airborne battalion made the first assault. The LZ was secured and became a fire support base when six 105mm and three 155mm howitzers were flown in shortly afterward. The guns were manned by the 111th Armored Cavalry Regiment. A second A.R.V.N. airborne battalion in a 42-ship lift, supported by 22 Bell AH-1 HueyCobra gunships, began its combat assault on a second objective around

Above: American citizens leave a U.S. Marine CH-46 Sea Knight helicopter after landing on the deck of the U.S. Amphibious Command Ship U.S.S. *Blue Ridge* during the evacuation of Saigon, 29 April 1975.

Far left: UH-1D helicopters from the 173rd Aviation Company, 11th Combat Aviation Battalion, fly in formation during a surveillance mission, Vietnam, 1969. The 1D was a distinguished member of the Huey dynasty and in pushing for its production along with the larger-sized Chinook, the U.S. Army accelerated its airmobility program by years.

Following pages, main picture: The 173rd Airborne Brigade take part in a search-and-secure mission north of the Ai Lao River, northwest of Bong Song (1970). The first U.S. Army combat unit into Vietnam in 1965, the "Sky Soldiers" saw over six years of active service in the war before being de-activated on 17 December 1971.

Following pages, inset: An air cavalryman fires a jeep-mounted M-2 ·50 caliber machine-gun in defense of Landing Zone "English," 1969.

Far left: Troopers of the 3rd Brigade, 82nd Airborne Division have mounted a 105-mm howitzer gun in exposed lowland terrain, 1968.

Left: Fire Base "Terry Linn", Cambodia, 1970. Lieutenant Colonel James L. Anderson shows newsmen captured enemy machine-guns.

Below: American engineers check out supply crates left behind by the fleeing enemy.

10.00 a.m. The D-day landings were further reinforced in the afternoon by the 2nd Battalion, 7th Cavalry, flying into "X-Ray" in the northern sector of the 3rd Brigade area of operations. The enemy was ill-prepared to deal with this maneuver, and tactical surprise was complete.

The invaders had a field day trying to trap fleeing N.V.A. soldiers. A large exodus of trucks going in all directions was hotly pursued by helicopters of the 1st Squadron, 9th Cavalry. On 4 May, "B" Troop of the Air Cavalry Squadron observed numerous bunkers and military structures in a densely vegetated area north-west of the early ground operations. Additional aerial reconnaissance teams further reported that these structures and bunkers were connected with bamboo-matted trails. One pilot also reported seeing numerous antennae in the southern part of the complex. On 5 May, in response to the aerial reconnaissance sighting reports, Company "C," 1st Battalion, 5th Cavalry displaced into the northern half of the complex, which had been dubbed "the city." Immediately upon entering the suspected area, the cavalry spotted the storage bunkers, which contained larger quantities of weapons and munitions, the enemy having evacuated the complex. Throughout the period 5-13 May 182 storage bunkers, 18 mess-halls, a training ground and a small animal farm were discovered in the area. The "Air Cav" had uncovered the supply depot of the 7th N.V.A. Division.

Throughout the Cambodian campaign, Allied forces would discover other major caches of weapons, munitions and equipment. The size of the N.V.A. logistics system in Cambodia adjoining III Corps Tactical Zone was vast. It had the capacity to move thousands of tons of matèriel by truck from various points in Cambodia to supply depots along the South Vietnamese border and move these supplies quickly over the network of roads that connected the various caches. By mid-May, the search had expanded eastward to the border area north of Phuoc Long Province, where on 8 May the 2nd Brigade discovered a significant cache site. This N.V.A. base camp, nicknamed "Rock Island East," eventually yielded 329 tons of munitions. As the operation continued, the 1st Brigade was moved to another sector of the O'Rang area east of the 2nd Brigade. Both cavalry brigades used the airstrip at Bu Gia Map as a forward logistics base. One rifle company patrolled out of the abandoned Special Forces camp there as a security for a refuel and rearm point, and the tons of palletized supplies which were offloaded from Lockheed C-130s and Fairchild C-123s.

Left: Cambodia, 1970. A captured enemy cache of arms. The weapons used by the N.V.A. and Viet Cong were usually of Russian origin, or Chinese-manufactured copies of Russian weapons.

Far left: A three-quarter view of a U.S. Army CH-47 Chinook taking off from an airfield during the Cambodian Offensive. At the left is an Army UH-1 on the ground, and at the right a U.S. Air Force C-7A lands.

The withdrawal of the 1st Cavalry Division from Cambodia was time-phased to allow for the redeployment of one fire support base each day. The evacuation involved Sikorsky CH-54s and Boeing Vertol CH-47s lifting portable bridges, 155mm howitzers, two-ton trucks and bulldozers. The CH-54s also recovered downed aircraft worth $7,315,000. On the final day of the operation, in the actual crossing of the border by all U.S. troops, every possible precaution was taken to pull out all the troops. Troop ladders, smoke ships, pathfinders and recovery aircraft were available to cover any contingency. The crossing proved uneventful with the last CH-47 aircraft leaving Cambodia in mid-afternoon, 29 June. The distinction of being the last U.S. Army aircraft out of Cambodia went to Company "B" of the 1st Squadron, 9th Cavalry, whose screening "Pink Team" reported re-entering Vietnam at 5.28 p.m. 29 June.

The 1st Squadron, 9th Air Cavalry, proved again during the Cambodian campaign how invaluable its expertise was to airmobile operations. During the period 1 May – 29 June 1970, the squadron had performed intensive ground and aerial reconnaissance operations almost every flyable hour. The squadron's assets were shifted as necessary, capitalizing on mobility, reconnaissance and firepower in order to determine enemy locations and escape routes. Using "Pink Teams" (one HueyCobra gunship and one Hughes OH-6A Cayuse observation helicopter), the air cavalry troops were able to cover large areas effectively. When the situation warranted, the aero-rifle platoon could be inserted to face the enemy until a larger force could be committed into the area. The intelligence provided by the 1st Squadron, 9th Cavalry, enabled the division to redeploy its helicopters and effectively destroy many of the enemy's large cache sites.

By the late fall of 1970 it became apparent to the South Vietnamese government that the N.V.A. planned to seize Vientiane, the capital of Laos, and overthrow the government. As in Cambodia, the Laotian communists had established bases in Laos and the South Vietnamese decided to send three divisions to the country in an attempt to block the N.V.A.'s entry points from North Vietnam and destroy their supply depots. Operation "Lamson 719" would cover an area roughly 35 by 60km (22 by 39 miles). The geography of this area varied dramatically. The Xe Pon River split the region and was roughly paralleled by Highway 9. Vegetation was

Far left: Cambodia, 1970. Sp 4 Phillip Stanbaugh, door gunner, Troop "C," 271st Helicopter Company, 16th Cavalry, mans an M-60 machine-gun mounted on a UH-1D helicopter as they near a landing zone in southern Cambodia.

mostly single or double canopy jungle along the river. Just south of the river rose a sheer escarpment leading to rugged mountainous terrain. Natural clearings were rare throughout the area and landing zones would have to be carved out of the dense undergrowth. Any relatively clear spaces available would be heavily defended.

The attack into Laos was launched on 8 February 1971 from bases established on the Khe Sanh Plain. The 1st A.R.V.N. Armored Brigade Task Force crossed the border at 10.00 a.m. and advanced 9km (5.5 miles) to the west along Highway 9 on the first day. At the same time, three battalions of the 3rd Regiment, 1st A.R.V.N. Infantry Division, air assaulted into landing zones south of Highway 9, while two battalions of the 1st A.R.V.N. Airborne Division air assaulted north of the highway. Some 105mm howitzer batteries were landed in both areas on D-day. On 10 February, the 1st A.R.V.N. Airborne Division air-landed a battalion into Objective "Aloni" and the armored task force linked up with this battalion. On the same day, the 1st A.R.V.N. Division landed a battalion at LZ "Delta" and the initial objectives of "Lamson 719" had been taken. After the attack on 8 February the enemy reacted violently to the offensive. N.V.A. reinforcements were rushed to Laos, and the South Vietnamese were forced to consolidate on the ground they so far held.

By 22 February, both Fire Bases 30 and 31 and the South Vietnam Ranger positions were under heavy attack. The enemy possessed tanks but they made slow progress through difficult terrain. On 25 February the N.V.A. managed to move armor stealthily over concealed routes to mount an attack. The defenders threw back two waves of the enemy but were forced to withdraw when three Soviet-made T-34 tanks (of World War II vintage) penetrated the fire base. The South Vietnamese were beginning to lose their hold in Laos but it was decided to attack the main objective of Tchepone with a series of rapid air assaults along the high escarpment to the south of the river using the 1st Infantry Division. After a Boeing B-52 bomber attack, the A.R.V.N. air assaulted successfully into Landing Zones "Lolo" and "Liz," and Fire Base "Sophia." At the same time two battalions were landed on LZ "Hope" north of Tchepone. The Hueys flew in on both occasions to a very hot reception from anti-aircraft fire, but only one was forced down after being hit. The A.R.V.N. succeeded in reaching Tchepone but it was then decided to withdraw from Laos before the weather worsened. The last elements of the 1st Infantry Division left Laos on 21 March. Thousands of tons of ammunition, petroleum, oils and lubricants (as well as other supplies and equipment) had been destroyed by "Lamson 719" forces, and approximately 14,000 of the enemy killed. An effective blow had been delivered on the N.V.A. supply bases in Laos.

After the last American troops left Vietnam on 29 March 1973, an unsettled peace reigned between North and South Vietnam for nine months. The war began again in January 1974 but it was not until the dry season, commencing the following September, that the communists were seriously onto the offensive. By January 1975 the N.V.A. was fewer than 160km (100 miles) from Saigon. Throughout April, as the final outcome of the Vietnam War left no reason for doubt, many Vietnamese and American officials and their families fled Saigon on scheduled flights. Others took ships. The U.S. Air Force was also called in to conduct massive airlifts using their giant Lockheed C-5A Galaxies and Lockheed C-141A StarLifters, and the ever-faithful C-130 Hercules. For humanitarian reasons, the American government decided that the first three days of aerial evacuation would be used for Operation "Baby Lift" – the airlifting of a fraction of the small children who had been orphaned by the war. "Baby Lift" was successfully accomplished, but one Galaxy with 250 children and 37 American personnel on board experienced massive structural failure a few minutes after climbing out of Tan Son Nhut airfield. Fighting for control of the aircraft, the captain made a safe landing and no one was killed.

After the first few days of the airlift, a deep and dark panic began to set in at Tan Son Nhut. The airfield was always overflowing with Vietnamese and to add to the confusion was the exodus from foreign embassies. Civil and military aircraft flew in from many countries. The American Evacuation Control Center now swung into action to implement air evacuation plans if the airfield should be closed by enemy action. It had been hoped to evacuate 1,000,000 people from South Vietnam by sea. Conditions aboard ship were awful and thousands died of thirst, starvation and other causes. The sealift came apart when N.V.A. troops poured into the port area of Nha Trang. In the event, fewer than 100,000 South Vietnamese escaped to a new life. Helicopters were the only answer to lifting up to 5,000 Americans and selected South Vietnamese from downtown Saigon.

Left: Vietnamese refugees watched over by U.S. Marines aboard the U.S. merchant ship *Green Port*, April 1975.

Above: Vietnamese refugees are seen aboard a mechanized landing craft from the Amphibious Cargo Ship U.S.S. *Durham*. These people have been evacuated from the Phan Rang area of South Vietnam, April 1975.

U.S. Ambassador Graham Martin gave the order for "Frequent Wind," Option IV. Rescue choppers were put on alert at Nakhon Phanom and at Ubon in Thailand, and aboard the carrier U.S.S. *Midway* in the South China Sea.

Six assembly areas were chosen where a dozen U.S. Marine Corps and U.S. Air Force Sikorsky CH-53s and HH-53s could land at one time. Landing pads were also hastily constructed on the rooftops of the American-occupied buildings, but their structures were strong enough to take only the Hueys. The air routes were carefully planned from Saigon to the armada of naval vessels holding off at Vung Tau.

On the afternoon of the 29 April 1975, with N.V.A. shells pouring into the city, the evacuation of Saigon began. U.S. Marine Corps Boeing Vertol CH-46 Sea Knights, Sikorsky CH-53 Sea Stallions and U.S. Air Force HH-53 Super Jollies rose from the *Midway* and flew to Saigon. At midnight the

weather and visibility remained good, so the evacuation continued. At that point 6,619 people had been carried out. At 3.00 a.m. CH-53s landed in the American embassy compound to pick up officials who were hastily burning secret documents. Within two hours, Ambassador Martin and his staff were on their way to the Fleet. As the sun came up there was panic among thousands of Vietnamese swarming around the embassy walls. They climbed the walls and over the barbed wire defenses only to have U.S. Marines ground security forces drive them back with rifle butts. At 7.30 a.m. the U.S. Marines slammed and barred the building's huge oak doors.

As they reached the last steps of the rooftop helicopter pad, panic-gripped Vietnamese smashed through the doors below and surged into the embassy and up the stairwell. The U.S. Marines climbed aboard Swift-22, the waiting CH-53. The turbines whined, the rotor blades moved round, picking up speed

with each revolution. The chopper lifted. Throughout the day they watched aboard the *Midway* as 48 South Vietnamese Hueys, three CH-47s and even a small, single-engined Cessna 0-1 observation plane brought out more Vietnamese refugees. The pilot of the 0-1, a Vietnamese air force major, had his wife and children on board. On 29-30 April 1975, 662 military helicopter missions were flown between the fleet and Saigon. U.S. Marine HueyCobras flew 24 armed sorties. Head-counts revealed that 57,507 people had been evacuated by air. Of these, 7,014 were moved by U.S.M.C., U.S.A.F. and Air America helicopters. (Air America, the Central Intelligence Agency's own airline, flew over 1,000 sorties in Hueys – truly an impressive accomplishment.)

The story of airmobility in the Vietnam War was seen by the U.S. Army as the first chapter of a new and dynamic fighting force. The glamor of airmobility has long passed, but the challenges are as great as ever. It is well

to remember, however, that the birth and early life of the airmobile concept did not take place in the framework of guerrilla warfare. It was originally conceived out of the necessity to disperse forces quickly on the modern battlefield under threat of nuclear weapons and still retain the ability to mass swiftly elsewhere for decisive action before dispersing again. The actualities of Vietnam have since obscured these origins and led many people to believe that the helicopter is a counter-guerrilla weapon. So indeed it is, but the chopper has a much wider application. In Vietnam, the helicopter overcame the obstacles of limited landing zones, primitive roadnets, restricted observation and high altitudes as no other fighting vehicle could. But, in the open countryside of Europe, flatlands of Asia or a desert in the Middle East, the airmobile force presents the land commander with far more flexibility and many more options than have hitherto existed in the history of warfare.

Above: A Huey helicopter is pushed over the side of the Amphibious Command Ship U.S.S. *Blue Ridge*, to make room for more helicopters landing with fugitives from Saigon, April 1975.

Enter the Green Berets

Shortly after World War II the U.S. Army recognized the need for a unit to parachute behind enemy lines to support friendly guerrilla fighters. The 10th Special Forces Group (Airborne) was consequently formed in 1952 at Fort Bragg. The 10th was posted to West Germany to help meet the threat of war with the U.S.S.R. The idea was that in the event of conflict, the Green Beret A-teams would drop in eastern Europe to teach military skills and donate weapons to a group of guerrillas who would fight the Soviets and their eastern bloc allies. In September 1961, the 5th Special Forces Group was activated at Fort Bragg. These were the Green Berets who were destined to serve in Vietnam. President John F. Kennedy took a great interest in the Special Forces, and it was he incidentally who in the fall of 1961 first authorized the wearing of the green beret. But the president saw Special Forces in the opposite role of fighting guerrillas and not helping them.

What were the special skills of the Green Berets and how did they operate? There were three operational arms of the Special Forces groups (the A-, B- and C-teams), but it was the Λ-teams that saw most of the action. The B- and C-teams were the higher echelons of authority who essentially gave the A-teams their tasks and supplied them with intelligence, equipment and rations in the field. A-teams consisted of 12 men with the following duties:

Commanding Officer (with the rank of Captain)
Executive Officer (Lieutenant)
Operations Sergeant
Heavy Weapons Leader
Medical Specialist
Radio Operator Supervisor
Engineer Sergeant
Assistant Medical Specialist
Chief of Research and Development Operator
Engineer
Intelligence Sergeant
Light Weapons Leader.

Each man in the A-team was an expert at his job and capable of imparting his knowledge to friendly forces. If a man was killed or wounded at least one other member of the team was trained to do his job. A-teams were designed so that they could be split into two six-man detachments if necessary.

U.S. Special Forces troops actually worked in South-East Asia for the first time in 1957. A small team was sent from the 1st Special Forces Group, which was raised in June of that year and based on Okinawa, to help train the South Vietnamese army. As a result of learning Special Forces skills, the South Vietnamese formed their own Special Forces. As the prospect of war between the North and South increased, more Green Berets were sent to Vietnam as instructors. With the Viet Cong to be found everywhere in the South, it was vital to prevent the communists from recruiting the people of South Vietnam to the northern cause.

This objective would be achieved by winning the "hearts and minds" of the people, a doctrine successfully pursued by the British army directed by the High Commissioner, General Sir Gerald Templer, during the seven-year Malayan Emergency in the 1950s. The

Above: Fort Bragg, North Carolina, 1962. A 12-man "A" team of the 5th Special Forces Group (Airborne) are seen in training at the U.S. Army Special Warfare Center, Fort Bragg, which was set up with the approval of President John F. Kennedy.

Far left: South Vietnamese paratroopers drop from C-123 Providers during a minor airborne operation against the Viet Cong, 1966.

Right: Fort Bragg, North Carolina, 1962. Sergeant Henry Cardinal of the "Green Berets" stresses the importance of keeping a weapon clean as he demonstrates the disassembly of a British Bren Mark I machine-gun.

Below: A group of Montagnard tribesmen receive instruction at the Special Forces Training Center at Pleiyit, 1963. The Montagnards or "mountain people" have a history in Vietnam dating back for at least four centuries. A nomadic people, the "Yards" were taught by the Green Berets how to organize village communities and how to defend them from the Viet Cong.

Green Berets assigned to the task began by working on the nomadic tribesmen, who roamed the Central Highlands and had done so for centuries. The Montagnards, as the French had called them, had in the Middle Ages been driven into the highlands by the southerners, who were not originally natives of Vietnam. The "mountain people," who were of diminutive stature, settled temporarily anywhere their livelihood could be secured, locating their rice fields near the rivers and springs. The most influential of the many Montagnard tribes were the Rhade (pronounced Rah-day), who accepted the Americans as they had done the French before them. Why not? The Americans had "round eyes" like the French, who had treated the tribesmen well.

The Green Berets started the campaign to win over the "hearts and minds" of the Montagnards with the Rhade. Permanent villages were established with an A-team in charge, and the people were taught skills that would improve their life as a community. The Rhade learned quickly and a strong bond of affection developed between master and pupil. In return the villagers were trained to defend their homes from Viet Cong attacks. Defenses were built around the villages, which were thus turned into minor forts. The able-bodied menfolk exchanged their medieval crossbows for modern weapons of war which they handled very well under the watchful eyes of their American instructors. One category of tribesmen – the young and the old – formed a unit purely to defend their village. Another of warrior age provided a strike force to patrol the surrounding jungle paths and set up ambushes. Later in the war the strike force idea was extended to an elite mobile strike ("Mike") force, which was parachute-trained and which could be lifted by air into battle to support ground forces anywhere in South Vietnam.

The Civilian Irregular Defense Group (C.I.D.G.) program established over 300 of these defended villages mainly in the highland border zones throughout the length of South Vietnam. Not all the camps were a success. The Viet Cong were a brave, well-organized enemy armed with modern weapons, but the C.I.D.G. camps were a major factor in the allied war effort in Vietnam. The Green Berets ran a parachute training school for South Vietnamese volunteers. They also undertook rescue missions and reconnaissance (recon or scouting) assignments. During the monsoons they floated their own navy in the Plain of Reeds in the Mekong delta, and in

the Tet offensive of 1968 when the North Vietnamese Army attacked the populated areas of South Vietnam for the first time, the mobile strike forces were everywhere in the thick of the fight.

The Green Beret Vietnam story really starts in February 1962. Captain Ronald A. Schackleton's Detachment A-IIB of the 1st Special Forces Group stationed in Okinawa had been preparing for duty in Laos. Instead Schackleton was ordered to Vietnam. He was disappointed: he had expected to see some action in Laos and he thought he was in for a dull time. The Central Intelligence Agency (C.I.A.) was already assessing means of recruiting the Montagnards to fight the Viet Cong. The Rhade inhabiting Darlac Province in Central South Vietnam were noted as being the most friendly of the 100 or so mountain tribes, so they were chosen for the launch of the C.I.D.G. program. Not all the Rhade were recruited by the Green Berets, some serving with the Viet Cong. Schackleton and his seven-man team were directed by the C.I.A. to set up camp in the village of Buon Enao in Darlac Province. The Rhade greeted the Americans with enthusiasm and were ready to work hard to improve their lifestyle and safeguard their homes from Viet Cong attack. Soon other villages in the vicinity

Above right: Another training shot of South Vietnamese paratroopers dropping from a C-123 Provider.

Above left: South Vietnamese paratroopers descend toward earth near Tan Son Nhut Air Base near Saigon during a training exercise.

Left: A newly-arrived Montagnard recruit checks in at a Special Forces Civilian Irregular Defense Group (C.I.D.G.) camp in Thua Thien Province.

Above: Sergeant 1st Class Robert Daniel, the heavy weapons expert of Detachment A-730, 7th Special Forces, gives Montagnards at the Thua Thien camp a lesson in the use of a 60-mm mortar.

by to protect military posts and communities throughout the world. An outer ring of bamboo fencing was erected, within which was a deep ditch filled with sharp pointed punji stakes, traps, firing positions and protective shelters. A radio was provided to keep in touch with the outside world.

By far the most popular member of the team was the medic. He could recognize and treat minor ailments and serious tropical diseases, and he could take out teeth and an appendix if necessary. Clinics in the C.I.D.G. villages were the center of local life and the medics advised on home hygiene. Civic action included advice on farming and useful handiwork such as carpentry. The Montagnards had been used to the "slash and burn" method of farming, clearing the brush with crude machetes and tilling the ground with simple hoes, before moving on to try their luck in a different valley in another season. The Americans flew in bulldozers and other modern equipment, dug irrigation ditches and wells, and laid on village water supplies. The success of the C.I.D.G. programs depended on the Americans understanding the Montagnard culture and way of life. The "Yards," as they were affectionately known by their "round eye" mentors, lived in "long houses" built on stilts. The Green Berets studied local customs and dialects, ate the tribal food when invited and wore the garb when participating in rituals and ceremonies.

More Special Forces C.I.D.G. camps sprang up, but not all were successfully defended. The first camp to be overrun was Hiep Hoa in the Plain of Reeds between Saigon and the Cambodian border. On 23 November 1963, the strike force (A-21) was under strength after Captain Doug Horne had led a small group out on patrol. Lieutenant Colby and three other Green Berets were left in charge of the main force, which had been infiltrated by a few communist sympathizers or "spies." All hell let loose at midnight when the garrison was awakened by mortar bomb explosions and the din of machine-gun and rifle fire. After blasting their way through the outer defense the Viet Cong shouted in Vietnamese "Don't shoot! All we want are the Americans and their weapons." With the defenders refusing to fight, the Green Berets were faced with the impossible task of saving Hiep Hoa. All four Americans were wounded, three of them overpowered, but Colby evaded capture by hiding in a sugar cane field as he nursed his wounds.

After the fall of Hiep Hoa, the Special Forces

were included in the Buon Enao defense program.

The Special Forces team first assembled a group of village defenders. These men were taught only the basics of weapon handling. They lived and worked in the villages and fields, and took up arms only if the Viet Cong attacked. The village defenders were usually very young, or older men who were unsuited to duty outside the village. The main military task of the A-team was to recruit and train a well-armed strike force, which could help the central village when under attack, reinforce another village in the defense system in time of trouble, and mount patrols to hunt elusive "Charlie" in the surrounding jungle. In pattern the lay-out of the defended areas resembled the fortifications that were built in days gone

took more camp security measures. Tough soldiers of fortune of Chinese extraction called Nungs were hired as special camp guards. Another Viet Cong assault on Nam Dong C.I.D.G. camp (A-726) two days later was not so successful. About 600 Viet Cong crept through the grass and cut the double ring of fences. Carefully positioned mortars lobbed bombs, creating havoc in the center of Nam Dong. When the mortar barrage ceased, waves of screaming Viet Cong charged into the camp. Captain Roger Donlon, the camp commander, was to the fore in marshaling the defenses. He dashed through a hail of fire and killed a Viet Cong demolitions team at the main gate. Wounded in the stomach,

he reached one of his own mortar positions and covered the withdrawal of wounded Special Forces soldiers. Seeing his team sergeant had been hit, Donlon carried him to a first aid post and was wounded. The Green Beret captain stumbled back to the mortar in great pain and directed the final defensive positions. After five hours the Viet Cong started to withdraw. Six Marine helicopters loaded with Special Forces and Nung troops flew in 45 minutes after the last Viet Cong had gone.

Wounded four times, Captain Donlon was largely responsible for saving Nam Dong. He became the first Medal of Honor winner in Vietnam.

Above: Sergeant Dale B. Winnie, 25th Medical Battalion, 173rd Airborne Brigade attempts to diagnose an ailment as he listens to a villager. The sergeant is a member of the U.S. Medical Civic Action Program (M.E.D.C.A.P.) team operating in the island village of Thai Hung, north-west of Bien Hoa on the Saigon River.

The War in the Central Highlands

In the period 1965-1969 the U.S. and South Vietnamese navies were engaged in an intense river war in the Mekong delta. Fast patrol boats policed in pairs or in massed formation to make amphibious assault raids by infantry on enemy strongpoints. One third of the Mekong delta is marsh, forest and swamp forest. In the north lies the Plain of Reeds, a virtually treeless, flat grassy basin during the wet season, which lasts from mid-May through early October. In the dry season, however, the plains dry out to the extent that the razor sharp reeds grow to 6.1m (20 ft) tall and grass fires are frequent. As a typical example of a Green Beret operation in the monsoon season in the Plain of Reeds, on 14 November 1966 a C.I.D.G. company, led by A-414 Operations Sergeant First Class Lyle D. Kimball, embarked in eight assault boats and 12 sampans, accompanied by an airboat platoon with Sfc. David S. Boyd in charge, and launched an assault north of Tuyon Nhon on the Cambodian frontier. The airboats were a Special Forces idea based upon the "swamp buggies" of the Florida Everglades.

The airboats moved ahead of the main C.I.D.G. force consisting of Cambodian and Cham tribesmen, who crossed marshland firing blindly into suspected Viet Cong hiding places. The maneuver triggered a hornet's nest and the Viet Cong responded in kind with automatic weapons, killing Boyd and throwing the airboats into disarray. The C.I.D.G. now formed an assault line, then advanced on the Viet Cong positions with all guns blazing. After a short but intense firefight that followed, Sergeant Kimball withdrew his force suffering several casualties in the process. When by mid-November the flood waters began to recede the airboats, reinforced by three U.S. Navy air cushion vehicles, dominated the delta. The skimmers, which were an awesome sight with shark's teeth painted on the bows, moved over both dry and flooded terrain, restricted only by the obstructions which caused them to stall. The "Green Beret Navy" grew in size with an increasing allocation of airboats and the expansion in numbers of the mobile strike forces.

The forerunner of the mobile strike force ("Mike") was the "Eagle Flight" Detachment which was formed at Pleiku on 16 October 1964 to react to emergency combat situations in the western highlands. The "Eagle Flight" consisted of five Green Berets of Detachment 334-B of the Special Forces Group and 36 Rhade tribesmen. These Montagnards were trained in various Special Forces' skills and underwent parachute training. The "Eagle Flight" troops received better pay than the ordinary strike force personnel and were given higher ranks. Six helicopters were available to the "Eagle Flight." The success of the mobile "Eagle Flight" persuaded the 5th Special Forces Group to raise the "Mike" forces. The Montagnards who only a few years previously had been armed with crossbows now carried M16 automatic rifles.

The concept of the "Mike" forces was that these units could be used as mobile units for any number of purposes – to reinforce a threatened camp, to patrol areas not covered

Far left: A U.S. Navy gunship helicopter fires a rocket in support of two river patrol boats (PBRs) of the Brownwater Navy in action in the Mekong Delta. The helicopter is from the Seawolves squadron (HAL3) based at Vinh Long, 1967.

Above: A sergeant first class of Detachment B-51, 5th Special Forces (Airborne) checks the equipment of an American parachute volunteer, who is about to make his first jump from a C-123 Provider, during basic airborne training, Dong Ba Thin, Vietnam, 1970.

by camp strike forces or other units, to run special missions in remote areas, bail camps out of trouble, or provide reinforcements for the battleground. The elite of the "Mike" forces were the Nungs, who formed a battalion in Da Nang in 1965. The Nungs were a tribal group from an area near the North Vietnamese-Chinese border. During the French regime, there had been an entire Nung division which earned a top reputation for professionalism and fighting quality. The division was later demobilized, and the Nungs settled in various places in South Vietnam. They were not active again till the C.I.A. and the Special Forces hired them to support the A-teams in the C.I.D.G. program.

A mobile strike force was authorized for each C-detachment in July 1965, with another allocated to Nha Trang under the operational control of the commanding officer 5th Special Forces Group, making five in all. Each "Mike" force was battalion sized, with a full strength of three 198-man companies, plus a small headquarters, totalling in all 598 men. Parachute training was carried out at a Special Forces training school near Nha Trang and five jumps were required to qualify for airborne wings. De Havilland Canada C-7 Caribous, Fairchild C-123 Providers and Lockheed C-130 Hercules were used for jump training. As we have learned, there was only one large-formation parachute assault in the Vietnam War (Operation "Junction City Alternate" in February 1967), but in 1967 the 5th Mobile Strike Force (Airborne) made two spectacular jumps in support of ground forces.

The first parachute drop took place at Bunard, on the site of the new Special Forces camp to be opened in Thuoc Long Province,

about 160km (100 miles) from Saigon. The A-team requested the assistance of two "Mike" force companies from Nha Trang to secure the area while installing itself at Bunard with its own "Mike" force. A plan to land the Nha Trang "Mike" force by helicopter was discarded in favor of dropping the troops by parachute straight into the compound. The operation became something of a demonstration piece. On 1 April a large pathfinder force jumped from helicopters, followed half-an-hour later by the main force jumping from fixed-wing aircraft. A few of the paratroopers missed the compound and disappeared into tall elephant grass.

The second airborne operation mounted by the 5th Mobile Strike Force (Airborne) centered on the Nhui Giai in the Seven Mountains region in the northern sector of the Vietnamese war zones. The "Mike" force climbed into six C-130 aircraft on 13 May, 36 hours after receiving their battle orders. A short while later the drop was made from 213m (700 ft). The Nhui Giai drop was intended as a diversion for a much larger operation of C.I.D.G. companies surrounding a Viet Cong stronghold in the Seven Mountains. The Nha Trang "Mike" force was in action for five days, destroying a Viet Cong base. The next significant factor to occur was that twice in six weeks Rhade tribesmen had proved they were first class airborne soldiers.

As the war grew more intense the Special Forces used the mountains to build a new kind of "fighting camp." These fortified camps were built primarily to prevent the infiltration of men and supplies from Laos and Cambodia into Vietnam. Once a site had been chosen the Green Berets recruited and trained a new civilian irregular defense group from the local tribesmen. The fighting camps were completed in six weeks and the C.I.D.G. ready to perform short-range missions. Designed as a miniature fortress, the camp was bounded by barbed wire and marked by a series of machine-gun bunkers. Mines were sewn in the intervals between these strongpoints. An inner concrete-surfaced perimeter contained the headquarters block which housed the A-team operations center. The central area also contained communications, medical and ammunition bunkers, and a helipad. A small barracks for the C.I.D.G. or "Mike" force companies was situated to the rear of the inner compound. The heavy machine-guns were augmented by 4·2 in mortars and 105mm howitzers, which lobbed their shells high over the fences into the camp approaches.

Special Forces fighting camps were of three principal types. In the first, where the soil was firm enough, the bunkers were placed underground. There were two basic varieties of the second type: in one kind vital facilities and bunkers were composed of concrete, logs, heavy timber or empty steel freight containers, while the second kind used salvaged containers for all important facilities and even for sleeping quarters. The third main variant was the floating camp which operated in the Plain of Reeds and in the lower Mekong delta in the monsoon. The fighting camps sprang up in 1967, and their effect on the N.V.A. and Viet Cong aggressors (and in controlling the local population) was impressive, but as usual there was no room for complacency. The Green Berets were already looking for the use of camps to launch long-range reconnaissance and strike missions deep into hostile territory.

A fierce battle took place at a fighting camp at Tong Le Chon in Binh Long "Peaceful Dragon" Province. Detachment A-334 opened this border surveillance camp in deep jungle along a bend in the Saigon River, on 24 March 1967. There was no village in this remote area, and the C.I.D.G. garrison lived in tents. Tong Le Chon had a dismal record of high desertion rates and poor morale. The camp defenses and living quarters were consequently in a poor state of repair. Skilled laborers were only obtained by high rates of pay, and most quit their jobs after only a few days. The men of the A-team were fearful of the consequences. The night of 6-7 August was hot and very humid. A-334's depleted strike force had been reinforced by two "Mike" forces, which totalled 573 men, from Bien Hoa and Nha Trang. Just after midnight, the south-eastern edge of the camp was hit by mortar fire, and this steadily increased in volume as the explosions spread into the camp's interior.

Captain Berg, A-334's commander, ordered counter-mortar fire and called for helicopter gunship fire support, which was prompt to arrive overhead. At shortly after 1.00 a.m., the enemy mortarmen had found the range of the camp's interior perimeter, and the command bunker took a direct hit. The night was lit by a furious blaze in the fuel and storage area. This time it was not the Viet Cong guerrillas who cut lanes in the wire and advanced but the 165th N.V.A. Regiment, which by far outnumbered the defenders. The attack might have succeeded but for the fact that the camp's mortar ammunition dump

Above: One of the "Brown Water" Navy's riverine patrol craft at speed. Note the guns fore and aft, the heavy caliber twin mount forward presumably being an ex-aircraft turret.

blew up in the midst of the assailants. The tremendous blast instantly dismembered the lead element and stunned and dazed the rest of the men. The A-team seized its chance in the suffocating smoke and dust.

Calling for a counter-attack, the Green Berets rallied the "Mike" forces and then threw out the North Vietnamese infantrymen in close combat. Artillery and mortar fire continued to be hurled against the camp and two hours later the N.V.A. made another mass charge against the south and east walls. Several effective air attacks helped to stop the attack. One N.V.A. rifle squad captured a machine-gun bunker, but this was mopped up shortly before dawn. By daytime the N.V.A. had gone. At day-break "dust-off" (medical evacuation) helicopters brought in both U.S. Army and U.S. Air Force medical personnel, and began evacuating the wounded. The A-team encountered trouble with some of the C.I.D.G. and "Mike" force soldiers when they feigned wounds to climb aboard the helicopters. That afternoon a relief battalion arrived at Tong Le Chon and the camp survived.

From the beginning, Special Forces had been charged with "recovery" operations. When commanded in 1966 and 1967 by Colonel Francis Kelly, a former Boston cop, the 5th Special Forces Group took every opportunity to rescue downed aircrew and stragglers. One recovery operation of a different kind took place over the Christmas period in 1966. A Lockheed U-2 "spy" plane assigned to photographing military locations in unfriendly zones from a great height, was brought down in the thick jungles along the Cambodian border. The pilot ejected safely and was rescued, but the stricken U-2

contained a secret "black box." The U.S. Air Force wanted that box back again before it revealed vital information to the enemy. General Westmoreland turned to the 5th Special Forces Group in Nha Trang for help. The 3rd Mobile Strike Force, commanded by Captain James G. "Bo" Gritz, was selected for the job.

Stationed at Bien Hoa, and consisting of three companies of 150 men each and three reconnaissance platoons of 35 men each, the 3rd Mobile Strike Force was headed by a 12-man A-team in command of the "Mike" Force. For this mission, Gritz alerted one company and a recon platoon, with the other units held on standby reserve. The jungle into which the U-2 had crashed was not as thick in most other places in Vietnam. There were numerous bamboo clumps and areas with 3m (10 ft) high elephant grass, but the forests were small with relatively thin trees some 7.6-9.1m (25-30 ft) high. Visibility on the trails, which were numerous, was guaranteed to be good in the hours of daylight. Gritz and his men studied the area map provided by the U.S. Air Force, together with photos of the U-2 indicating the position of its vital black box. After dropping by helicopter, the "Mike" force company was sufficiently strong in numbers and well enough armed to take boldly to the jungle trails. The men trekked back and forth for three days, broadening their search, as they plunged deeper into Viet Cong territory.

By no more than a stroke of luck on the third day, they found the U-2. To their alarm the black box was missing. Gritz correctly surmised that the Viet Cong had got there first, but that they could not have gone far with the magic box. He concluded that he needed a prisoner who knew who was holding it. After several attempts, the "Mike" force men grabbed a P.O.W. who was persuaded to guide them to a Viet Cong base camp in a jungle clearing. The entire force raced through the camp with their M16s blazing. The Viet Cong fled, some diving into tunnels, leaving the camp to the "Mike" force troopers. A hasty search turned up the black box, and the "Mike" force quickly withdrew and headed for home, stopping only briefly to rendezvous with a helicopter which picked up the black box, their wounded, and the wounded Viet Cong guide. Gritz and the rest of his men walked out of the jungle several days later, the Viet Cong failing in furious attempts to destroy them on the way.

The 5th Special Forces Group knew that the Viet Cong had numerous secret bases and complete freedom of movement through certain areas of South Vietnam. Shortly after the "Mike" forces were created SF decided to go a step further and form small bands of C.I.D.G. troops led by A-teams to attack the Viet Cong in their bases in the remote areas of the country. The mobile guerrilla force was the brainchild of Colonel Francis Kelly, who used the code word "Blackjack" for these deep penetration missions. "Blackjack" Kelly's mobile guerrilla force was a direct development of the mobile strike force, but the former's assignments were of a more complex and varied nature. The mobile guerrilla forces were engaged in numerous "Blackjack" operations until they were merged with the "Mike" forces in May 1968.

The first guerrilla mission was "Blackjack 21," launched in October 1966. After five weeks of training and planning, the month-long combat sweep was conducted through the mountains and valleys of the Plei Trap region in south-western Kontum Province. Led by Captain James A. Fenlon, Task Force 777 consisted of 15 Special Forces troopers and 249 Montagnards. The enemy were North Vietnamese soldiers, and the task force was soon at work planting mines on jungle paths and laying ambushes. On 5 November, one ambush team killed three N.V.A. soldiers who were carrying tin boxes containing grenades and walking bicycles with their loads strapped on. The N.V.A. retaliated by killing two Montagnards, but the ambush team escaped to link up with a nearby Special Forces platoon. Task Force 777 remained for a full month in the Plei Trap area. The men waded waist deep in streams, trudged through bamboo and jungle, and struggled across the dense vine tangle of untended rice fields. The operation was invaluable as a test for the mobile guerrilla forces. Casualties were light, and some success was obtained in gathering information about enemy units.

In April 1967 an extended reconnaissance and mobile guerrilla force operation was ordered in support of the 1st Infantry Division, operating in rugged country north-west of Saigon in Binh Duong Province near the Cambodian border. This formation's 1st Infantry Brigade was allocated an area based on Phuoc Vinh and needed information on where to strike with its combat troops, artillery and air cover. Task Force "Blackjack 33" consisted of three "Mike" force companies, a Mobile Guerrilla Force (A-303), seven Special Reconnaissance Teams and nine Road Runner Teams. (The roadrunners were South Vietnamese soldiers who disguised themselves in the black pajamas worn by the Viet Cong, and openly walked the trails gathering intelligence.) "Blackjack 33," which numbered 26 Green Beret officers and sergeants as well as nearly 700 Montagnards and South Vietnamese soldiers, was airlifted from Bien Hoa airbase to Phuoc Vinh in C-123 and C-130 transport aircraft on 24 April 1967.

The 1st Infantry Brigade briefed the task force, which prepared for action after an aerial survey of its operational area had been completed. The recon teams inserted by helicopter obtained the pieces that made up the jigsaw pattern of enemy strength in the area. Sometimes these four-man squads found trail-watching unrewarding when no enemy was seen, but at other times the sighting of a lone Viet Cong would lead to a helicopter probe to find his base. Recon Mission 8, infiltrated at dawn on 9 May, observed 200 Viet Cong moving in a south-westerly direction toward the 1st Infantry Brigade's position.

The recon team did not attract the attention of the Viet Cong and an air attack was called in to disperse the column. In the melee the recon team was split up but all four troopers were picked up by helicopter two days later.

In spite of their disguise, the roadrunners were usually quickly spotted by the Viet Cong. Recon Mission 33 on 15 May made contact with a 30-man Viet Cong squad. One team-member threw a M26 rifle grenade when the Viet Cong were only a short distance away, and killed five of them. The roadrunners then dived into old fox-holes and killed four more Viet Cong before being rescued by helicopters under fire.

Recon Mission 25 on 19 May made contact with three Viet Cong, killing one of them and capturing a home-made weapon. The team then withdrew to the helicopter landing zone under rifle grenade fire from the Viet Cong. Turning on the helicopters the Viet Cong succeeded in shooting down two of them. Three Americans and two South Vietnamese were wounded. The U.S. Air Force later recovered the helicopters. On 20 May, Mobile Guerrilla Force (M.G.F.) 957 contacted an elite multi-battalion-sized force, which was well armed with Soviet and Chinese weapons. There were many Chinese soldiers, who wore khaki uniforms, fighting in this unit. The Viet Cong were either wearing black uniforms with camouflaged soft hats, or blue uniforms. The enemy unit was well trained and inflicted casualties on the M.G.F. "Blackjack 33" ended on 24 May when the Green Beret detachment command elements returned by helicopter to their base at Nha Trang. The main body of the task force was transported in C-130s the same day to Bien Hoa airbase. "Blackjack 33" had lasted a month and the 1st Infantry Division had gained enough intelligence to launch offensive action over the coming months.

MACV/SOG: Tet-68 and the Green Berets

The U.S. Special Forces could justly claim in Vietnam that they had earned the title "Special," but there was another unit associated with SF that was considered "extra special." Military Assistance Command, Vietnam, sponsored the Special Operations Group (M.A.C.V./S.O.G.), which was charged with highly secret operations throughout South-East Asia. M.A.C.V./S.O.G. was a joint service task force assigned to stop unconventional warfare in North and South Vietnam and in neighboring countries that harbored bases for the supply of the North Vietnamese Army (N.V.A.) and the Viet Cong. Special attention was paid to Laos and Cambodia. Although M.A.C.V./S.O.G. was not the responsibility of the 5th Special Forces Group, the former relied on the Green Berets for their fighting personnel. Cross-border patrols into Laos by mixed U.S. and South Vietnamese Special Forces teams began in September 1965. On these highly dangerous missions the Special Forces fought the N.V.A. and Pathet Lao in open battle, assessed Boeing B-52 bomb damage and directed air attacks though the main objective was still to prevent N.V.A. units from passing through Laos into South Vietnam.

As early as 1963, Special Forces had identified Cambodia as a likely Viet Cong sanctuary and source of supply. Most Special Forces border surveillance efforts in the Vietnam War were directed against Cambodia, and only half a dozen faced Laos. In May 1965 Cambodia severed diplomatic relations with the United States and the way was clear for the North Vietnamese to use

the country. Before the creation of the Special Operations Group, the C.I.A. had used agents parachuted into Cambodia to observe military activity, but these undercover operators were soon captured and executed. By 1967-1968 the build-up of N.V.A. and Viet Cong units had increased to the extent that it was vital to send the S.O.G. recon teams deeper into Cambodian territory. The M.A.C.V./S.O.G. Special Forces recon missions were conducted in some of the most rugged terrain in South-East Asia. Each team consisted of three Green Berets and nine Vietnamese commandos. The team was supported by four transport helicopters, four helicopter gunships, a Douglas A-1E Skyraider aeroplane and a light observation aeroplane. A number of H.A.L.O. (High Altitude Low Opening) jumps were made in remote areas.

When enemy concentrations were spotted, the Special Forces commandos were quick to react, but movement on foot in thick jungle undergrowth was slow. Jungle trails had to be avoided and any team's pace was often restricted to less than 1.6km (1 mile) per day. The matted surfaces of the trees in thick forest cast darkness or a shadowy gloom on patrols cautiously approaching their targets. Sometimes the recon and approach marches covered a wide area. The point man or scout led the way, and was followed at short intervals by the rest of the team. Navigating with compass and map at night or in poor visibility daylight hours is a skilled business, and the troopers also had to guard against losing touch with each other. Blinds were built in the brush to watch movement

Above: These A-1H Skyraiders of the Vietnam Air Force could deliver prompt heavy weight close air support.

Far left: High-altitude low opening (HALO) parachutists demonstrate their "in flight" skills. By this technique small groups of clandestine operators can be dropped with great accuracy and secrecy from aircraft flying at sufficient altitude and speed to conceal their missions, especially at night-time, from enemy forces on the ground.

on trails, roads and rivers. Important sightings were reported by radio and strike aircraft screamed in to blast the enemy convoys and columns. B-52 bombers hit the larger concentrations of troop supply depots. The Special Forces raided enemy locations, blew up targets and took prisoners for interrogation. The cross-border raids were some of the toughest assignments of the Vietnam War, but the dangers matched the high stakes involved.

Six Medals of Honor were won by M.A.C.V./ S.O.G., and none was a more deserving recipient than Sfc. Fred W. Zabitovsky. A tall six-footer of impressive physique and with a mop of black hair, he was not a man to seek the limelight. In February 1968, when the spotlight was turned on him, Zabitovsky was already the veteran of two previous Vietnam tours. On 19 February Zabitovsky led a nine-man team from Dak To across the border into the Attopeu area in the south-eastern corner of Laos. The terrain alternated between thick jungle, 3m (10 ft) high elephant grass and bamboo thicket, but there were many clearings where helicopters could land. The helicopter flight descended into the target zone but only one of the "slicks" carried a recon team. With the choppers flying one behind the other, the leading helicopter touched down momentarily then rose up again and joined the flight. The process was repeated so that when the commandos jumped out the enemy was confused as to where the actual landing took place.

This was Zabitovsky's fourteenth cross-border raid into Cambodia and Laos. He was the most experienced man in the team but he did have under his command two Nungs who had fought in the French Indochina War. The helicopter ruse was a familiar deception by the crews, but was not such a success this time. Within minutes of stepping out onto the landing zone the recon men were attacked by a large force of North Vietnamese regulars. Zabitovsky was cool enough to call in two Skyraiders to strafe the enemy, using as a marker white smoke produced by white phosphorus grenades attached to a Claymore mine, which was electronically detonated. The Skyraiders dropped napalm bombs which wiped out the first wave of attackers. Zabitovsky then put another Claymore mine in position and took on the second wave with his CAR-15 automatic rifle. The second mine burst among the N.V.A. and this brought the Skyraiders back, this time dropping high explosive bombs. Still the N.V.A. poured more men into the clearing. They looked fit

and their clean uniforms suggested that they were reinforcements who had not been long in the area.

Zabitovsky realized that the odds were against him and radioed for choppers to evacuate the team, but none was available so the Special Forces men had no alternative but to stand and fight. Fortunately, the nine-man team was still intact. The sergeant directed his men to defensive positions in the clearing and waited for the next onslaught. Twenty-two enemy attacks were broken up with the help of two Skyraiders. Finally two helicopters landed to evacuate the commandos and Zabitovsky climbed aboard the second one to leave. The chopper lifted off the ground and was 23m (75 ft) in the air when it was hit by a well-aimed rocket grenade. The sergeant was thrown out of the door and regained consciousness 6·7m (22 ft) from the helicopter, which had crashed and was burning fiercely. Although in pain with crushed vertebrae and ribs he pulled out the pilot, who was only dazed, and then was pulling out the co-pilot when the fuel cells exploded, throwing them clear of the burning wreck. They were all successfully evacuated but the co-pilot later died of his wounds.

The Special Operations Group had many other brave men whose feats are deserving of much wider knowledge. These stories now lie buried in dusty army archives, and many of the M.A.C.V/S.O.G. missions are still secret and will remain so for a long time to come.

In the Tet offensive of 1968 attacks were launched against towns and cities that were thought to be impregnable. The onslaught by the N.V.A. and the Viet Cong was finally defeated by the allies, but not before bitter fighting had resulted in serious loss of life on both sides. When the enemy struck, many of the Special Forces in the C.I.D.G. camps had taken passes and gone out for the night believing the northerners would observe the truce as they had done in previous years. The "Mike" forces were hastily assembled and went into action on 30 January with street fighting in Pleiku. Detachment B-24 fought in defense of its own compound in Kontum from 30 January to 4 February, assisted by a C.I.D.G. company from Dak Pek (A-242) and two platoons of the 7th Squadron, 17th Cavalry. The Viet Cong attacks commenced with rockets and mortar bombs exploding inside the camp's perimeter followed by probes by foot soldiers. Gunships hovering overhead repulsed the Viet Cong, but panic was caused when howitzer shells fired by a South Vietnamese artillery regiment plunged into the compound. The Vietnamese commander denied that his guns were in error but the shelling stopped immediately when B-24's detachment commander threatened to fire back using his own heavy mortars.

The Green Berets' heaviest engagement with the enemy was at the Special Forces border camp at Lang Vei near the U.S. Marine Corps combat base close to Khe Sanh. By January 1968, several N.V.A. divisions had encircled Khe Sanh, placing the Lang Vei camp in imminent danger. Lang Vei was set aside Highway 9 – only 2.4km (1.5 miles) from the Laotian border, and the Green Berets learned with alarm that N.V.A. tanks were heading their way. Captain Frank C. Willoughby's Detachment A-101 was busy turning Lang Vei into a fighting camp when Kha tribesmen of a Laotian volunteer battalion, retreating with their families and belongings, confirmed the presence of armor in the area. Anti-tank defenses had not been put in place but A-101 was hastily air-supplied with 100 Light Anti-Tank (LAW) weapons. The Laotian battalion commander, who was a lieutenant colonel, refused to take orders from the American captain and Lieutenant Colonel Daniel F. Schungel flew in on 6 February to provide an American officer of equal rank. First Lieutenant Paul R. Longgreat's Hre tribal 12th Mobile Strike Force also flew in to reinforce the defenders.

That evening mortar bombs started falling on Lang Vei and at midnight on 7 February N.V.A. tanks and infantry mounted the first assault. Sfc. James W. Holt destroyed two PT-76 amphibious tanks, whose headlights lit up a portion of the center wire, with his hand-held weapon. Assisted by Staff Sergeant Peter Tiroch, the assistant intelligence sergeant, as loader, Holt knocked out another tank before running to the ammunition bunker to pick up more LAWs. A shell hit the bunker, which instantly exploded: Holt must have been blown to pieces as he was never seen again. The Green Beret officers and sergeants, led by Lieutenant Colonel Schungel, personally tried everything they could to stop the tanks. When the LAW rockets malfunctioned or bounced off the tanks without exploding, the Americans leapt on to the hulls of the tanks, opened the hatches and dropped in grenades.

N.V.A. engineers armed with explosives, tear-gas grenades and flame-throwers fought their way through the C.I.D.G. trenches and captured the opposite ends of the narrow-shaped bunker. Forced back into the inner compound, each man fought his own desperate battle with enemy tanks and infantry. The inner compound contained underground bunkers which the N.V.A. threatened to blow up. When the South Vietnamese surrendered and walked out with their hands up, they were executed by the N.V.A. soldiers. The enemy ruthlessly pressed home the attack, dropping explosives and gas grenades down the bunker air vents. At dawn the camp had been overrun, and the surviving Special Forces officers and sergeants escaped outside the wire and took refuge in a creek bed. The Green Berets took with them as many of the "Mike" forces tribesmen as could move. Eventually the escapees made their way down Highway Nine. Casualties in the Lang Vei battle had been extremely heavy. Among the Americans, ten were missing, while 13 others were wounded. Although their fates were unknown at the time, three of the missing were prisoners.

The U.S. Special Forces served 11 years in Vietnam. In the aftermath of the Tet offensive, the Green Berets were increasingly involved in handing over responsibility for the C.I.D.G. and fighting camps, "Mike" forces and recon missions to the South Vietnamese Special Forces. The Green Berets found this a difficult task to perform as the South Vietnamese forces were beginning to display an uncertain posture toward the enemy. (In fairness to the government of the Republic of Vietnam units it must be said that though the South Vietnamese felt that they were being "let down" by the gradual withdrawal of American forces, the A.R.V.N. as a whole fought on bravely almost to the last before the fall of Saigon in 1975.)

Since Buon Enao in 1962, a strong bond of affection and loyalty had existed between the Americans and the Rhade and other Montagnard tribes. Once the Americans had gone, the tribesmen feared that no matter if the war was won by the North or the South, they would be persecuted and driven from their new homes. Tales of the Green Berets, both fact and fiction, are now popular, everyday viewing on movie and TV screens. When fact takes over from fiction, who is to say what hair-raising yarns lie hidden in secret files and in the now-forgotten jungles of Vietnam?

Students of the Vietnam War today will truthfully say that the Special Forces' most important contribution to the conflict was the making of over 300 Civilian Irregular Defense Group units.

Main picture: A Skyraider peels off to bomb a target in the Vietnam jungle in 1966.

The fortunes of Bellerophon, the first airborne warrior, were spiced with both triumph and disaster. Greek legend tells us that the erring son of Glaucus captured and tamed the winged horse Pegasus, and as an act of atonement took off on his loyal steed to slay the fire-breathing dragon Chimera. Bellerophon's mission was successful: the monstrous creature was destroyed by aerial attack with bow and arrow; and the Prince of Corinth was all set for a brief spell of military glory. Not long after killing the Chimera, Bellerophon was made to fall to earth from his winged mount, and he spent the rest of his life as a pathetic cripple.

Fortunately for the world airborne forces of the 20th century, their luck has never descended to such a depressing level, but the deployment of parachute and glider troops in World War II saw both triumph and disaster. Airborne troops of that era were vulnerable in the air, and with their light scale of infantry support weapons, were also at a disadvantage in action on the ground. It is certainly true that the global air transport fleet of the U.S. Air Force now adds significantly to the strategic air mobility of the U.S. Army and Marine Corps, and that the U.S. Army's helicopters – as in the Vietnam war – will have a major impact on tactical movement by air on future battlefields. So is the status of airborne forces today so very different?

Even if the Lockheed Galaxy, in its latest C-5B marque, can lift two main battle tanks with an assortment of other military vehicles, just how many Galaxies of the U.S.-based strategic reserve would be needed to reinforce Western armor in Europe in time to have a telling effect in a crucial battle? And would they get through to the scene of operations anyway? While the Western establishment of airborne forces remains modest, the Soviet Union, on the other hand, can paradoxically afford the luxury of at least 11 airborne divisions – probably more, not counting those of the Soviet allies of the communist bloc. At the turn of the decade, East-West tension is gradually diminishing and the former communist satellites are actively seeking multi-party democracy. If conventional forces are scaled down, will parachute troops be the first to go?

The U.S. 82nd Airborne Division has now been maintained for more than 30 years at full combat potential to take its part in the many possible eventualities of conflict in various parts of the world. Kept at a high peak of training in the mountains, deserts, plains and Arctic wastes of North America, the "All Americans" have now annually demonstrated their capability of emplaning at Fort Bragg in Starlifters and flying in one major lift without refueling to drop zones in West Germany for a number of years. In May 1965, the 82nd played a role in keeping the peace in the Dominican Republic. In 1968, a brigade of the 82nd was in Vietnam, the "crisis" year of that long and bitter war and was involved in tough fighting well into 1969. In 1981, the division took part in the "Bright Star" one-lift parachute drop from Fort Bragg into Egypt. Two significant operations are worth looking at in more detail. The first was in Grenada in 1983 and the second in Panama in 1989.

Above: Troopers of the 82nd Airborne Division aboard a C-141 Starlifter grasp their static lines. A few minutes later they will be on the ground. Exercise "Reforger," West Germany, September 1980.

Far left: These paratroopers of the 82nd Airborne Division forming part of the Rapid Deployment Force have flown non-stop in C-141 Starlifters from Fort Bragg to take part in a NATO exercise in West Germany. The occasion is Exercise "Reforger," West Germany, September 1980. The soldier in the foreground on Lhuende drop zone is an air traffic controller.

The Coconut Invasion

The Caribbean island of Grenada, first discovered by Christopher Columbus in 1498, for centuries formed part of the British Empire. Given its independence within the framework of the Commonwealth in 1974, Grenada's first Prime Minister, Sir Eric Gairy, held office for five years until overthrown in a bloodless coup led by Maurice Bishop. The new leader set up Grenada's Provisional Revolutionary Government (P.R.G.) based on communist principles. Bishop alarmed the Western powers when he invited a large contingent of Cuban workers to build a new international airport at Point Salines. The purpose of the project was two-fold: 1) to attract tourists to Grenada; and 2) to provide the Cubans with a staging airfield for their troops en route to fight for the communist cause in Africa. In October 1983, the People's Revolutionary Army (P.R.A.) took over Grenada: Maurice Bishop and four of his ministers were shot by a firing squad; another, Jacqueline Creft, was beaten to death.

On 21 October, the leaders of the six small nations forming the Organization of Eastern Caribbean States met in Bridgetown, Barbados to consider collective action against Grenada. The United States responded immediately to an appeal for help, the primary American concern being the safety of about 1,000 U.S. citizens in Grenada, 800 of them students. The naval task forces sailing for the Mediterranean were diverted to Grenada. Task Force 124 was built around the helicopter carrier U.S.S. *Guam* and four landing ships of Amphibious Squadron Four, in which were embarked 1,700 combat-ready Marines of the 22nd Marine Amphibious Unit (M.A.U.), together with landing craft, tanks and amphibious tractors. *Guam* also carried aircraft of Marine Medium Helicopter Squadron (Reinforced) 261 (HMM-261). The second naval task force was the Carrier Battle Group headed by the U.S.S. *Independence* with the aircraft of Carrier Wing 6 (CVW-6) and its cruiser and destroyer escorts.

No major airborne assault was planned, but two battalions of U.S. Army Rangers would be dropped onto the old Pearl's Airport in the north-east of the island, which hopefully by that time would have been taken by the Marines. Small teams of U.S. Navy SEALS and Delta Force troopers were also assigned to jump ahead of the main sea air assault using HALO (High Altitude, Low Opening) free-fall parachutes to carry out raids and reconnaissance tasks, which included checking out the state of progress with the new 3,050m (10,000 ft) runway at Point Salines. The 1/75th and 2/75th Ranger Battalions were alerted at Fort Lewis, Washington and Fort Stewart, Georgia.

The "Ready Brigade" of the 82nd Airborne Division at Fort Bragg was ordered to standby for airlift into Grenada. The airlift would therefore consist of Marines, Rangers and the 82nd Division paratroopers. The mission after capturing Pearl's was to secure the capital, St. George's, and to rescue the governor-general; to locate and evacuate the U.S. nationals; and to clear the 344km² (133 sq mile) island of the People's Revolutionary Army. This last task included fighting the Cubans, who were likely to join with the P.R.A. in defending the new runway at Point Salines, which was long enough to take the Lockheed C-141A Starlifters designated to pull out the U.S. civilians.

On the night of 23-24 October, the first American invaders to land in Grenada were Navy SEALS, who went ashore in rubber Sea Fox raiding boats. The SEAL and Delta Force free-fallers jumped the same night, but a four-man SEAL team assigned to land at Point Salines somehow dropped into the sea and drowned entangled in their parachutes in the surf. At 5.00 a.m. on 25 October the

Below: Members of the 82nd Airborne Division board a C-141 during Operation Urgent Fury, Grenada, 4 November 1983.

Marines headed by Battalion Landing Team (B.L.T.) 2/8 (2nd Battalion, 8th Marine Regiment) and an artillery group landed in amphibians in preparation for the assault on Pearl's Airport and the initial objective of the securing the northern part of the island. They met with "no resistance of substance" according to Major Pat Coulter, a U.S. Army public relations officer, and the airfield had been taken by the Marines by 7.25 a.m., in good time for the jump by the Rangers from Lockheed C-130 transports later that morning.

The C-130s were so full of light artillery, jeeps and weapons containers that the Rangers rode in considerable discomfort. The DZ at Pearl's Airport was long but narrow, and was bordered on one side by water. A strong wind was blowing over the island, so a low-drop altitude was indicated with the Rangers carrying as much ammunition as possible in their rucksacks. Rifles and grenade launchers were clipped to the parachute harnesses with snap-links. The new MC-1 parachutes had been rejected for the old T-10s which were thought to be safer at a low height, and at the last minute the Rangers were ordered to dump their reserve parachutes, to enable them to jump with heavier loads than usual. As the time to jump approached, with the 2nd Battalion leading, the Rangers – because of the crowded cabins – found it impossible to carry out the normal "station rigging" and had to resort to the "buddy system" of helping each other assemble and check their equipment. On the run in aboard the lead aeroplane, Lieutenant Colonel Ralph Hagler, who commanded the 2nd Ranger Battalion, observed that anti-aircraft fire and mortar rounds from the Cuban camp were impacting on the west side of the airport. Hagler took a brief look back at his men and shouted "Rangers, be hard!" before leaping out at 153m (500 ft) into a 40km (25 mph) wind force. Resistance was at first spirited until two Marine companies were back-loaded into 13 amphibious assault vehicles and landed at Grand Mal in the rear of the enemy force. The two Ranger battalions now headed for the Cuban camp, which they captured without difficulty. The combined Marine-Ranger force then moved south to assemble north of St. George's before the Marines took over the governor-general's residence and the Rangers took the radio station.

The revolutionaries now concentrated their forces in the island on Forts Ruppert, Matthew and Frederick, the latter being the P.R.A.'s command center. All efforts to dislodge them on the first day failed. On the second day of the invasion the Marines and Rangers made a combined helicopter assault on the campus south of St. George's where the majority of the American students were to be found. Marine Boeing Vertol CH-46 Sea Knights were used to evacuate the students from the college compound. Meanwhile, a company of Marines successfully attacked the Fort Frederick command center. Resistance by the revolutionaries was now becoming sporadic and disorganized.

The 2nd Brigade of the 82nd Airborne Division, led by Major General Edward L. Trobaugh, had touched down at Point Salines at 2.00 p.m. on D-day and was by now busy sweeping the island. When all three elements of the U.S. ground forces met in St. George's on the third day of the operation, the fighting was virtually over. During that day a final 202 students were picked up in the city. After the fall of Pearl's Airport, Marines of the 22nd M.A.U. launched a combined helicopter/amtrac assault on an island, 32km (20 miles) north of Grenada. Their mission completed, by 1 November the Marines were on their way to their original destination at Beirut.

A few weeks later, President Ronald Reagan addressed Marines and their families and friends at Camp LeJeune, Cherry Point, North Carolina. In a moving speech, in which the president also paid tribute to the Marine heroes of Lebanon, he said: "On Grenada, our military forces moved quickly and professionally to protect American lives. . .

"This was no invasion, it was a rescue mission . . . American forces on Grenada were responding to an urgent request from the Organization of Eastern Caribbean States. . . Only days before our action, Prime Minister Maurice Bishop had been brutally murdered along with several members of his cabinet and unarmed civilians . . .

"With 1,000 Americans, including 800 students on that island, we weren't about to wait for the Iran crisis to repeat itself, only this time in our own neighborhood – the Caribbean."

The American community was lifted intact and in comfort in Starlifters from Point Salines, Grenada. Eleven U.S. soldiers, three Marines and four Navy SEALs died during the battle, and 116 American servicemen were wounded. Grenadian casualties amounted to 45 dead and 35 wounded; the Cubans lost 35 dead and 59 wounded.

The Assault on Panama: December 1989

On the evening of 17 December 1989, President George Bush was entertaining 50 old friends to a Christmas party at the White House when the unexpected arrival of Joint Chiefs of Staff Chairman, General Colin Powell, Secretary of Defense, Richard Cheney, and National Security Adviser, Brent Snowcroft, meant that it was "business as usual." President Bush, who, since taking over the presidency from Ronald Reagan had so far seen out 1989 without indulging in controversial actions, was faced with decisions which could not wait until the morning.

On 16 December, an off-duty U.S. Marine lieutenant had been shot dead by Panamanian Defence Force (P.D.F.) troops and on the 18th a U.S. Army officer had wounded a Panamanian police corporal near U.S. installations in the Canal Zone area. Panama had been a sharp thorn in Washington's side for well over a year. Drug-trafficking from the country into the United States had reached enormous proportions. On 9 May a general election had been held in which the victory of President Manuel Antonio Noriega's favored party had been countered by allegations by its opponents, led by Guillermo Endera, that the ballots had been rigged.

George Bush could no longer exercise his customary restraint and stated summarily: "This guy [Noriega] is not going to lay off. It will get worse." There was no option for the U.S. but to launch an invasion of Panama. U.S. objectives in taking over military control of the country were three-fold: 1) To overpower resistance by Noriega's forces; 2) to capture the dictator and bring him to trial in the U.S.A. on drug-running charges, from which criminal activity he had amassed a considerable personal fortune; and 3) to install a stable government, under the leadership of Endera, who claimed he had won the May election.

The United States already had 13,000 troops with tanks, armored cars and helicopters stationed at several bases in the Panama Canal Zone, 2,000 of the troops having been sent there as reinforcements earlier in 1989. U.S. Southern Command Headquarters were situated a few miles west of Panama City. Other important locations were the P.D.F.'s HQ, also west of the city, the palatial Presidential Palace built on the western promontory of Panama Bay, nearby Howard Air Force Base, Allbrook Air Force Station to the north, and Tocumen International Airport, about 20 miles to the east of the canal.

Some 11,000 troops were despatched by air from the U.S. for the invasion. There was never any doubt that the P.D.F. (a combination of soldiers and armed policemen) would not fight. The main fear in Washington was that Noriega, a one-time, paid-up member of the Central Intelligence Agency (C.I.A.), would escape to the jungle and conduct Vietnam-style guerrilla warfare, which could continue for years. In addition, Bush, whose avowed intention was to put Endera's party in power, had no wish to be regarded as a puppet-master and was concerned that there might be an adverse reaction in Latin America to U.S. involvement in Panama's political affairs.

Below: 1st Ranger Battalion, Hunter Army Airfield, Georgia, wait to emplane for Operation "Just Cause."

Bottom: Army Rangers, 1st Ranger Battalion. Operation "Just Cause."

The fly-in by U.S.A.F. transports carrying troops and equipment commenced at 1 a.m. local time on the night of 20-21 December and the airborne troops advancing on Panama City immediately went into action. The units involved were the 5th Infantry from Ford Polk; Army Rangers, 7th Infantry from Ford Ord; and 82nd Airborne from Fort Bragg. Rangers and "All-American" paratroopers were dropped at key positions and, although no details are available, a U.S. Navy SEAL team was reported to have been dropped in Panama Bay to attack the Presidential Palace and prevent Noriega's escape in the event of him being there. As soon as the attack began, Guillermo Endera was sworn in by a Panamanian judge, within the grounds of a U.S. base.

At daybreak waves of U.S. strike aircraft, tanks, armored cars and paratroopers assaulted Panama City, while light tanks surrounded and set alight the Comandancia, the P.D.F.'s headquarters, as many loyal supporters of Noriega fled for their lives. Two battalions secured a power station, the Madden Dam and a prison at Gamboa, where 48 former P.D.F. members had been imprisoned for taking part in an attempted coup to overthrow Noriega in October. U.S. ground attack aircraft flew an effective sortie to pin down Panamanian troops at Fort Amador, southwest of the city, and parachute troops were dropped onto an airstrip nearby to secure the area.

While the fighting to capture Noriega's headquarters continued, the U.S., against thin opposition, blocked the Pacora River Bridge, cutting off Panama City and wrecking P.D.F. Navy boats that were attempting to escape. Scenes within parts of the city limits were chaotic. From the balconies of Panama City's tall blocks of flats, clouds of billowing smoke and the glow of flames could be seen above one sector of the city, while traffic continued normally in other places. The

Below: Paratroopers from the 82nd Airborne Division, Fort Bragg, wait to board C-141s at Torrijos International Airport, Panama. The troops were on the way home after participating in Operation "Just Cause."

heaviest fighting revolved around the Comandancia, from which area the sounds of machine-gun fire echoed across Panama Bay. More aircraft came in for the attack and artillery shells arched over the city without hitting specified targets.

The artillery barrage now shifted to the old part of the city, known as Chorrillo and a bright orange glow appeared at the foot of Ancon Hill, where Noriega's HQ and barracks were located. Where usually the bay was lit with the steady glow of street and dock lights, now bright red trails of shells were reflected in the water. Later, gunfire could be heard on the east side of Panama City. There was little fighting in the city's main business district. The conflict now turned to the old part of the city, where the skyline is shaped by small houses, not skyscrapers. Traffic gradually came to a standstill and Panamanian looters were soon out in force, foraging amongst ruined homes and shops.

Throughout the long night of 21/22 December, machine-gun bursts and explosions continued sporadically. The main hospital reported 50 dead and 100 wounded and civilians sought refuge in the building. To the north, at Allbrook Air Force base, sporadic bursts of artillery shells could be seen tracing their curved trajectories across the sky. All the time the drone of aircraft could be heard overhead, and flares were dropped in the neighborhood of the Comandancia, where flames erupted, leaping 50 feet high. By 5.30 a.m. the inferno at Noriega's headquarters had subsided, and gunfire had not been heard for 20 minutes, though aircraft still flew overhead.

The end of the fighting was in sight but more parachute troops were dropped to help "mop-up" the P.D.F. forces and helicopter gunships fanned over the capital to knock out isolated pockets of resistance. At dawn, a pall of smoke shrouded Panama City and the Panamanian forces were fast disintegrating. Manuel Noriega, however, was nowhere to be found. The resourceful former dictator had not – no doubt wisely in view of his declining support – taken the option of escaping to the jungle but sought instead and was granted the sanctuary of refuge in the Panama City nunciature – the papal embassy.

The events leading up to Christmas had been dramatically dominated by the revolution taking place in Romania and the arrest of the Romanian president Nicolae Ceausescu and his wife Elena, who were executed at an Army camp near Bucharest on Christmas Day. Over the "holiday" the only sounds of commotion in Panama City were caused by U.S. forces bombarding the Vatican compound with rock music. The Papal Nuncio complained that he was being kept awake while Noriega slept soundly in his bed. Within a few days the deposed dictator surrendered and on 4 January Noreiga was delivered to a Miami jail, where – at the time of writing – he awaits what promises to be a sensational trial. Altogether, 23 G.I.s were killed and about 300 wounded in the Panama invasion; the Panamanian dead numbered 600 men.

Below: Members of the 82nd Airborne Division are reunited with their families at Fort Bragg, following more than three weeks in Panama supporting Operation "Just Cause."

GENERAL INDEX

Figures in *italics* refer to illustrations

INDEX OF AIRCRAFT